AIM Higher!

FCAT Mathematics Review

Level H

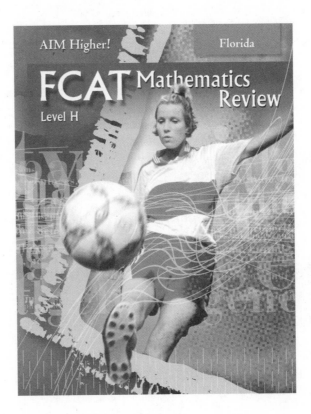

Diane Perkins Castro
and Mark Roop-Kharasch

aim higher!®
Great Source Education Group
Wilmington, MA

Editorial

Diane Perkins Castro
Mark Roop-Kharasch
Robert D. Shepherd
Barbara R. Stratton

Consultants

Todd Bersaglieri*
Matthew Beyranevand*
Sheri Ann Cheng*
Annie Sun Choi†
Rosalie Fazio∆
Sharon Greenwald∆
Sylvia D. Leonard*
Matt Stuck*

* *Mathematics Teacher*
† *Mathematics Editor*
∆ *Mathematics Teacher/ Facilitator*

Design & Production

Diane Perkins Castro
Paige Larkin
Marie Anne St. Arnaud

Cover Design

Seann Dwyer,
Studio Montage

Cover Photo

Duomo/Corbis:
William Sallaz

aim higher! More than just teaching to the test™

First Edition

Printed in the United States of America

1 2 3 4 5 6 7 8 9 10   DBH   07 06 05 04 03

International Standard Book Number: 1-58171-392-4

CONTENTS

Mathematics Pretest

On pages 2–28, you will find a practice test with 55 questions. Taking this test will show what you know about math and help you see what you still need to work on. To help you answer the questions, you may use a calculator and the Mathematics Reference Sheet on page 311.

This test contains four types of question. For multiple-choice questions, choose the **best** answer and fill in the bubble next to that answer. Give yourself about a minute to answer each multiple-choice question. Those questions are worth 1 point each. Other questions include a grid where you should record your answer. Short-response and extended-response questions require you to write your own answers.

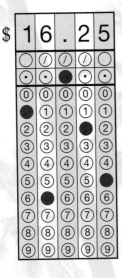

For gridded-responses, write your answer in the spaces at the top of the grid. Then fill in the correct bubble in each column. You can grid whole numbers up to five digits. When you grid fractions, use the slash symbol as the fraction bar between the numerator and the denominator. You can also grid decimals by putting a decimal point in the right position. If an answer should be a percent, there will be a percent sign after the grid. If an answer should be in dollars and cents, there will be a dollar sign before the grid. The example to the left shows how to grid the answer "$16.25." Allow a minute and a half to answer each gridded-response question. Those questions are worth 1 point each.

Extended Response

This symbol appears next to questions that require long answers. Allow 5–15 minutes to answer each of these questions. They are worth 4 points each.

Short Response

This symbol appears next to questions that require short answers. Allow 3–5 minutes to answer each of these questions. They are worth 2 points each.

Read each question carefully. Be sure to fill in each bubble correctly. Reread your short and long answers to be sure that they make sense.

1

MATHEMATICS PRETEST

Directions: *There are 55 questions on this test. Read each problem carefully. Think about ways to solve the problem before you try to answer each question. Then write or mark your answers in the book.*

1. Rajeev drew the following design on a graph. Which of these lines is a line of symmetry?

    Ⓐ $x = 1$

    Ⓑ $y = 1$

    Ⓒ $x = y$

    Ⓓ $x = {}^-y$

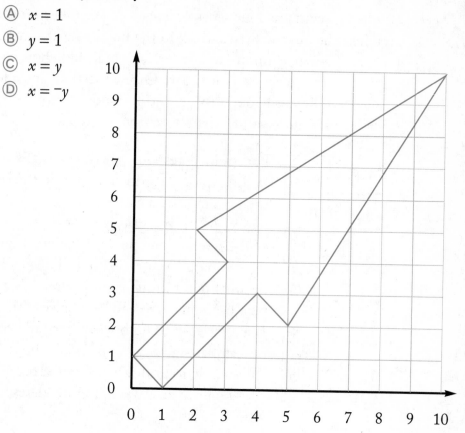

2. Which of the following inequalities is true if $x = 8$?

    Ⓐ $5x + 35 < 75$

    Ⓑ $28 - 3x < 3$

    Ⓒ $4x - 5 > 25$

    Ⓓ $2 + 4x > 46$

Name_____ Class _____ Date _____

3. Kent made up a new ball game for his friends. Goals are worth
4 points each. Teams lose 1 point for each foul. The red team
scored 4 goals but committed 6 fouls. The blue team scored
5 goals but committed 8 fouls. What was the score for each team?

Ⓐ red team = 24   blue team = 40
Ⓑ red team = 22   blue team = 28
Ⓒ red team = 16   blue team = 20
Ⓓ red team = 10   blue team = 12

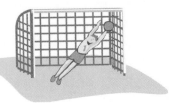

4. What is the value of the following expression
when $x = 13$? Express your answer as an
improper fraction in the lowest terms.

$$\frac{3x - 9}{x + 2(x - 15)}$$

5. The Earth is hurtling around the sun at a rate of 6.7×10^4 miles
per hour. About how far does the Earth travel in 1 day?

Ⓐ 1.6×10^4 miles
Ⓑ 1.6×10^5 miles
Ⓒ 1.6×10^6 miles
Ⓓ 1.6×10^7 miles

6. Franco's car gets about 23 miles per gallon of gas. He puts 17 gallons into the tank. About how many miles can he go on 17 gallons of gasoline?

7. The area of a circular lid to a container is 113 square inches. What is the radius of the lid, to the nearest inch? Use 3.14 as an approximation of π.

Ⓐ   6 inches

Ⓑ   18 inches

Ⓒ   36 inches

Ⓓ   72 inches

8. Use the following function table to find the value of *y* when
   x equals 10.

x	y
2	5
4	9
6	13
8	17
10	

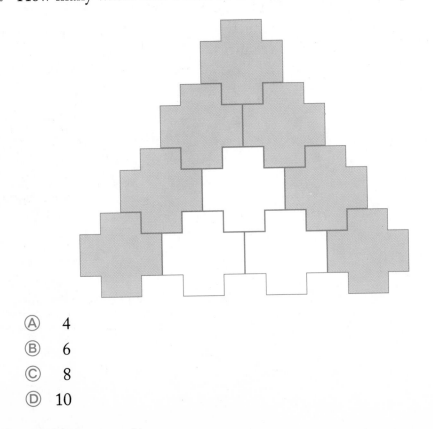

9. How many white tiles would be in the tenth row of this pattern?

Ⓐ 4

Ⓑ 6

Ⓒ 8

Ⓓ 10

10. Philippe is 3 years older than his sister Adrienne. Their parents give each child a base allowance of $5.00. In addition, they give each child $1.00 for each year of his or her age. If x represents Adrienne's age, which equation expresses how many dollars Philippe receives?

Ⓐ $5 + x$

Ⓑ $5 + x + 3$

Ⓒ $x + 3$

Ⓓ $5 + x - 3$

11. Juanita wants to buy 4 CDs. They have the following prices: $9.10, $13.40, $17.50, and $7.60. She has a coupon for 20% off the total. If she has $50.00, how much change will she receive after buying the 4 CDs with the discount?

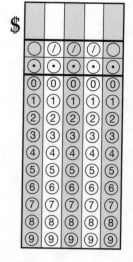

12. Jesse and Grant have a reading competition over the summer. They get a certain number of points for each comic book and each chapter book that they read.

Jesse read the following:
    3 comic books
    8 chapter books

Grant read the following:
    10 comic books
    6 chapter books

Part A Write an expression to show how many points Jesse received. Use x to represent the point value of the comic books and y to represent the point value of the chapter books.

Part B Using the same variables, write another expression to show how many points Grant received.

Part C If each comic book is worth 1 point and each chapter book is worth 5 points, calculate how many points each boy received.

Jesse's points _____

Grant's points _____

13. The people who plan the meals for the school cafeteria poll a sample of students to find out their favorite meals. They survey sixth-, seventh-, and eighth-grade students. Which of the following sample groups would give the meal planners the most accurate idea of the meal preferences of the students?

Ⓐ all the basketball players in the school

Ⓑ 20 students from each grade

Ⓒ the vegetarian students

Ⓓ the sixth-grade cooking class students

14. Triangle *ABC* is a right triangle. What is the measure of angle *A*?

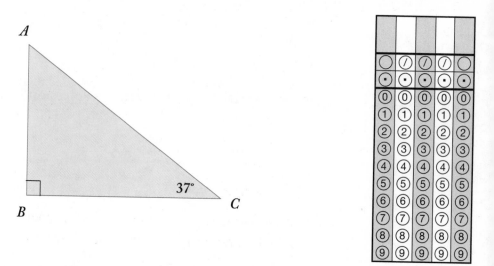

15. In the inequality below, *x* represents any whole number. What values for *x* make the inequality true?

$-3x \leq -4$

Ⓐ $x > 1$

Ⓑ $x \geq 0$

Ⓒ $x < -1$

Ⓓ $x \leq 3$

Name_____ Class _____ Date _____

Use the chart below to answer questions 16 and 17.

TOWN SOCCER TEAMS	
Team	**Team Members**
Tigers	14
Lions	18
Bats	16
Cougars	14
Jaguars	14
Iguanas	15
Raptors	18
Hawks	14
Eagles	15

16. The town community center keeps a record of the number of players on each soccer team. On the town's soccer teams, what number of players is the mode?

Ⓐ 14

Ⓑ 15

Ⓒ 16

Ⓓ 18

17. What is the mean number of players on a soccer team? Round to the nearest tenth.

© GREAT SOURCE. COPYING IS PROHIBITED.

18. Laura's quilt is made up of alternating light blue triangles and dark blue quadrilaterals. If angle *A* of the light blue triangle measures 35°, then what is the measure of angle *B* of the dark blue quadrilateral?

Ⓐ   55°

Ⓑ   65°

Ⓒ   145°

Ⓓ   155°

19. Gwen proposes the hypothesis that about 70% of graduates from her high school go on to college right after high school. The data for last year's graduating class at her school is as follows:

Short Response

Number of graduates: 598

Number who went to college the next fall: 293

Explain whether or not these numbers support her hypothesis.

20. What is the **best** description of how the two shapes below are related?

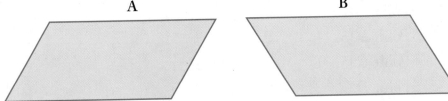

A   B

Ⓐ Shape A is perpendicular to shape B.

Ⓑ Shape A is a reflection of shape B.

Ⓒ Shape A is a tessellation of shape B.

Ⓓ Shape A is a translation of shape B.

21. The following equation compares the lengths of two pieces of wire, A and B.

$B = \frac{1}{2}A + 10$ feet

Which of the following statements is true for any value of A?

Ⓐ Wire B is shorter than Wire A.

Ⓑ Wire B is 10 feet longer than half the length of Wire A.

Ⓒ Wire B is half the length of a wire that is 10 feet longer than Wire A.

Ⓓ Wire B is longer than Wire A.

Go On   11

22. Plot the following ordered pairs on the grid below. Connect the points, beginning and ending with Point A.

Short Response

Point A (2, 3)   Point E (−2, −3)

Point B (5, 1)   Point F (−5, −1)

Point C (5, −1)   Point G (−5, 1)

Point D (2, −3)   Point H (−2, 3)

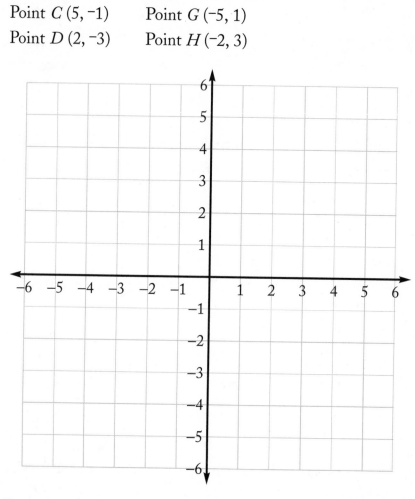

Describe the shape that is drawn.

23. How much fencing does a rancher need to construct a round pen that has a diameter of 65 meters? Use 3.14 as an approximation of π. Round your answer to the nearest meter.

24. Genevieve is making a round picture frame with the dimensions shown below. What is the area of her frame (the blue portion of the diagram)?

   Ⓐ 36π square inches

   Ⓑ 21π square inches

   Ⓒ 16π square inches

   Ⓓ 4π square inches

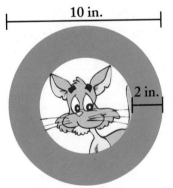

10 in.

2 in.

25. A telephone pole that was 24 feet tall fell over in the street. A town worker cuts it into 18-inch logs. What is the maximum number of 18-inch logs she can get from the telephone pole?

   Ⓐ 13 logs

   Ⓑ 14 logs

   Ⓒ 15 logs

   Ⓓ 16 logs

26. Geraldo bought 20 pounds of oranges. If the average weight of an orange was 8 ounces, how many oranges did Geraldo buy?

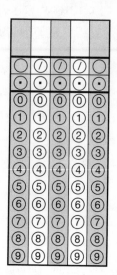

27. Petra feeds her dog about 4 pounds of food a week. ESTIMATE how many 25-pound bags of food her dog would eat in a year. Show your work.

Short Response

Name_____ Class _____ Date _____

28. Which of the following expressions is equal to 12?

Ⓐ $1 + 3^2 - (2 + 4)$

Ⓑ $(1 + 3)^2 - (2 + 4)$

Ⓒ $1 + 3^2 - 2 + 4$

Ⓓ $(1 + 3)^2 - 2 + 4$

29. Which of the following types of wave has the **shortest** wavelength?

Ⓐ blue light wave = 4×10^{-9} meters

Ⓑ microwave = 1×10^{-4} meters

Ⓒ FM radio wave = 1×10^{-1} meters

Ⓓ red light wave = 7×10^{-9} meters

30. On her hike in the Mojave Desert, Ms. Wang brings $3\frac{3}{4}$ quarts of water. How many cups did she bring? (Hint: There are 2 cups in a pint and 2 pints in a quart.)

© GREAT SOURCE. COPYING IS PROHIBITED.

31. Janelle is decorating her room. The dimensions of the room are given in feet (ft). She wants to divide one of the walls diagonally in half. She will paint the upper half gray and the lower half blue. Then she will add a strip of wallpaper border between the gray and the blue areas.

Extended Response

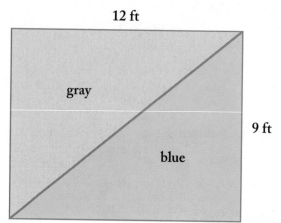

12 ft

gray

9 ft

blue

Part A How much area, in square feet, will be covered by gray paint?

Part B How many feet long does Janelle's strip of wallpaper border need to be?

32. An average healthy person has about 5×10^6 red blood cells in every cubic millimeter of blood. An average 14-year-old has about 4×10^6 cubic millimeters of blood. About how many red blood cells does an average 14-year-old have altogether?

Ⓐ 9×10^{36}

Ⓑ 9×10^{12}

Ⓒ 2×10^{13}

Ⓓ 2×10^{12}

Name _____ **Class** _____ **Date** _____

33. The radius of the circle below is 5 inches. The area of the white space is 27 square inches. What is the area, in square inches, of the blue portion of the circle? Use 3.14 as an approximation of π. Give your answer to the nearest square inch.

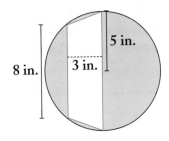

8 in. 3 in. 5 in.

34. Joe is making a scale model of the Grand Canyon for the science fair. The Grand Canyon is about 29 kilometers wide at its widest and 446 kilometers long. If Joe uses the scale 1 centimeter = 4 kilometers, how wide and how long will his model be, to the nearest centimeter?

Ⓐ 116 centimeters × 1784 centimeters

Ⓑ   7 centimeters × 112 centimeters

Ⓒ   15 centimeters × 223 centimeters

Ⓓ   29 centimeters × 446 centimeters

35. Avi bought a shirt on sale for $15.60. It had been marked down by 35%. What was the original selling price?

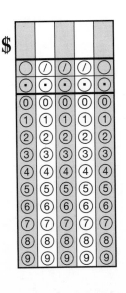

$

36. Mr. Delpero's eighth-grade music class has 25 students. The table below lists their music preferences. What is the probability that a student chosen from the class at random will be a country music fan? Express your answer as a decimal.

MUSIC PREFERENCES OF 8TH-GRADE MUSIC STUDENTS	
Music Preference	**Number of Students**
Rock	11
Country	9
Classical	3
None	2

37. Ayesha has twice as many trading cards as Belinda. Carlo has 5 more cards than Ayesha. Belinda has 25 cards.

Short Response

Let *a* represent how many cards Ayesha has.
Let *b* represent how many cards Belinda has.
Let *c* represent how many cards Carlo has.

Write two equations that you can use to find how many cards each person has. Solve the equations to find the number of cards each person has.

Ayesha: _____ cards

Belinda: _____ cards

Carlo: _____ cards

38. On the graph below, which line represents the equation $y = \frac{1}{2}x + 1$?

Ⓐ line AB

Ⓑ line CD

Ⓒ line EF

Ⓓ line GH

39. Alexa ran in an 880-yard race. How many miles did she run?
(Hint: There are 1,760 yards in a mile.)

Ⓐ 8 miles

Ⓑ 6 miles

Ⓒ 2 miles

Ⓓ $\frac{1}{2}$ mile

Go On

40. The manager of Rolling Along, a sporting goods store, has created a table showing the number of bikes and scooters the store has sold from the year 2000 to 2003. She wants to know which item has increased more in popularity.

Extended Response

BIKE AND SCOOTER SALES		
Year	Bikes	Scooters
2000	508	257
2001	621	243
2002	570	378
2003	490	752

Part A Using the information in the table, construct a line graph on the next page to show how sales of the two items have changed over that four-year period. Remember to label both axes of your graph and to give it a title.

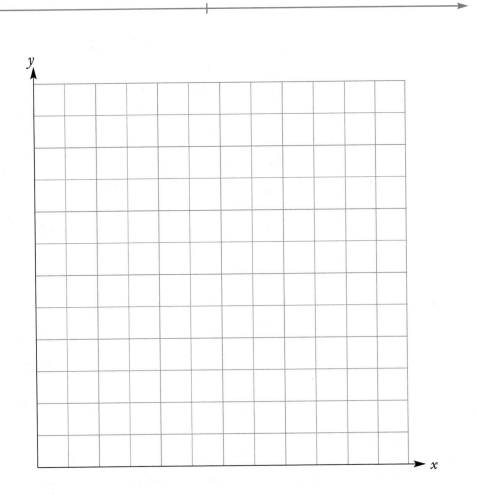

Part B Compare the information provided by the table and the graph. Which item has increased more in popularity? Use the data from both the table and the graph to explain your answer.

41. The community swimming pool is 15 feet wide and 30 feet long. The depth of the water is 4 feet. How many gallons of water does the pool hold? Express your answer to the nearest 100 gallons. (Hint: Calculate the volume of the pool first. Then find its capacity, in gallons.)

1 cubic foot of water is approximately 7.5 gallons

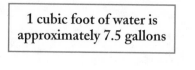

42. There are 36 students in the International Club. Twenty-nine of the members are going on a field trip. What percentage of the members are NOT going on the field trip? Round to the nearest percent.

Ⓐ 18%

Ⓑ 19%

Ⓒ 20%

Ⓓ 81%

43. This year, Duane has read 3 less than twice as many books as Ayala. Together, Duane and Ayala have read 18 books. How many books has Duane read?

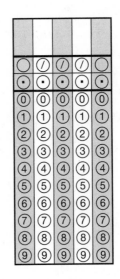

44. An architect makes a model of a town. The scale of the model is 1 inch : 8 feet. If the bank in town is 40 feet tall, how many inches tall should the bank in the model be?

Ⓐ   2 inches

Ⓑ   4 inches

Ⓒ   5 inches

Ⓓ   10 inches

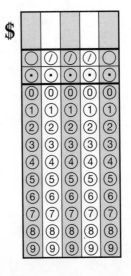

45. Mary is buying dinner rolls for a party. Each roll costs 25¢. How much will she pay for 50 rolls?

Go On

46. The line on the graph below represents the equation $y = 3x - 1$.

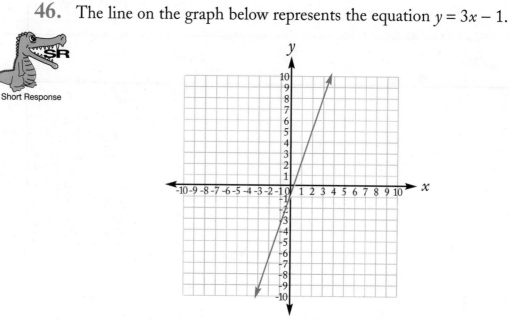

Short Response

Write an equation for a line that is parallel to the line on the graph and passes through the point $(0, -7)$.

47. What is the sum of all the interior angles of the polygon below?

Ⓐ   180°

Ⓑ   360°

Ⓒ   900°

Ⓓ 1,260°

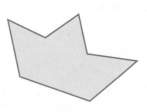

48. A hardware store owner faced with rising costs decides to increase the prices of all his products. The chart below shows the price increases for some products. If all the prices are increasing by the same percent, what will be the new price of Product C?

	Old Price	**New Price**
Product A	$34.00	$37.40
Product B	$27.00	$29.70
Product C	$51.00	

49. Jolene and Roger marked off a large square to play a game. The square is 16 feet by 16 feet (ft), as shown below. If Jolene and Roger stand on opposite corners of the square, how far apart are they? Give your answer to the nearest foot.

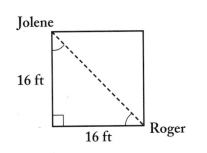

Jolene

16 ft

16 ft

Roger

50. Last year, 12 students from Washington Junior High School participated in the math league. This year, 15 students are participating. What is the percent increase of students in the math league from last year to this year?

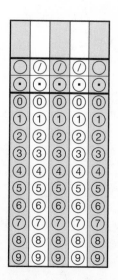

51. Jelani, Tamira, and Clint plant flowers. Jelani plants 6 less than half the number of flowers Tamira plants. Clint plants 8 more than Jelani. If they plant 48 flowers altogether, how many flowers does Tamira plant?

Ⓐ 7

Ⓑ 26

Ⓒ 30

Ⓓ 38

52. A fenced pasture is 650 feet long and 250 feet wide. The owner wants to double the area of the pasture. If the length stays the same, what will the new width of the pasture be, in feet?

53. The area of the trapezoid below is 36 square inches. Angles A and B are equal to each other. Lengths are given in inches (in.).

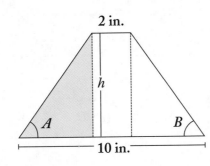

Part A Calculate the height (h) of the trapezoid.

Part B Calculate the area of the shaded portion of the figure.

Part C Explain what would happen to the area of the trapezoid if the lengths of the top and bottom were doubled.

54. What is the sum, in degrees, of the angles *A*, *B*, *C*, *D*, and *E* in the figure below?

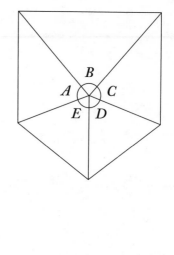

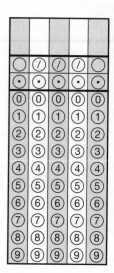

55. After conducting a survey, a salesperson claims that 7 out of 10 people in Florida prefer Fizzy Fresh Cola over Peppy Pop Soda. A smart shopper finds out that the salesperson surveyed only 50 people.

Short Response

Part A Calculate how many people in the survey preferred Fizzy Fresh Cola.

Number of people who preferred Fizzy Fresh Cola _____

Part B Explain why the salesperson's claim is misleading.

UNDERSTANDING THE FCAT MATHEMATICS EXAM

Students often ask, "Why do I have to study math?" There are two good answers to this question. The first is that math can be incredibly beautiful and interesting in and of itself. The second is that math is an amazingly useful tool. Almost every job these days requires some mathematics.

To help make sure that Florida students learn the math skills that they will need for success in later life, the state Department of Education has created standards for mathematics. **Standards** are general statements of expected student achievement. For every standard, there are specific **benchmarks** that tell what a student is expected to know and be able to do at each grade level.

The **Sunshine State Standards** in mathematics are divided into five major categories, called **strands:** Number Sense, Concepts, and Operations; Measurement; Geometry and Spatial Sense; Algebraic Thinking; and Data Analysis and Probability. The **Florida Comprehensive Assessment Test** (**FCAT**) in mathematics was created to test your skills in each of these five areas. Passing this test will show that you have learned the skills and concepts described in the state standards and that you are ready for more advanced study in mathematics and in math-related fields such as science and business.

Format of the FCAT Math Exam

The FCAT math exam contains four question types:

Multiple-choice bubbles

- For each **multiple-choice** question, you select the correct answer from among the four choices given. Fill in the bubble of the answer you choose.

- For **gridded-response** questions, you must solve a problem and then fill in your response on a grid. You can grid numbers up to five digits long. You can grid fractions by using a slash mark for the fraction bar between the numerator and denominator. You can also grid decimals using the decimal point. Write your answer in the boxes at the top of the grid. Then shade in the correct bubble under each digit. If your answer is a fraction or a decimal, shade in the correct fraction bar or decimal point. The grid for percent problems is followed by a percent sign. If the answer should be in dollars and cents, there will be a dollar sign before the decimal grid.

Examples of Grids

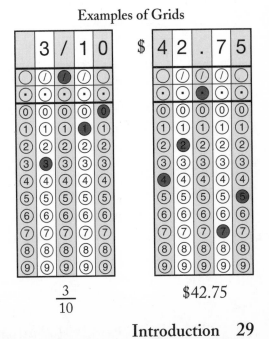

$\frac{3}{10}$

$42.75

- For **short-response** questions, you have to write your own answers. Show your work in the space provided. On the FCAT, these items are called **Short Think, Solve, and Explain** questions.

Short Response

- For **extended-response** questions, you may be asked to write an explanation in your own words or to show the steps in solving a math problem. Sometimes you have to create a graph, chart, or diagram. On the FCAT, these items are called **Long Think, Solve, and Explain** questions. Be sure to answer each part of the problem completely. It is also important to write neatly; you won't get credit for your answers if the graders can't read your writing!

Extended Response

How to Use this Book to Prepare for the FCAT Math Exam

To get the most out of this book, you should familiarize yourself with its contents. The **Pretest,** on pages 1 through 28, gives you experience with questions in all the categories and of all different formats. If you did not do well on the Pretest, don't panic! The lessons in this book will teach you the skills you need in order to do well on the FCAT. This Introduction explains the format of the FCAT, gives guidelines for preparing for tests, and shows how to develop general mathematical reasoning skills. The lessons in the other units teach you specific skills and concepts you must know.

Each lesson begins with a problem, called **The Challenge,** next to a picture of a rocket taking off. The Challenge problem is to be solved using the skills taught in the lesson. Next comes **Learning the Ropes,** an explanation of the concepts and skills covered in the lesson. The examples in this section help you see how to apply the skills. **Meeting the Challenge,** designated by an astronaut who has reached the goal, takes you through the process of solving the Challenge problem, one step at a time. Every lesson contains special features to enhance learning. **Math in History** tells interesting historical facts related to the lesson. **Math in Use** shows how math is used in fields like science and business, how mathematical concepts are found in nature, and how you can apply mathematical ideas to everyday situations. **Another Way** helps you to approach the concept in the lesson from a different angle, which may be easier for you to understand.

At the end of each lesson are two pages called **Try It Yourself.** Doing these exercises lets you practice your new skills. Following the last lesson in each unit are two pages of extended-response questions for **Extra Practice.** At the end of the last unit, there is a **Cumulative Review** section with more extended-response questions covering all of the units. If you have trouble with any of these practice problems, review the lessons indicated in the box at the end of the problem.

After you finish the lessons, take the **Posttest,** found on pages 281 through 310. Compare your Posttest to your Pretest to see how much you have learned!

Also take time to check out other features of the book. Look through the **Table of Contents** on pages iii–v. The **Appendices** at the back of the book include helpful information such as a **Reference Sheet** with formulas and measurement conversions. Take the **Diagnostic Test** to discover any problems you may have with basic math facts and operations. The **Glossary** defines nearly three hundred mathematical terms. Use the **Index** at the back of the book to find topics and terms in the book.

APPROACHING TESTS WITH CONFIDENCE

If you feel nervous about taking tests, you are not alone—many other students feel the same way. The goal of this book is to build your confidence and skills in math. The skills you develop in math will help you do well on math tests and will be useful in solving problems throughout your life. Follow the strategies outlined in this box to overcome anxiety about taking tests so you can perform at your best, not only on the FCAT, but on every test you take.

Before the Test

✔ **Prepare and practice.** Would you try to give a piano concert without practicing? Of course not! You would practice your piece until you knew every note by heart, and then you could go out and play with confidence. In the same way, you should practice the skills that you need to know for the FCAT exam. You can do this by using math in everyday activities like shopping, cooking, and traveling. Practice using mental math, rounding, and estimation to get quick answers. By studying the lessons and doing the exercises in this book, you will be able to go into the test with confidence.

✔ **Think positively.** Positive thoughts can help you to succeed. Remind yourself of times you have succeeded before and of what you are doing to prepare yourself.

✔ **Break problems down into steps.** You may be overwhelmed when you face a big task, but if you break it down into small, manageable tasks, you can handle it, one step at a time. Similarly, when you face difficult math problems, break them down into smaller problems that you can tackle one step at time. Make sure that you understand and can explain each step in a problem before moving on to the next step. The step-by-step process outlined in each Meeting the Challenge section in this book will help you learn to think in a systematic way.

✔ **Try different problem-solving methods.** There is often more than one way to solve a problem. The Another Way sections in this book give different approaches that may be easier for you to understand.

✔ **Practice explaining your reasoning.** For Think, Solve, and Explain questions, the FCAT may ask you to explain your thinking. You will have to describe the steps you take to arrive at your answer. Practice writing out answers to problems step by step.

✔ **Try to understand *why* formulas work.** It will be easier to remember a formula if you know how it works or why it is true.

✔ **Practice using a calculator daily.** You are allowed to use a calculator for the FCAT math exam. You should be able to do simple addition, subtraction, multiplication, and division automatically and very rapidly in your head, but you should practice using a calculator for lengthy calculations. The more you practice, the more useful your calculator will become to you.

✔ **Don't forget the practical steps.** The night before the exam, gather all the materials you will need. Fix yourself a healthful snack to eat during a break if that is allowed. Get a good night's sleep, and get up in time to eat a nutritious breakfast. Be sure to go to the bathroom before entering the test room.

During the Test

✔ **Be honest.** Cheating isn't worth it. You will end up hurting yourself.

✔ **Pay attention to directions.** Listen carefully to instructions given by the test administrator. Read all written directions before you begin. Make sure that you know what you are supposed to do.

✔ **Pace yourself.** Look at the whole test to get an idea how long it is. Budget your time so that you can finish in a reasonable time. You may encounter more difficult problems toward the end of the test. Do not get bogged down on a difficult question. Leave it and go on; you can come back to it later. Plan to spend time checking your work at the end of the test. Do not waste time, but do not rush.

✔ **Write neatly and show all your work.** You cannot get credit for answers that are illegible. Reread each answer to be sure that it makes sense.

✔ **Develop a system for marking multiple-choice answers.** You might put a light ✗ next to answers that you have ruled out. If you need to move on and come back to the question later, you can see immediately which choices are left. When you decide upon your answer, fill in the circle neatly. Erase any other marks besides the correct answer.

✔ **Pay attention to key words in questions.** Words in boldface type, like **greatest** or **least,** or in all-capital letters, like NOT or ESTIMATE, are important clues to what you need to do.

✔ **Choose the *best* answer.** If one possible answer to a multiple-choice question is partly right and another is completely right, choose the one that is completely right.

✔ **Check your answers.** Estimate to make sure that your answers are in the right ballpark.

✔ **Record your answers carefully.** Check to be sure that you are writing each answer in the correct place. Make sure that the number circles you fill in for a grid match the numbers you have written in the boxes at the top of the grid.

✔ **Take a break.** If you are allowed to take a break, get up and move around. If there is no break, take a mental break. Close your eyes, relax for a few moments, and gather your thoughts before you go on.

REASONING ABOUT WORD PROBLEMS

All the questions that you will find on math exams—not to mention many problems that you will have to solve in your life—require you to reason mathematically. To be successful on math exams, as well as in life, you need to develop the ability to think logically and to work with numbers. You may not think of yourself as a mathematician, but you use math every day; using money, reading music, counting calories, making a budget, keeping score, baking bread, and countless other tasks involve math. Many of the decisions you make will be based on conclusions you draw by using mathematical reasoning.

Most of the questions on math exams are in the form of **word problems.** Each one describes a situation and presents a problem that must be solved by applying math skills. This lesson will teach you how to approach these problems. The next lesson will teach you a number of problem-solving techniques. The last lesson in this Introduction teaches vocabulary that will help you to read word problems with greater understanding. Later in this book, you will learn how to translate word problems into mathematical equations with unknown quantities and then how to solve these equations to find the unknowns. Throughout this book, you will learn terms that will help you to express yourself mathematically, along with skills that will enable you to solve problems using mathematical reasoning.

Here are the steps to take when approaching a word problem:

1. Set your goal. Your first step in solving a word problem should always be to read the problem through to learn what you are being asked to find or to do. Usually, a problem will require that you find a particular number that is the problem's answer, or **solution.** For example, you might be asked to find the number of hours that it takes a plane to travel a particular distance at a particular speed, or you might be asked to find the total price of a group of items being purchased. Here are some other kinds of solutions that you might be asked to find or produce:

COMMON NON-NUMBER SOLUTIONS TO WORD PROBLEMS	
• a graph	• a drawing
• a table	• a sentence or two
• a figure or shape	• a mark (such as circling or underlining)
• a word or group of words	• an explanation of a procedure

Before beginning a problem, always make sure that you understand what you are supposed to find or do.

2. Think about the nature of the solution. Should the solution be a particular kind of number, such as a decimal, a fraction, a percent, or a square root? Should it be in particular units, such as square inches (in.²), miles (mi), quarts (qt), degrees Fahrenheit (°F), or cubic meters (m³)? Before beginning the problem, always make sure that you understand what the solution should be like.

3. Check the problem for essential information. Once you understand what the solution should be like, read the problem carefully to find out what essential, or key, information it contains. That is, after asking yourself, *What am I being asked to find?* and *What should the solution look like?*, ask yourself, *What do I know?* Pay particular attention to words that indicate the key elements or variables involved. For example, a problem might deal with area, length, and width. It might deal with distance, time, and speed.

EXAMPLE   A rectangular backyard patio is 12 feet by 8 feet. What is the area of the patio?

THINKING ABOUT THE PROBLEM   *What am I being asked to find?* The area of the patio. *What should the solution look like?* It should be in square feet (ft²). *What essential information does the problem provide?* The patio is rectangular. It is 12 feet long and 8 feet wide.

4. Make a plan of attack. Decide what operations you need to use. The charts in Lesson 5 of this Introduction describe key words associated with each of the four basic operations (addition, subtraction, multiplication, division). Create an equation or come up with a step-by-step procedure for solving the problem. It may be useful for you to think about similar problems that you have seen in the past and to remember the equations and/or procedures that you used to solve those problems. Another possibility is to use the problem-solving techniques described in Lesson 4.

5. Show your work as necessary. For open-ended questions, it is particularly important to show all your work. If you show all your work, you may be able to get some credit even if your final answer is not correct. Work in appropriate units, and do conversions as necessary. In order to do some problems, you may have to convert the units that you are given. For example, a problem might give information in hours and parts of hours and ask for the answer in minutes. In such cases, you will have to convert the units. For information on converting units, see Unit 4, Lesson 4.3, "Converting Customary and Metric Units."

6. Always check your answer. After solving a problem, check the answer. Make sure that
   • you have provided the type of answer that the problem calls for,
   • you have answered all parts of the question,
   • you have labeled your answer,
   • you have shown your work and provided any explanations required, and
   • your answer makes sense.

For example, if your answer to a problem is that a loaf of bread weighs 28 kilograms, you need to recheck your calculations because that is an unlikely weight for a loaf of bread. It often pays to estimate your answer first, to check your answer against the estimate, and to recheck your calculations. Sometimes, you can check your calculations by reversing them. For example, suppose that you have calculated the difference 524 − 167 = 357. By adding 167 and 357 to get 524, you can check to make sure that your calculation is correct.

Name _____ Class _____ Date _____

Try It Yourself

A. Use the word problem below to answer the multiple-choice questions. Fill in the circle next to the correct answer to each question.

Two hundred light bulbs are packed into cartons. Each carton has a volume of 248 cubic inches. If each carton has a length of 12 inches and a width of 6 inches, what is its height?

1. What are you being asked to find?
   Ⓐ the height of a carton
   Ⓑ the length of a carton
   Ⓒ the number of light bulbs that fit in a carton
   Ⓓ the area of the bottom of a carton

2. What information from the problem will you need in order to solve it?
   Ⓐ the number of light bulbs that are packed in the carton
   Ⓑ the length, width, and weight of the cartons
   Ⓒ the material that the cartons are made of
   Ⓓ the length, width, and volume of a carton

3. How should the solution be expressed?
   Ⓐ in square inches (in.²)   Ⓒ in square feet (ft²)
   Ⓑ in inches (in.)   Ⓓ in cubic inches (in.³)

B. Complete the three parts below. Show all your work. Use additional paper if necessary.

At a car wash, an eighth-grade class raised $520, which was 65% of its goal. How much did the students hope to raise?

Part A What should the solution to this problem look like?

Part B Describe how you would solve the problem.

Part C How can you check that your answer is correct?

Try It Yourself

A. Use the word problem below to answer the multiple-choice questions. Fill in the circle next to the correct answer to each question.

James collects tropical fish. He has a large fish tank that holds about 50 gallons of water and can house 65 fish. The base of the tropical fish tank is 62 centimeters long. The perimeter of the base is 1.92 meters. How wide is the base in meters?

1. What are you being asked to find?
   - Ⓐ the area of the base of the fish tank
   - Ⓑ the capacity of the fish tank
   - Ⓒ the height of the fish tank
   - Ⓓ the width of the base of the fish tank

2. What information from the problem will you need in order to solve it?
   - Ⓐ the length and perimeter of the base of the fish tank
   - Ⓑ the length and area of the base of the fish tank
   - Ⓒ the number of fish in the tank and the number of gallons of water it holds
   - Ⓓ the area of the base and the volume of the fish tank

3. Which step can you take in order to solve the problem?
   - Ⓐ convert the length of the base to meters
   - Ⓑ divide the volume of the tank by the length
   - Ⓒ divide the area of the base by the length of the base
   - Ⓓ convert the volume of the tank to cubic meters

B. Complete the three parts below. Show all your work. Use additional paper if necessary.

A 120-pound carton is unloaded from a truck carrying $5\frac{1}{2}$ tons of cargo. What percent of the total cargo does the carton represent?

Part A What should the solution to this problem look like?

Part B Describe how you would solve the problem.

Part C How can you check that your answer is correct?

PROBLEM-SOLVING STRATEGIES

Types of Thinking in Mathematics and in Everyday Life

In both mathematics and in everyday life, people continually draw conclusions, or **inferences**, from what they have observed or from what they already know. Two types of reasoning that people use to draw conclusions are induction and deduction.

Inductive Reasoning. When you use **inductive reasoning,** you draw a general conclusion based on specific facts. Here is an example of inductive reasoning:

> Observation: Yolanda's cat has a long tail.
>
> Observation: Javier's cat has a long tail.
>
> Conclusion: Therefore, all cats have long tails.

Most of what we learn about the world is based on inductive reasoning. Unfortunately, induction can sometimes lead to **overgeneralizations**—conclusions that are too broad. If you were to decide, based on observation of a couple of cats, that all cats have long tails, you would be right most of the time; however, there are some cats in the world, such as the bobcat and the manx, that have very short tails or no tails at all.

Despite the potential for overgeneralization, inductive reasoning has an important place in mathematics. Thinking inductively can help you to observe mathematical patterns and to solve problems. Consider the following problem:

EXAMPLE Find the next number in the sequence: 1, 2, 4, 7, …

To answer this problem, you might first note specific facts, and then make a guess. For example, if you look at the first two numbers, 1 and 2, you might guess that each number in the sequence is double the one before it, because 2 is twice 1. If you look at the next two numbers, 2 and 4, the guess holds true; the number 2 is twice the number 4. The same pattern does not apply, however, to the next two numbers. The number 7 is not twice the number 4, so doubling the last number will not always give you the correct answer.

Going back to the first two numbers, you might notice that if you add 1 to the first number, you get the second number. If you add 2 to the second number, you get the third number. If you add 3 to the third number, you get the fourth number. Considering a few specific examples can lead you to a general conclusion: each time, add 1 more than you did the time before.

$$1 + 1 = 2 \qquad 2 + 2 = 4 \qquad 4 + 3 = 7 \qquad 7 + 4 = 11$$

By induction, or looking at specific examples, you can draw the general conclusion that to get the next number in the sequence, you have to add 1 more than you added the previous time.

Here is another example of inductive reasoning in mathematics: an **even number** is any number that can be divided by 2 without a remainder. Examples include 2, 4, 6, 8, 10, 12, 14, 16, and 18. A **prime number** is any whole number larger than 1 that can be divided without a remainder only by 1 and itself. Examples include 2, 3, 5, 7, and 11. Now consider these examples:

$$12 = 7 + 5 \qquad 18 = 11 + 7$$

Based on specific facts like these, you might draw the general conclusion that every even number, such as 12 or 18, can be written as the sum of two primes. This idea is known as the **Goldbach Conjecture,** named for a German mathematician, Christian Goldbach, who lived from 1690 to 1764. No one has ever found an exception to Goldbach's rule, but neither has anyone proved that it is always true. When you do inductive reasoning—when you make a generalization based on specific examples—you can discover important rules of thumb. Inductive reasoning does not lead to absolute certainty, however.

Deductive Reasoning. Mathematicians sometimes use inductive reasoning, but mathematics itself is based primarily on deductive reasoning. When you use **deductive reasoning,** you draw a conclusion that has to be true if

- the assumptions that you made are true, and
- each step in your reasoning is valid.

Here is an example of deductive reasoning:

> Assumption: Socrates is a man.
>
> Assumption: All men are mortal.
>
> Conclusion: Socrates is mortal.

You can tell that this is a piece of deductive reasoning because if the assumptions are true, then the conclusion has to be true.

Here is an example of deductive reasoning with algebraic equations:

> Given: $a = b$
>
> Given: $b = c$
>
> Conclusion: $a = c$

Again, if the given facts are true, the conclusion has to be true, so this is a piece of deductive reasoning. Proper deductive reasoning leads to absolute certainty and is the foundation of mathematical thinking. Mathematicians use deductive reasoning to create proofs of their conclusions. A **proof** is a logical argument showing that the conclusion must be true.

Reasoning about Math Problems

Usually, in real life and in mathematics, you cannot simply sit down and quickly think up a complete deductive argument that leads to an absolutely certain conclusion. Real problems, in mathematics and in life, tend to be messier. You start off being uncertain and perhaps confused about how to proceed. Then you try out some approaches to solving the problem, and eventually you hit on one that works.

Solving problems in mathematics and in life can be a lot easier if you use a problem-solving strategy, or **heuristic.** A heuristic is simply a way to go about tackling a problem. The following chart describes some possibilities:

PROBLEM-SOLVING STRATEGIES (HEURISTICS)

Divide-and-Conquer Method. Break the problem into parts and solve the parts separately.

EXAMPLE Maria's point total during the basketball game was 20 points higher than the average for the other players on her team. If the other players scored 2, 12, 7, and 23 points, what was Maria's score?

To solve the problem, break it into two parts. First, figure out the average for the other players:

$$2 + 12 + 7 + 23 = 44$$
$$44 \div 4 = 11$$

The average score for the other 4 players is 11.

Second, figure out Maria's score by adding 20 to the other players' average:

$$11 + 20 = 31$$

Simplification Method. Simplify the elements in the problem first. Then do the calculation.

EXAMPLE In a recent election in Centerville, USA, 450 people went to the polls, and 150 of those people voted for the Democratic candidate for mayor. If 3,600,000 people in the state vote in the race for governor, and if the proportion of Democratic voters in the state is the same as in Centerville, approximately how many votes will be cast for the Democratic candidate for governor?

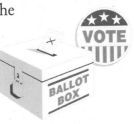

To solve this problem, first set up a fraction. One hundred fifty people out of 450 voted Democratic in the race for mayor; that's $\frac{150}{450}$. If you simplify that fraction by dividing both the top and bottom by 150, you find that 1 out of 3, or one-third, of the voters voted Democratic. To get the answer, you simply have to divide the total number of voters in the state by 3: $3,600,000 \div 3 = 1,200,000$.

Diagramming Method. Draw a diagram or sketch to represent the problem.

EXAMPLE Tricia plants a rectangular garden that measures 25 feet by 40 feet. She puts up a fence around three sides of the garden. One long side does not need a fence because Tricia's garage walls off that side of the garden. How much fencing does Tricia use?

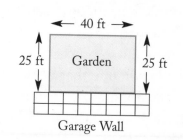

Make a sketch of the problem situation to see how much fencing Tricia needs for three sides of the garden. Label the number of feet of fencing used on each of the three sides. Then add up the number of feet of fencing used. The solution is 25 + 40 + 25 = 90, or 90 feet of fencing.

Trial-and-Error Method, or Back-Solving. Try various possibilities in turn, one after the other. For example, you might try the various answers given in a multiple-choice question to see which one makes an equation true.

EXAMPLE A theater company held 5 performances of a play. At each performance, the audience was twice as large as the audience at the previous performance. If the total number of people who attended the play was 6,200, how many people came to the first performance?

(A) 2   (B) 20   (C) 40   (D) 200

One way to solve this problem would be to make an equation. If you let a equal the number of people in the audience on the first night, then the total number would be

$$a + 2a + 4a + 8a + 16a = 6{,}200$$

You might find it easier just to try each answer to see which one makes sense.

$2 + 4 + 8 + 16 + 32 = 62$

$20 + 40 + 80 + 160 + 320 = 620$

$40 + 80 + 160 + 320 + 640 = 1{,}240$

$200 + 400 + 800 + 1{,}600 + 3{,}200 = 6{,}200$

Answer D, 200, is the correct answer.

Goal Analysis Method. Think about the **initial state** (what you know) and the **goal state** (what you want to accomplish or find). Then, take steps to change the initial state into the goal state.

EXAMPLE Solve this equation: $x + 23 = 2x - 7$

The initial state is given. The final state that you want to reach is one in which you have x by itself on one side and some number on the other side of the equation.

> Given: $x + 23 = 2x - 7$ Goal: $x = $ _?_

Take steps to change one into the other:

STEP 1: Eliminate the -7 by adding 7 to both sides.

$$x + 23 + 7 = 2x - 7 + 7$$
$$x + 30 = 2x$$

STEP 2: Eliminate the x on the left by subtracting x from both sides.

$$x + 30 = 2x$$
$$x - x + 30 = 2x - x$$
$$30 = x$$

Estimation Method. Often it will help to **estimate,** or make an approximate guess about, what the answer will be. Then you can solve the problem and check whether your solution is close to your estimate. If the solution and the estimate are very different from one another, you will need to check your work to see if or where you have made an error in your calculations.

EXAMPLE What is the sum of $28 + 71 + 133 + 299$?

Ⓐ 481   Ⓑ 531   Ⓒ 571   Ⓓ 591

You can estimate the sum by quickly adding $30 + 70 + 130 + 300$, which is 530. This is closest to answer B, so B is probably correct.

Equation Method. Often, to solve a problem, you will need to create your own **equation**—a number sentence containing variables and an equals sign. A **variable** is a letter, such as x, y, a, b, A, or B, that stands for a numerical value. It usually stands for the unknown quantity in the problem.

EXAMPLE Paula spent a total of $61 on a trip to a museum. She spent $8 for the admission ticket and $5 on food, and she bought 4 books at the gift shop. All the books were the same price. Find the price of each book.

Start by choosing a variable to stand for the unknown amount you want to find. Since you want to find the price of each book, let b stand for the unknown quantity in this problem. Then write an equation representing the information given in the problem:

ticket	+	food	+	books	=	total spent
$8	+	$5	+	$(4 \times b)$	=	$61

Your equation is $8 + 5 + 4b = 61$. If you solve this equation for b, you will have the answer to the problem. The price of each book is $12.

Try It Yourself

A. Use the word problem below to answer the multiple-choice questions. Fill in the circle next to the correct answer to each question.

The area of a square room is about 800 square feet. What is the length of one side of the room?

1. Assume you were given four answer choices for the problem. How could you use the trial-and-error method (back-solving) to choose the best answer?
   - Ⓐ Square each answer choice and see which one comes closest to 800.
   - Ⓑ Multiply each answer choice by 4 and see which one equals 800.
   - Ⓒ Divide each answer choice into 800 and see which answer is the largest.
   - Ⓓ Divide each answer choice into 800 and see which answer is the smallest.

2. If s = the length of one side of the room, which equation could be used to solve the problem?
   - Ⓐ $2s = 800$ Ⓑ $s^2 = 800$ Ⓒ $800 \div s = 2$ Ⓓ $4s = 800$

3. Which of the following is the best estimate for the size of the room in the problem?
   - Ⓐ 8 ft by 8 ft   Ⓑ 10 ft by 10 ft   Ⓒ 28 ft by 28 ft   Ⓓ 35 ft by 35 ft

4. A student drew a diagram for the problem. She drew a square and labeled each side 800. What is wrong with this student's technique?
   - Ⓐ She should have drawn a rectangle instead of a square.
   - Ⓑ The area 800 is not the square of a whole number, so you cannot use a diagram.
   - Ⓒ The area is 800 square feet. The length of each side is not 800.
   - Ⓓ The area of the square is the unknown and should be marked x.

B. Complete the two parts below. Use additional paper if necessary.

Last year, Ruthie ran a marathon in 4 hours, 6 minutes, and 38 seconds. This year, her finishing time was 3 hours, 58 minutes, and 10 seconds. How much did her time improve?

Part A Explain how to use estimation for this problem.

Part B Find the exact solution. Show your work.

Try It Yourself

A. Fill in the circle next to the correct answer to each multiple-choice question.

1. How can you use estimation to solve this problem?

    The price of a computer decreased $410.50. If the price last year was $1,609, what was the percent of decrease?

    Ⓐ $410.50 is less than half of $1,609, so the answer is about 50%.

    Ⓑ $1,600 − $400 is $1,200, so the price went down about $1,200.

    Ⓒ $400 is 25% of $1,600, so the answer will be a little more than 25%.

    Ⓓ Four times $400 is $1,600, so the answer will be about 40%.

2. Use trial-and-error to find the solution of the equation $-5x - 1 = 3x + 15$.

    Ⓐ −2　　　　Ⓑ −1　　　　Ⓒ 0　　　　Ⓓ 1

3. Eve wants to build a tower out of blocks. There will be 1 block at the top, 4 blocks arranged in a square on the next layer down, 9 blocks on the third layer, 16 on the fourth layer, and so on. The tower is going to be 10 blocks high. Which of the following is the best strategy for determining the number of blocks she will need on the bottom layer?

    Ⓐ Trial-and-Error: Try different possibilities for the number of blocks on the bottom.

    Ⓑ Diagramming: Draw a picture of the tower and count the number of blocks on the bottom.

    Ⓒ Estimation: If there are 14 blocks in the first three layers, estimate that there would be about 3 times as many blocks in 10 layers.

    Ⓓ Inductive Reasoning: Find the pattern for the number of blocks in each layer. Layer 1 has 1 block (1^2); layer 2 has 4 blocks (2^2); layer 3 has 9 blocks (3^2). You could draw the conclusion that layer 10 has 10^2 blocks.

B. Complete the two parts below. Use additional paper if necessary.

Carrie and Kurt were eating at a restaurant. They spent $16 for their entrees, $4 for drinks, and $5 for dessert. They gave the server a 20% tip. How much did they pay altogether?

Part A Explain how to divide and conquer to solve this problem.

Part B Solve the problem. Show your work.

UNDERSTANDING MATHEMATICAL LANGUAGE

Your first step in solving any word problem is to read the problem carefully and identify what you are being asked to find. Notice any special mathematical language that could provide clues to the calculations you will need to perform. Understanding terms such as *area*, *simplify*, and *exponent* may be important in planning your solution. Key mathematical terms such as these are in bold type throughout this book. They are also defined in the Glossary.

In addition to mathematical terms, word problems can include common, everyday words such as *more*, *left*, *share*, and *total*. Although words of this type are not included in the Glossary, they often help you to solve problems because they can indicate which operation is appropriate. The four most common operations are addition, subtraction, multiplication, and division.

Words and Phrases Associated with Addition. Addition is the joining together of quantities or groups. Here are examples of addition situations. Notice how the boldfaced words provide clues to the operation you are to perform.

Addition Words and Phrases	Example
and	What is the weight of a 950-pound horse **and** a 98-pound rider? (950 + 98)
combine	The jeweler **combined** 1.2 ounces of gold with 3.4 ounces of silver. (1.2 + 3.4)
in all	Val bought a total of 18 tomato plants, 20 squash plants, and 35 bean plants. How many plants did she buy **in all**? (18 + 20 + 35)
increased by	Precipitation in the area was only 1.5 inches in 1998, but it **increased by** 2 inches the following year. (1.5 + 2)
more, more than	Alex's score on the second exam was 14 points **more than** his score of 63 on the first. (14 + 63)
sum	The **sum** of the terms in the infinite sequence $1, \frac{1}{2}, \frac{1}{4}, \frac{1}{8}, ..., \frac{1}{n}$ is 2. $(1 + \frac{1}{2} + \frac{1}{4} + \frac{1}{8} + ... + \frac{1}{n} = 2)$
tally	John wrote 4 songs. Andrea wrote twice as many as John. The director **tallied** the number of songs. $[4 + (2 \times 4)]$
total	Six European countries signed the treaty, as did 3 Asian countries. What was the **total** number of signatories? (6 + 3)

Words and Phrases Associated with Subtraction.

Subtraction situations involve removing or taking away quantities. They may also compare two amounts by finding their difference.

Subtraction Words and Phrases	Example
decrease	The zookeeper **decreased** the amount of hay, h, that he fed the elephants by 2 bales. $(h - 2)$
deduct	Jon asked that $12.00 be **deducted** from his wages, w, each month for a company savings plan. $(w - 12)$
difference	The **difference** between 9 and 5 is 4. $(9 - 5 = 4)$
diminish	There were 48 eagles in the park. By the next year, that number had been **diminished** by 7. $(48 - 7)$
fewer	There are 24 students in Ms. Polazzo's class. There are 3 **fewer** in Ms. Goldstein's class. $(24 - 3)$
left, left over	Sid had saved $423. He used $85 for a new jacket. How much was **left**? $(423 - 85)$
less, less than	The gas tank of car A holds 20 gallons of fuel. The tank of car B holds 4 gallons **less**. $(20 - 4)$
more, more than	Hal collected $258 for the fund-raising drive. Shari collected $314. How much **more** did Shari collect? $(314 - 258)$
take, take away	There are 12 canoes at the camp. If you **take away** 3 canoes, there are 9 left. $(12 - 3 = 9)$
reduce	The original plan was for a 2,800 ft² house. The owners decided to **reduce** the size of the house by 800 ft². $(2,800 - 800)$
remain, remainder	If 4 of the 96 teachers at the school leave, how many will **remain**? $(96 - 4)$
remove	The instrument had 36 strings. Clio **removed** half of them. $(36 - 18)$

Key words and phrases are one clue to help you choose an operation, but you should always read the entire problem carefully to understand the context of the clue words. Compare these uses of the key word *more:*

1. The membership goal is 125 new members. So far, 65 have signed up. How many more people are needed to meet the goal? (subtraction: $125 - 65$)

2. Jared bicycled 20 miles on Saturday. On Sunday, he bicycled 4 miles more than he had on Saturday. How many miles did he bike on Sunday? (addition: $20 + 4$)

3. Fiona has finished $\frac{7}{8}$ of the homework assignment. Alex has finished $\frac{2}{3}$. Who has completed more of the assignment? (comparison: $\frac{7}{8} > \frac{2}{3}$)

Words and Phrases Associated with Multiplication. Addition and multiplication both involve finding a total amount. The operations differ in that multiplication adds only equal groups or equal amounts; it is really a special, fast way to add like quantities. Here are some examples of multiplication situations.

Multiplication Words and Phrases	Example
double, triple, quadruple, etc.	Ellen planned to make 4 gallons of punch. Ivan thought they should make **double** that amount. (4×2)
factor	The **factors** of 10 are 1, 2, 5, and 10. ($2 \times 5 = 10$; $1 \times 10 = 10$)
multiple	The number 12 is a **multiple** of 1, 2, 3, 4, 6, and 12. ($1 \times 12 = 12$, $2 \times 6 = 12$, $3 \times 4 = 12$)
of (with a fraction)	Two-thirds **of** the 480 students in the school voted for Javier. ($\frac{2}{3} \times 480$)
product	The **product** of 9 and 9 is 81. ($9 \times 9 = 81$)
squared, cubed	Ten **cubed** is 1,000. ($10 \times 10 \times 10 = 1,000$)
times	Twenty **times** $\frac{1}{4}$ is 5. ($20 \times \frac{1}{4} = 5$)
twice, three times, four times, etc.	**Twice** 114 is 228. ($114 \times 2 = 228$)

Many geometric formulas require multiplication. Here are some of the most frequently used formulas that involve multiplication.

To Find	Use This Formula
area of rectangle	$A = lw$
area of square	$A = s^2$
area of parallelogram	$A = bh$
area of triangle	$A = \frac{1}{2}bh$

To Find	Use This Formula
volume of rectangular box	$V = lwh$
volume of cube	$V = s^3$
circumference of circle	$C = \pi d$
area of circle	$A = \pi r^2$

Words and Phrases Associated with Division. A division problem may involve finding the number of equal parts or finding the size of one of those equal parts. Situations in which people are sharing equally are often division problems. Like multiplication, division may be needed in problems about area, speed, rate, and percent. Also, remember that fractions and ratios are ways of indicating quotients, so they also involve division.

Division Words and Phrases	Example
average	Ruth scored 96 points in 8 basketball games. What is her **average** score? $(96 \div 8)$
distributed equally or evenly	Alana **distributed** the 24 party favors **evenly** among the 6 guests. How many did each guest get? $(24 \div 6)$
half, third, fourth, etc.	**Half** of 14 is 7. $(14 \div 2 = 7)$
out of	There were 16 **out of** 64 club members present. $(16 \div 64 = 0.25 = 25\%)$
per	The rate of defects was 86 **per** thousand. $(86 \div 1,000)$
quotient	Find the **quotient** of 120 and 8. $(120 \div 8)$
separate	The teacher **separated** the 24 students into 3 equal groups. $(24 \div 3)$
shared equally, divided equally	The three investors **shared** a profit of $24,000 **equally**. $(24,000 \div 3)$
split, split up	Eight slices of pizza were **split** 4 ways. $(8 \div 4)$
unit price or cost	Find the **unit price** if 9 apples cost $4.50. $(\$4.50 \div 9)$

Many problems involve more than one operation. Make sure that you apply the correct operations in the correct order.

EXAMPLES Identify the necessary operations and explain how to solve each problem.

1. Oliver bought 3 shirts for $17 each. How much money did he have left from $60? (Multiply 3 times $17. Subtract the answer from $60.)

2. Arnie and 2 friends spent a total of $22 at the movies. Arnie paid $6 for snacks, and his 2 friends shared the rest of the cost equally. How much did each of Arnie's friends spend? (Subtract $6 from $22. Divide the answer by 2.)

Name _____ Class _____ Date _____

Try It Yourself

A. Fill in the circle next to the correct answer to each multiple-choice question.

1. What expression can be used to solve this problem?

   Sam's test scores were 90, 88, 96 and 94. What was his average?

   Ⓐ $(90 + 88 + 96 + 94) - 4$ Ⓒ $(90 + 88 + 96 + 94) + 4$

   Ⓑ $(90 + 88 + 96 + 94) \div 4$ Ⓓ $(90 + 88 + 96 + 94) \times 4$

2. What expression can be used to solve this problem?

   Two-thirds of the 420 students in the school play intramural sports. How many students participate in intramurals?

   Ⓐ $\frac{2}{3} \div 420$ Ⓑ $420 \div \frac{2}{3}$ Ⓒ $\frac{2}{3} \times 420$ Ⓓ $420 - \frac{2}{3}$

3. Matt has a part-time job. He works a total of 12 hours during the week and 8 hours on weekends. Which question can be answered using multiplication?

   Ⓐ How many more hours does he work during the week than on the weekends?

   Ⓑ If he is paid $9.50 per hour, how much does he make on the weekends?

   Ⓒ How many hours in all does he work per week?

   Ⓓ What is his average number of hours per day?

4. Which expression can be used to solve this problem?

   A scale model of a truck is $\frac{1}{10}$ the actual size. If the truck is 8 feet long, how long is the model?

   Ⓐ $8 \div \frac{1}{10}$ Ⓑ $\frac{1}{10} \div 8$ Ⓒ $\frac{1}{10} \times 8$ Ⓓ $8 - \frac{1}{10}$

B. Identify the operations you need, and explain how to solve each problem.

1. The area of a rectangular room is 120 square feet. How much larger is this room than a kitchen with an area of 100 square feet?

2. What is the cost per ounce of a 42-ounce bottle of dishwashing liquid that is priced at $2.59?

Try It Yourself

A. Fill in the circle next to the correct answer to each multiple-choice question.

1. What expression can be used to solve this problem?

   A taxi charges $1.20 per mile. How long was a ride that cost $12?

   Ⓐ 1.20×12 Ⓑ $1.20 \div 12$ Ⓒ $12 \div 1.20$ Ⓓ $1.2 - 1.20$

2. Which is the best operation to use to solve this problem?

   Each of the six faces of a cube has an area of 25 square centimeters. What is the total surface area of the cube?

   Ⓐ addition Ⓑ subtraction Ⓒ multiplication Ⓓ division

3. Kyle runs every day to train for a marathon. He runs 30 miles during the week and 20 miles each weekend. Which question can be answered using division?

   Ⓐ How many fewer miles does he run on the weekends than during the week?

   Ⓑ If he runs a 10-minute mile, how much time does he spend running per week?

   Ⓒ What is the average number of miles he runs per day during the week?

   Ⓓ At this rate, how many miles would he run per year?

4. Which expression can be used to solve this problem?

   A theater was $\frac{7}{8}$ full. If the theater can seat 522 people, how many seats were filled?

   Ⓐ $\frac{7}{8} \times 522$ Ⓑ $7 \times 8 \times 522$ Ⓒ $7 \div 8 \div 522$ Ⓓ $7 \times 8 \div 522$

B. Identify the operations you need, and explain how to solve each problem.

1. Janine drove at an average speed of 50 miles per hour for $2\frac{1}{2}$ hours. How far did she drive?

2. The area of a rectangle is 221 square feet. If the length of the rectangle is 13 feet, what is the width?

DISCOVERING NUMBERS

This lesson addresses Benchmarks MA.A.1.2.1, MA.A.1.3.2, and MA.A.1.3.3 of the Sunshine State Standards.

The Challenge

Can subtraction be done using just whole numbers? Explain why or why not.

Learning the Ropes

Natural Numbers. No one knows where and when numbers were first discovered. Until recent times, some hunting and gathering tribes had names only for "one," "two," and "many." At some time in the remote past, thousands of years ago, people figured out that they could pair up things in the world with abstract symbols and count them. The earliest numbers were the **counting numbers,** also known as the **natural numbers:**

Natural numbers: {1, 2, 3, 4, ...}

Whole Numbers. Between 500 B.C. and A.D. 600, some unknown genius improved the number system by creating a symbol to stand for nothing: the number zero (0). Robert Kaplan, author of *The Nothing That Is: A Natural History of Zero,* thinks that the shape of the number might be due to the fact that early people in Babylon, India, and Greece counted by placing pebbles on sand. When a pebble was picked up, what was left was a zero-shaped indentation in the sand.

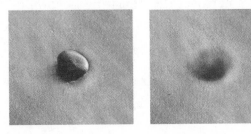

Early people noticed that a round hole in the sand where a pebble had been showed the absence of the pebble. For this reason, they may have started using a round-shaped character to indicate zero, or the absence of a quantity.

By adding zero to the natural numbers, we get the **whole numbers:**

Whole numbers: {0, 1, 2, 3, 4, ...}

The discovery of zero made possible the development of decimal numbers like 10, 100, and 1,000, which use zero as a placeholder.

Math in History

In some languages, the names for natural numbers are based on tens because people counted on their ten fingers. In other languages, the names are based on twenties because people counted on their ten fingers and ten toes. In Inupik, the language of Greenland, there are specific names for the first five natural numbers. The next five are named *second hand, second hand two, second hand three,* and so on. The next five are *first foot, first foot two,* and so on, followed by *second foot, second foot two,* and so on. For example, the word for "nineteen" in Inupik is *arfersaheq-sisamat,* which literally means "second foot four."

Integers. Around A.D. 650, people in India discovered numbers that are less than zero, which they used in bookkeeping to keep track of debts. If we add these negative numbers to the whole numbers, we get the set of numbers known as the **integers:**

Integers: {..., ⁻4, ⁻3, ⁻2, ⁻1, 0, 1, 2, 3, 4, ...}

The number-line model below shows numbers of feet above and below sea level.

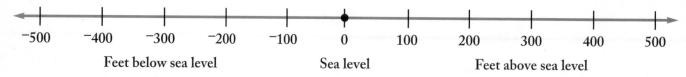

| ⁻500 | ⁻400 | ⁻300 | ⁻200 | ⁻100 | 0 | 100 | 200 | 300 | 400 | 500 |

Feet below sea level   Sea level   Feet above sea level

Fractions. Around 569 B.C., a boy was born in ancient Greece who would grow up to become the famous philosopher and mathematician known as Pythagoras. Pythagoras started a secret society. His disciples were sworn to vegetarianism and were taught that all things in nature could be described using whole numbers or ratios of whole numbers known as **fractions.** You will learn more about fractions later in this unit. For now, it is enough to say that a fraction is a number written using two numbers, one above the other, separated by a line:

Examples of fractions: $\frac{1}{2}, \frac{3}{4}, \frac{6}{2}, -\frac{2}{1}, \frac{214}{17}$

Rational Numbers. Any number that can be expressed as a fraction in which the top number and the bottom number are both integers and the bottom number is not 0 is called a **rational number.** A rational number can be expressed as a **repeating decimal,** one that has a digit or sequence of digits that repeats indefinitely. To **convert,** or change, a fraction into a repeating decimal, simply divide the top number by the bottom number:

Examples of repeating decimals: $\frac{1}{3} = 1 \div 3 = 0.3333...$, or $0.\overline{33}$

$\frac{1}{7} = 1 \div 7 = 0.142857142857...$, or $0.\overline{142857}$

$\frac{284}{99} = 284 \div 99 = 2.8686...$, or $2.\overline{86}$

A repeating decimal is indicated by a bar over the repeating portion of the decimal, as shown in the examples above. You can also use **ellipsis points** (...) for repeating decimals. You should include the repeated pattern at least two times.

You can locate rational numbers on a number line. Each point on the number line represents a number that is greater than any number to its left. For example, $-1\frac{1}{2}$ is greater than ⁻2 and less than ⁻1.2.

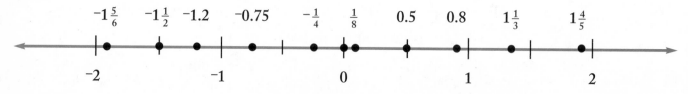

| $-1\frac{5}{6}$ | $-1\frac{1}{2}$ | ⁻1.2 | ⁻0.75 | $-\frac{1}{4}$ | $\frac{1}{8}$ | 0.5 | 0.8 | $1\frac{1}{3}$ | $1\frac{4}{5}$ |

⁻2   ⁻1   0   1   2

Irrational Numbers. As you saw on the previous page, some numbers are **infinite decimals**—they have an infinite number of decimal places. Repeating decimals are infinite decimals with digits that keep on repeating forever. Some infinite decimals, however, do not repeat; the digits keep on changing forever. Here are some examples: 1.12134516… and 0.37037003700037…. The ellipsis points (…) show that the numbers go on forever. Such numbers, ones that can be expressed as decimals that do not repeat, are called **irrational numbers.**

According to legend, some followers of Pythagoras were traveling by ship when one person among them discovered irrational numbers. The other Pythagoreans were so upset by the discovery that they threw the inventor of irrational numbers overboard and swore the others on the ship to secrecy! Who would have thought that doing math could be such a dangerous activity!

Examples of irrational numbers: $\sqrt{2}$, π, 3.14159…, 1.93860275…, 222.2275601…

It is impossible to write an irrational number exactly in decimal form since it has an infinite number of nonrepeating decimal places. To show that the number is *approximately* equal to another, you can use the symbol ≈. For example, 3.14159… ≈ 3.14.

Numbers such as the square root of 2 are irrational numbers. You can estimate the value of the square root of 2 as being between the square root of 1 and the square root of 4. Since the square root of 1 is 1 and the square root of 4 is 2, the square root of 2 is between 1 and 2.

Real Numbers. The rational numbers plus the irrational numbers make up the set of **real numbers.** The set of real numbers includes every single point on a number line. All the math that you will do in this book will deal with real numbers.

```
◄──┼────┼────┼────┼────┼────┼────┼────┼────┼────┼────►
  -5   -4   -3   -2   -1    0    1    2    3    4    5
```

Math in Use: Bookkeeping   To see how integers can be used in bookkeeping to make a budget, suppose that you have a part-time job at which you earn $40 a week. During the next two weeks, you plan to spend about $25 on a pair of new pants, $8 on a movie ticket, and $4 a week on snacks from the school cafeteria. You might make a budget for yourself that looks like this:

		Balance
Beginning Balance		$ 0
Earnings, Week 1	+$40	40
Snacks, Week 1	−4	36
Movie Ticket	−8	28
Earnings, Week 2	+40	68
New Pants	−25	43
Snacks, Week 2	−4	39

Your budget, using positive and negative numbers, shows that you will have about $39 left at the end of the two weeks.

Unit 1: Number Sense, Concepts, and Operations

Meeting the Challenge

Sometimes math questions require you to explain your answers. The Challenge question at the beginning of this lesson is an example of the kind of question you might see. To answer the Challenge, follow these steps:

STEP 1: Recall what the whole numbers are. Whole numbers are zero plus the natural numbers: {0, 1, 2, 3, 4, …}.

STEP 2: Try some subtraction problems to see if they can be done using just whole numbers.

$7 - 3 = 4$ This operation can be done using just whole numbers.

$7 - 8 = {}^-1$ This operation cannot be done using just whole numbers. The answer is $^-1$, which is an integer but not a whole number.

STEP 3: Write your answer, describing all the steps in your thinking. The answer to the Challenge is that subtraction cannot be done using just the whole numbers, because some subtraction problems require negative numbers, which are not part of the whole numbers. For example, 7 minus 8 equals $^-1$.

Another Way As you have seen in this lesson, to convert a fraction into a decimal, you divide the denominator into the numerator. This is easy to do when using a calculator. Sometimes, however, you will not have a calculator handy. An easy way to convert some fractions to decimals is first to change the fraction into an equivalent one that has a power of ten (10, 100, 1,000, and so on) as its denominator. For example, to convert $\frac{1}{2}$ into a decimal, multiply the top and the bottom by 5 to get $\frac{5}{10}$. Then rewrite the numerator by moving the decimal point over one place to the left for each zero in the denominator. The answer is $\frac{1}{2} = 0.5$.

Try It Yourself

A. Fill in the circle next to the correct answer to each multiple-choice question.

1. Which of the following is the smallest set of numbers that you need in order to count the number of people in a crowded soccer stadium?
   Ⓐ the natural numbers   Ⓒ the integers
   Ⓑ the whole numbers   Ⓓ the rational numbers

2. Which of the following is the smallest set of numbers that you need in order to keep track of how many dollars you have or you owe to other people?
   Ⓐ the natural numbers   Ⓒ the integers
   Ⓑ the whole numbers   Ⓓ the rational numbers

3. Which of the following is NOT a rational number?
   Ⓐ 4   Ⓑ $\frac{4}{2}$ Ⓒ $\frac{4}{0}$ Ⓓ $\frac{444}{-4}$

4. Which of the following is an irrational number?
   Ⓐ 0.22222…   Ⓑ 0.323232…   Ⓒ 0.1121231234…   Ⓓ 0.285714285714

5. Which of the following shows the numbers $1.3, -\frac{1}{8}, -2, -1\frac{1}{2}, \frac{5}{8}, 2$ in order from least to greatest?
   Ⓐ $-\frac{1}{8}, -1\frac{1}{2}, -2, \frac{5}{8}, 1.3, 2$ Ⓒ $-1\frac{1}{2}, -2, -\frac{1}{8}, \frac{5}{8}, 1.3, 2$
   Ⓑ $-2, -1\frac{1}{2}, -\frac{1}{8}, \frac{5}{8}, 1.3, 2$ Ⓓ $-2, -\frac{1}{8}, -1\frac{1}{2}, \frac{5}{8}, 1.3, 2$

B. Each of the following fractions represents a repeating decimal and is a rational number. Use a calculator to determine what that decimal is. Write your answers on the lines provided.

Example: $\dfrac{2}{9} = 0.2222…$

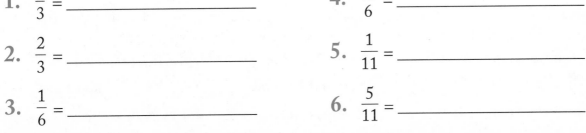

1. $\dfrac{1}{3} =$ _____

2. $\dfrac{2}{3} =$ _____

3. $\dfrac{1}{6} =$ _____

4. $\dfrac{5}{6} =$ _____

5. $\dfrac{1}{11} =$ _____

6. $\dfrac{5}{11} =$ _____

Name_____ Class _____ Date _____

Try It Yourself

A. Fill in the circle next to the correct answer to each multiple-choice question.

1. Which of the following is NOT a natural number?
   Ⓐ 0   Ⓑ 1   Ⓒ 2   Ⓓ 3

2. Which of the following fractions does NOT represent an integer?
   Ⓐ $\frac{1}{1}$ Ⓑ $\frac{3}{1}$ Ⓒ $\frac{330}{11}$ Ⓓ $\frac{145}{999}$

3. Which of the following numbers is a natural number?
   Ⓐ 9,562,125   Ⓑ −6   Ⓒ $\frac{1}{256}$ Ⓓ 3.14159…

B. Complete the three parts below. Show all your work.

Use your knowledge of number sets to answer the following questions.

Part A What pattern do you notice when you divide each of the natural numbers from 1 through 8 by 9? For example, what is $\frac{1}{9}$, $\frac{2}{9}$, $\frac{3}{9}$, $\frac{4}{9}$, and so on? Do these numbers belong to the set of rational numbers or irrational numbers? Explain your answer.

Part B Which of the following is the smallest set that contains all the numbers that result from multiplying whole numbers? Explain your answer.

     Natural Numbers   Whole Numbers   Integers

     Rational Numbers   Irrational Numbers   Real Numbers

Part C Which of the following is the smallest set that contains all the numbers that result from dividing whole numbers? Explain your answer.

     Natural Numbers   Whole Numbers   Integers

     Rational Numbers   Irrational Numbers   Real Numbers

ABSOLUTE VALUE

This lesson addresses Benchmarks MA.A.1.3.1, MA.A.1.3.2, and MA.A.1.3.3 of the Sunshine State Standards.

The Challenge

Your class divides into three teams to play an estimation game. The teams try to guess how many pennies are in a jar. Each team member submits one guess. When all the entries have been submitted, your teacher records the results by writing how much each guess was above (+) or below (−) the actual number of pennies. Here are the results:

Team A	Team B	Team C
1. +121	1. + 59	1. +291
2. +186	2. − 251	2. − 156
3. + 82	3. − 86	3. + 99
4. +112	4. − 130	4. + 84
5. − 197	5. − 117	5. − 122
6. − 44	6. +209	6. + 45
7. + 38	7. +232	7. − 210

You can calculate who won in two different ways. One way is to find the sum of each column and divide by 7 to find the average for the *whole* team. Another way is to add up the absolute values of the numbers in each column and divide by 7 to find the average error for *each* team member. Try it both ways.

Learning the Ropes

The **absolute value** of a number refers to its **magnitude**—that is, its size—without consideration of its positive or negative nature. You can also think of absolute value as the distance of a number from zero. The symbol for absolute value is a pair of straight lines, one on either side of the number.

EXAMPLES   the absolute value of 45 = $|45|$ = 45

the absolute value of negative 78 = $|^-78|$ = 78

the absolute value of negative 4.689 = $|^-4.689|$ = 4.689

the absolute value of negative 3 plus 1 = $|^-3 + 1|$ = $|^-2|$ = 2

When you calculate absolute value, first find the value of the expression inside the lines. Then take its absolute value, as in the last example.

Unit 1: Number Sense, Concepts, and Operations

Meeting the Challenge

To answer the Challenge, you must use the concept of absolute value to look at a set of data in different ways.

STEP 1: To determine which team's *average* came closest to the actual value, first add all seven guesses, taking into consideration the positive and negative signs. Divide each sum by 7 to find out how much the average of all the guesses for each team differed from the actual value.

Team A $\quad 121 + 186 + 82 + 112 - 197 - 44 + 38 \ = \ +298 \qquad\qquad 298 \div 7 \ \approx \ +43$

Team B $\quad 59 - 251 - 86 - 130 - 117 + 209 + 232 \ = \ -84 \qquad\qquad -84 \div 7 \ = \ -12$

Team C $\quad 291 - 156 + 99 + 84 - 122 + 45 - 210 \ = \ +31 \qquad\qquad 31 \div 7 \ \approx \ +4$

The members of Teams A and C generally guessed too high (+), and members of Team B generally guessed too low (−). The average of the guesses for Team A was off by about 43, for Team B by 12, and for Team C by only about 4. If the winner were determined this way, Team C would win.

STEP 2: To determine which team's *individual* guesses were closest to the actual number, add the absolute values of all the guesses for each team. Then divide the totals by 7.

Team A $\quad |121| + |186| + |82| + |112| + |{-}197| + |{-}44| + |38| \ = \ 780 \qquad 780 \div 7 \approx 111$

Team B $\quad |59| + |{-}251| + |{-}86| + |{-}130| + |{-}117| + |209| + |232| \ = \ 1{,}084 \qquad 1{,}084 \div 7 \approx 155$

Team C $\quad |291| + |{-}156| + |99| + |84| + |{-}122| + |45| + |{-}210| \ = \ 1{,}007 \qquad 1{,}007 \div 7 \approx 144$

The individual guesses on Team A were closest to the actual number; on average, they were off by only about 111.

The answer to the Challenge is that the average of Team C's guesses was closest to the correct value, but the members of Team A made the closest individual guesses. Using the positive and negative values for the guesses lets you find how far off the average of each team's guesses was. Some of Team C's guesses were way too high and some were way too low, but the *average* of all their guesses was off by only about 4. Using absolute value lets you see the *magnitude* of each error, not whether the guess was too high or too low. Most of Team A's guesses were too high (+); there were not enough low guesses (−) to balance out the average. In terms of absolute value, however, their guesses were closer to the correct number than were the other teams' guesses.

Another Way Absolute value is a way to compare numbers without letting the positive and negative signs get in the way. Another way to determine the absolute value of a number is to remove any positive or negative sign from the number and simply consider the magnitude of the number itself, without thinking about whether it is to the left or right of zero on a number line.

Name_____   Class _____   Date _____

Try It Yourself

A. Fill in the circle next to the correct answer to each multiple-choice question.

1. Which of the following expressions is equal to 10?

    Ⓐ |18 − 5| + |⁻3| Ⓑ |18 − 5| − |3| Ⓒ 18 + |5 − 3| Ⓓ 18 + |⁻5| + |⁻3|

2. Cassie rode her mountain bike from a valley 30 feet below sea level (−30) to a point on a mountain slope 910 feet above sea level (+910). Which expression shows how many feet she climbed?

    Ⓐ |910| − |⁻30| Ⓑ |910| − |30| Ⓒ |910| + |⁻30| Ⓓ |⁻910| − |30|

3. What is the absolute value of 234 − 589?

    Ⓐ ⁻355   Ⓑ 355   Ⓒ 823   Ⓓ ⁻823

4. Which value below is NOT equal to the others?

    Ⓐ |12 − 7| Ⓑ |12| − |7| Ⓒ |7 − 12| Ⓓ |7| − |12|

5. The contestants on a game show had to guess the prices of a stereo system and of a TV. Brian's guess for the stereo was $300 too low (−300). His guess for the TV was $50 too low (−50). How far off were his two guesses altogether?

    Ⓐ |⁻300| + |⁻50| Ⓑ |⁻300| − |⁻50| Ⓒ |⁻300| − |50| Ⓓ |300| − |50|

B. Complete the activity below.

Write the letter of each expression below at the appropriate place on the number line. The first one has been done for you.

A |⁻4 + 5| F |9 − 1|

B |4 − 8| G |⁻6| − |8|

C −|7 − 2| H |7| + |⁻3|

D |5| − |⁻5| I |⁻1| − |⁻9|

E |⁻3 − 6| J −|2 + 8|

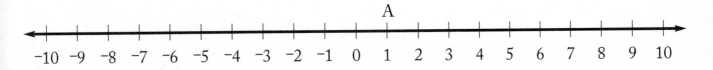

Unit 1: Number Sense, Concepts, and Operations   **59**

Try It Yourself

A. Fill in the circle next to the correct answer to each multiple-choice question.

1. Kalil played three rounds of golf. On his first round, he was 5 over par (+5). On his second round, he was 2 under par (−2). On his third round, he was 4 under par (−4). Which expression shows his total score over or under par for the three rounds?

   Ⓐ $|5| + |^-2| + |^-4|$ Ⓑ $5 - 2 - 4$ Ⓒ $|5 - 2| + |^-4|$ Ⓓ $5 - |2 - 4|$

2. Freda wanted to write three equal expressions using absolute value. Which value below is NOT equal to the others?

   Ⓐ $|18 - 9|$ Ⓑ $|18| - |9|$ Ⓒ $|^-18 + 9|$ Ⓓ $|^-18 - 9|$

3. Which set corresponds to the values of the following expressions?

   $3 \times |3|$ $|^-3 - 3|$ $|^-3| - |^-3|$ $-|^-3 - 3|$

   Ⓐ $^-9, 6, ^-6, ^-6$ Ⓑ $^-9, ^-6, 0, ^-6$ Ⓒ $^-9, 6, 0, ^-6$ Ⓓ $9, 6, 0, ^-6$

4. Which set corresponds to the values of the following expressions?

   $3 \times |^-3|$ $\dfrac{^-3}{|^-3|}$ $\dfrac{3}{|^-3|}$

   Ⓐ $^-9, ^-1, 1$ Ⓑ $9, ^-1, 1$ Ⓒ $9, 1, 1$ Ⓓ $9, ^-1, ^-1$

B. Complete the two parts below. Show all your work.

In the countdown for launching a space shuttle, the time before the launch is stated as a negative number, and the time after launch is stated as a positive number. For example, T − 25 minutes means there are 25 minutes before launch. T + 36 minutes means the space shuttle was launched 36 minutes ago.

Part A Sandra works near the Kennedy Space Center in Florida. At T − 57 minutes, she took a lunch break to watch the launch. She watched the space shuttle launch, and continued to watch until T + 8 minutes. How many minutes in total did Sandra take off from work to watch the launch?

Part B Enrique arrived at the launch at T − 11 minutes and stayed for half an hour. What time did he leave?

PRIME AND COMPOSITE NUMBERS

This lesson addresses Benchmark MA.A.5.3.1 of the Sunshine State Standards.

The Challenge

In the book *Contact* by Carl Sagan, astronomers received radio signals from an intelligent life form in a distant galaxy. The aliens sent out pulses of sound in a pattern that was a series of prime numbers. The aliens were communicating in what they considered to be the universal language, the language of mathematics. On the chart below, circle each prime number and mark each composite number with an ✕. The first prime number has been circled for you.

1	②	3	4	5	6	7	8	9	10
11	12	13	14	15	16	17	18	19	20
21	22	23	24	25	26	27	28	29	30
31	32	33	34	35	36	37	38	39	40
41	42	43	44	45	46	47	48	49	50

Learning the Ropes

In Lesson 1.1, you learned about natural numbers: {1, 2, 3, …}. All natural numbers are either prime or composite (except for 1, which is neither prime nor composite). The number 2 is the only even prime number.

A **prime number** is a number larger than 1 that can be evenly divided only by itself and the number 1. Some prime numbers are 2, 17, and 31.

A **composite number** is one that can be divided, without a remainder, by numbers other than itself and the number 1. For example, the number 6 is composite because it can be evenly divided by 1, 2, 3, or 6.

One important fact in mathematics is that all natural numbers greater than 1 are either prime or can be expressed as a product of prime numbers in only one way. This fact is known as the **Fundamental Theorem of Arithmetic.** Consider the composite number 12. This number can be written as a product of primes: $12 = 2 \times 2 \times 3$.

Math in History
One of the greatest mathematicians who ever lived was Euclid (about 300 to 260 B.C.). One of the inventors of the branch of mathematics known as geometry, Euclid proved that the number of primes is infinite. He did so by assuming the opposite (that the number of primes is *not* infinite), and showing that such an assumption leads to a contradiction, which means that the assumption must be wrong. In other words, there must be an infinite number of primes. This result from Euclid is known as the **Prime Number Theorem.**

Thus, every number either is prime or can be broken down into a group of **prime factors** that is unique to that number. One way to break down a composite number into its factors is to make a **factor tree.** Write the number as the product of two **factors**, and keep finding factors of the factors until you have only prime numbers left. For example, the number 400 written as the product of prime numbers is $5 \times 5 \times 2 \times 2 \times 2 \times 2$.

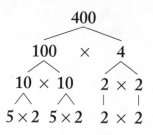

Two numbers are **relatively prime** if the only whole number by which they can both be divided is 1. For example, the numbers 4 and 9 are not prime, but together they are relatively prime because the only whole number that is a factor of *both* is 1.

The term **perfect number** refers to a number that is equal to the sum of all its different factors (prime and composite) except itself. For example, the factors of 6 are 1, 2, 3, and 6. The sum of all the factors (except 6) is 6, so 6 is a perfect number.

Meeting the Challenge

To answer the Challenge, you must identify all the prime and composite numbers up to 50. Here is a simple method for eliminating composite numbers to leave the prime numbers. This method is called the Sieve of Eratosthenes, after an ancient Greek mathematician.

STEP 1: Start by circling 2, which is prime. Then cross out every second number after 2. This will get rid of all multiples of 2. A **multiple** of 2 is any number that results from multiplying 2 by a whole number. Multiplying by any whole number greater than 1 will give a composite number.

STEP 2: Next, move on to 3, which is prime. Circle it. Cross out every third number after 3. This will get rid of all multiples of 3.

STEP 3: The multiples of 4 have already been crossed out because you have crossed out the multiples of 2, so you can move on to 5. Circle 5, and cross out every fifth number after 5. Continue in this way until you have crossed out all the numbers that are multiples of other numbers. The numbers left (not crossed out) will be the primes.

The completed table is shown to the right.

1	2	3	4	5	6	7	8	9	10
11	12	13	14	15	16	17	18	19	20
21	22	23	24	25	26	27	28	29	30
31	32	33	34	35	36	37	38	39	40
41	42	43	44	45	46	47	48	49	50

Another Way   To help you find factors, keep in mind the tricks that identify multiples of 3 and of 9. If the sum of the digits in a number is divisible by 3, then that number is a multiple of 3. For example, the sum of the digits in the number 597 is 21, which can be divided by 3. Therefore, you know that 3 is a factor of 597, so 597 cannot be a prime number. If the sum of the digits in a number is divisible by 9, then that number is a multiple of 9. For example, the sum of the digits in 891 is 18, which can be divided by 9. Therefore, 891 has 9 as a factor and is not prime.

Name____________________ Class __________ Date __________

Try It Yourself

1.3 Prime and Composite Numbers
Practice Exercises

A. Make factor trees for the following numbers:

1. 36
2. 51
3. 61
4. 84

B. Tell which of the following numbers are prime and which ones are composite. Break down the composite numbers into prime factors.

1. 3 ____________
2. 6 ____________
3. 7 ____________
4. 15 ____________
5. 20 ____________
6. 31 ____________

C. Complete the activity below. Show all your work.

Remember that a perfect number is one that is equal to the sum of all its different factors except itself (for example, 6 = 1 + 2 + 3). One of the numbers below is the next perfect number after 6. Test these numbers by finding all their factors and adding the factors. Tell which of the numbers is perfect. The number 12 has been done for you.

~~12~~ 15 18 20 23 28 30 36

The factors of 12 are 1, 2, 3, 4, 6, and 12.
The sum of the factors (except 12) is 1 + 2 + 3 + 4 + 6 = 16.
The sum of the factors is *not* equal to the number, so 12 is not a perfect number.

Name______________________ Class ________ Date ________

Try It Yourself

1.3 Prime and Composite Numbers
Assessment Practice

A. Fill in the circle next to the correct answer to each multiple-choice question.

1. What are the prime factors of 12?

Ⓐ 6, 2 Ⓑ 3, 2 Ⓒ 4, 3 Ⓓ 8, 4

2. Gabriela wants to give each of her friends the same number of marbles. What number of marbles could be divided equally among 2 or more friends?

Ⓐ 31 Ⓑ 41 Ⓒ 51 Ⓓ 61

3. Identify one prime factor of 56.

Ⓐ 4 Ⓑ 7 Ⓒ 8 Ⓓ 56

B. Find the smallest composite number that is a multiple of each number in the following sets of three numbers. Write your answer at the top of the grid and fill in the numbered circles.

1. 2, 4, 7

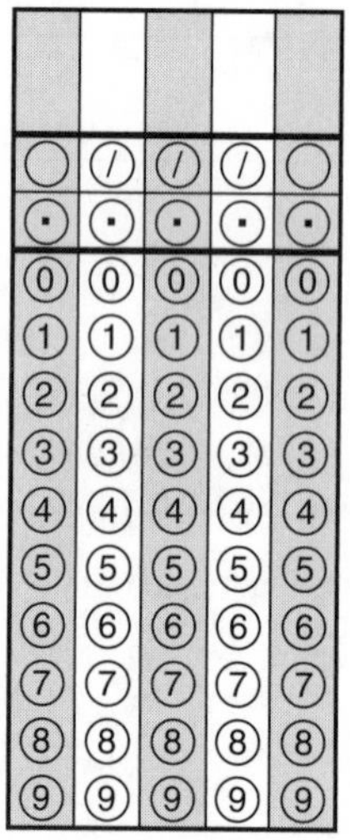

2. 3, 5, 9

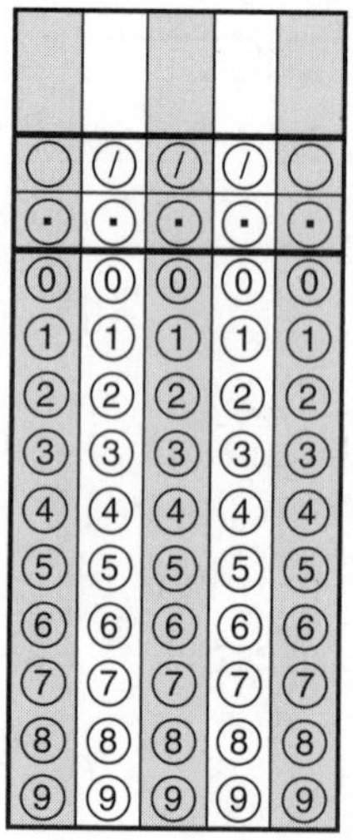

3. 4, 6, 10

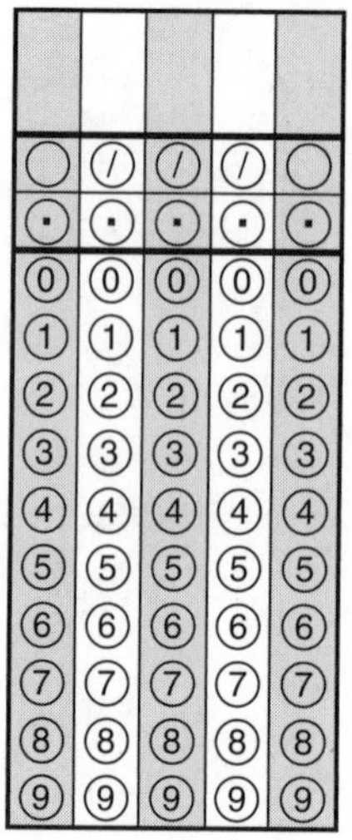

C. Complete the two parts below. Show all your work.

Part A On the table to the right, cross out each composite number and circle each prime number. (Hint: There are 10 prime numbers between 51 and 100.)

51	52	53	54	55	56	57	58	59	60
61	62	63	64	65	66	67	68	69	70
71	72	73	74	75	76	77	78	79	80
81	82	83	84	85	86	87	88	89	90
91	92	93	94	95	96	97	98	99	100

Part B On your own paper, explain the process you used to rule out the composite numbers.

FRACTIONS, RATIOS, AND PROPORTIONS

This lesson addresses Benchmarks MA.A.1.3.1, MA.A.1.3.2, MA.A.1.3.3, MA.A.3.3.1, and MA.A.3.3.3 of the Sunshine State Standards.

The Challenge

Francine goes to a museum that has an exhibit with a giant's house. The giant's book is 27 inches tall. The giant's toothbrush is 18 inches long, and the giant's cup is 12 inches tall. A sign says that the objects in the giant's house are produced on a scale of $3:1$. Francine calculates that in real life, the book would be 9 inches, the toothbrush would be 6 inches, and the cup would be 3 inches high. Are her calculations correct?

Learning the Ropes

A **fraction** is a number that names parts of a whole. The bottom number, or **denominator,** tells the number of parts that make up one whole. The top number, or **numerator,** tells how many of those parts you are talking about. For example, in the fraction $\frac{5}{8}$, the denominator, 8, tells how many parts are in the whole, like a whole pie divided into 8 slices. The numerator, 5, tells how many parts out of the whole you are referring to, like 5 of the 8 slices of pie. The fraction bar means to divide the numerator by the denominator.

A **ratio** is a comparison between two numbers when one is divided by another. Ratios can be written as fractions, like $\frac{1}{2}$, or in the form $1:2$ or 1 to 2.

A **proportion** is an equation showing two ratios that are equal. Equivalent fractions are proportional, meaning that the numerator and denominator of each are in the same ratio. For example, $\frac{5}{7} = \frac{10}{14}$. You could also say that 5 to 7 equals 10 to 14.

Comparing Fractions. To check if two fractions are equivalent, multiply the numerator of the first by the denominator of the second. Then multiply the denominator of the first by the numerator of the second. Put the products above the numerators. If the products are the same, the fractions are equivalent. If they are different, the bigger product will be above the bigger fraction.

EXAMPLES

$$\overset{24}{\underset{}{\frac{2}{3}}} \times \overset{24}{\underset{}{\frac{8}{12}}} \qquad 2 \times 12 = 3 \times 8$$
$$\text{so } \frac{2}{3} = \frac{8}{12}$$

$$\overset{36}{\underset{}{\frac{3}{4}}} \times \overset{40}{\underset{}{\frac{10}{12}}} \qquad 3 \times 12 < 4 \times 10$$
$$\text{so } \frac{3}{4} < \frac{10}{12}$$

Math in History

In 1666, when he was only 22 years old, Isaac Newton discovered the law of gravitation. This law states that the gravitational force that one body exerts on another body is directly proportional to its mass. Since the moon is much smaller than Earth, it exerts less gravitational force, and objects on the moon weigh less than on Earth. In fact, an object on the moon weighs only about $\frac{1}{6}$ what it does on Earth. Suppose that you weigh 96 pounds. Your weight on the moon would be $\frac{1}{6}$ what it is on Earth, or $\frac{1}{6} \times 96$. On the moon, you would weigh only about 16 pounds! Notice that multiplying by $\frac{1}{6}$ is the same as dividing by 6.

The U.S. Congress is divided into two houses, the Senate and the House of Representatives. Each state in the country has two senators; therefore, each state has equal voting power in the Senate. In the House, however, the number of representatives is based on each state's population. States with larger populations have more representatives, and thus more votes, than states with smaller populations. The system used to determine the number of representatives in the House is called **proportional representation** because the number of representatives is proportional to the population. In recent years, states in the Northeast have lost representatives, while states in the South and West have gained representatives, affecting the balance of power among the states.

Multiplying Fractions. To multiply fractions, multiply the numerators and the denominators.

EXAMPLES $\dfrac{3}{8} \times \dfrac{1}{2} = \dfrac{3 \times 1}{8 \times 2} = \dfrac{3}{16}$ $\qquad$ $7 \times \dfrac{3}{4} = \dfrac{7}{1} \times \dfrac{3}{4} = \dfrac{7 \times 3}{1 \times 4} = \dfrac{21}{4}$

Dividing Fractions. To divide any number by a fraction, multiply the number by the **reciprocal** of the fraction. To make the reciprocal of a fraction, just switch the numerator and denominator.

EXAMPLES $\dfrac{1}{3} \div \dfrac{4}{5} = \dfrac{1}{3} \times \dfrac{5}{4} = \dfrac{5}{12}$ $\qquad$ $2 \div \dfrac{1}{6} = 2 \times 6 = 12$

Simplifying Fractions. It is often easiest to work with **simplified fractions,** ones that are expressed with the simplest numbers possible. To simplify a fraction (sometimes called **reducing** a fraction), find a number that is a factor of both the numerator and the denominator. Divide both the numerator and the denominator by that factor. If you divide both parts of a fraction by the *greatest* number that is a factor of both the numerator and the denominator, you will simplify the fraction to its **lowest terms.** The numerator and denominator of a fraction in lowest terms are **relatively prime** because they have no common factor except 1.

EXAMPLE $\dfrac{16}{24}$ Factors of 16: 1, 2, 4, 8, 16
$\qquad\qquad$ Factors of 24: 1, 2, 3, 4, 6, 8, 12, 24

> The **greatest common factor (GCF)** is 8.

$\dfrac{16 \div 8}{24 \div 8} = \dfrac{2}{3}$

> The fraction $\frac{2}{3}$ is in lowest terms.
> The numbers 2 and 3 are relatively prime.

Adding and Subtracting Fractions with Like Denominators. When two fractions have the same denominator, you can add or subtract them by performing the operation on the numerators and keeping the denominator the same.

EXAMPLES $\dfrac{2}{7} + \dfrac{3}{7} = \dfrac{5}{7}$ $\qquad$ $\dfrac{8}{9} - \dfrac{7}{9} = \dfrac{1}{9}$

Adding and Subtracting Fractions with Unlike Denominators. If you want to add or subtract fractions with different denominators, you must change them into fractions with the same denominator. **Equivalent fractions** have the same value but use different numbers. Equivalent fractions are formed by multiplying the numerator and the denominator by the same number. The examples below show two different fractions that are equivalent to $\frac{2}{3}$.

EXAMPLES $\dfrac{2}{3} \times \dfrac{2}{2} = \dfrac{4}{6}$ $\qquad$ $\dfrac{2}{3} \times \dfrac{8}{8} = \dfrac{16}{24}$

Finding Common Denominators. To find a **common denominator**—a number that can be used as a denominator of each fraction you are working with—look at the multiples of the denominators. Any multiple shared by both denominators can be a common denominator.

EXAMPLE   Find a common denominator of $\frac{3}{5}$ and $\frac{1}{4}$.

$\frac{3}{5}$ multiples of 5: 5, 10, 15, 20, 25, … $\frac{1}{4}$ multiples of 4: 4, 8, 12, 16, 20, …

When a common denominator has been found, convert the original fractions into equivalent fractions, each having the common denominator as its new denominator. To do this, multiply both the numerator and the denominator by the factor that produces the common denominator.

$$\frac{3}{5} \times \frac{4}{4} = \frac{12}{20} \qquad \frac{1}{4} \times \frac{5}{5} = \frac{5}{20}$$

Once two fractions have the same denominator, they can be added or subtracted easily. To simplify your work, use the **lowest common denominator (LCD)**, the least number that can be a denominator for all the fractions you are working with.

EXAMPLE $\frac{2}{3} + \frac{1}{2} = ?$ multiples of 3: 3, 6, 9, 12, 15, …   multiples of 2: 2, 4, 6, 8, 10, …

$$\frac{2}{3} \times \frac{2}{2} = \frac{4}{6} \qquad \frac{1}{2} \times \frac{3}{3} = \frac{3}{6} \qquad \frac{2}{3} + \frac{1}{2} = \frac{4}{6} + \frac{3}{6} = \frac{7}{6} = 1\frac{1}{6}$$

Working with Proportions. Proportions show that one ratio is equal to another; they express equivalent fractions, like $\frac{1}{2} = \frac{50}{100}$. To check if ratios are equal, you can use **cross products,** or **cross multiplication.** To do this, multiply the numerator of the fraction on the left by the denominator of the fraction on the right. Then multiply the numerator of the fraction on the right by the denominator of the fraction on the left. If the two products are equal, the ratios are the same.

EXAMPLE   Are the two ratios $\frac{3}{4}$ and $\frac{9}{12}$ the same?

Cross-multiply

$3 \times 12 = 4 \times 9$ Since these products are equal, the ratios are the same, and $\frac{3}{4} = \frac{9}{12}$ is a proportion.

If the ratios are expressed with colons, multiply the outside numbers and compare the product to the product of the inside numbers:

$3:4 = 9:12$ Since 3×12 equals 4×9, the ratio of 3 to 4 is the same as 9 to 12.

Proportions are very useful when you are dealing with any quantities that are in a constant relationship to one another. For example, distances on a map are proportional to distances in real life. The dimensions of a model are proportional to the dimensions of the real object. If something is moving at a constant rate, the ratio of the distance to the time is always the same.

Meeting the Challenge

To solve the Challenge, you must check whether or not Francine's calculations are correct by setting up proportions.

STEP 1: Write a proportion expressing that the ratio between the giant's book and the book in real life is equal to the scale of the giant's house to a real house (3 : 1).

$$\text{book} = \frac{\overbrace{27 \text{ inches}}^{\text{giant's book}}}{\underbrace{9 \text{ inches}}_{\text{real book}}} = \frac{3}{1}$$

STEP 2: Use cross multiplication to see if the proportion is true.

$$\frac{27}{9} \underset{=}{\times} \frac{3}{1} \qquad 27 \times 1 \overset{?}{=} 3 \times 9$$

$$27 = 27 \qquad \text{Francine's calculation is correct.}$$

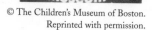

© The Children's Museum of Boston.
Reprinted with permission.

STEP 3: Follow the same steps for the toothbrush.

$$\text{toothbrush} = \frac{18 \text{ inches}}{6 \text{ inches}} = \frac{3}{1} \qquad 18 \times 1 \overset{?}{=} 3 \times 6$$

$$18 = 18 \qquad \text{Francine's calculation is correct.}$$

STEP 4: Follow the same steps for the cup.

$$\text{cup} = \frac{12 \text{ inches}}{3 \text{ inches}} = \frac{3}{1} \qquad 12 \times 1 \overset{?}{=} 3 \times 3$$

$$12 \neq 9 \text{ Francine's calculation is } not \text{ correct.}$$

The answer to the Challenge is that Francine's calculations of the sizes of the book and toothbrush in real life are correct. Her calculation of the cup's height, however, is incorrect. The real height of the cup would have to be 4 inches in order to make the proportion true.

$$\text{cup} = \frac{12 \text{ inches}}{4 \text{ inches}} = \frac{3}{1} \qquad 12 \times 1 = 4 \times 3$$

$$12 = 12$$

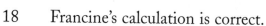

Another Way   Here is another method for finding the lowest common denominator: First, factor the two denominators and find their greatest common factor (GCF).

$$\frac{4}{6} + \frac{2}{9} = ? \qquad 6 = 2 \times 3 \qquad 9 = 3 \times 3 \qquad \text{GCF} = 3$$

Multiply the two denominators, and then divide by their greatest common factor: $\frac{6 \times 9}{3}$.

Simplify the fraction. $\frac{6 \times \cancel{9}^{3}}{\cancel{3}_{1}} = 6 \times 3 = 18$

Thus, 18 is the lowest common denominator: $\frac{4}{6} + \frac{2}{9} = \frac{12}{18} + \frac{4}{18} = \frac{16}{18} = \frac{8}{9}$.

Name_____   Class _____ Date _____

Try It Yourself

A. Complete each grid. Write your answer at the top and fill in the numbered circles. Express your answer as a fraction simplified to its lowest terms.

1. $\frac{3}{4} + \frac{1}{2} =$

2. $\frac{12}{36} \div \frac{8}{12} =$

3. $\frac{3}{5} - \frac{9}{15} =$

B. Fill in the circle next to the correct answer to each multiple-choice question.

1. Adam and his uncle are playing basketball using two adjustable basketball hoops. Adam is 4 feet, 8 inches (56 inches) tall and his basketball hoop is set at 7 feet (84 inches) high. If Adam's uncle is 6 feet (72 inches) tall, how high should his hoop be set to make the game fair?

Ⓐ 96 in.   Ⓑ 102 in.   Ⓒ 108 in.   Ⓓ 114 in.

2. Tia and Chamique are playing a board game in which players collect plastic stars for bonus points. All of the stars are worth the same number of points. If Tia gets 56 bonus points for 8 stars, how many stars will Chamique need to collect to earn 84 bonus points?

Ⓐ 10 stars   Ⓑ 12 stars   Ⓒ 24 stars   Ⓓ 36 stars

C. Complete the activity below. Show all your work.

Triangle *ABC* is similar to triangle *DEF*. Lengths are given in centimeters (cm).

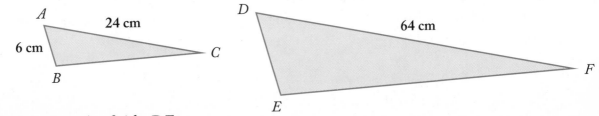

Find the length of side *DE*.

Unit 1: Number Sense, Concepts, and Operations   69

Name_____ Class _____ Date _____

Try It Yourself

A. Fill in the circle next to the correct answer to each multiple-choice question.

1. The school government is made up of representatives from each grade. There are 254 students in sixth grade, 302 students in seventh grade, and 325 students in eighth grade. If there is 1 student representative for every 25 students, how many representatives will the eighth grade select?

   Ⓐ 32　　　　Ⓑ 27　　　　Ⓒ 21　　　　Ⓓ 13

2. Jamal read $\frac{1}{6}$ of a novel on Monday and $\frac{3}{10}$ of it on Tuesday. Altogether, how much of the novel did he read? Express the answer as a fraction simplified to its lowest terms.

   Ⓐ $\frac{1}{4}$　　　Ⓑ $\frac{2}{15}$　　　Ⓒ $\frac{7}{15}$　　　Ⓓ $\frac{14}{30}$

3. The distance between the school and the shopping mall is 18 miles. The distance between the two locations on a map is 6 inches. What is the scale of the map?

   Ⓐ 1 inch : 3 miles　　　　Ⓒ 1 inch : 6 miles
   Ⓑ 1 mile : 3 inches　　　　Ⓓ 6 inches : 3 miles

4. Which of the following ratios is equivalent to 35 : 56?

   Ⓐ 3 : 5　　　　Ⓑ 5 : 8　　　　Ⓒ 7 : 11　　　　Ⓓ 8 : 5

B. Complete the two parts below. Show all your work.

Andy and Laura are architects who are making a scale model of a parking garage and a hospital. The scale of their model is 50 feet : 1 inch. The hospital is 400 feet long, 100 feet wide, and 50 feet tall. The parking garage is 250 feet long, 100 feet wide, and 50 feet tall.

Part A How many inches should each dimension of the hospital be on the scale model?

Part B Laura says that the parking garage on the scale model should be $2\frac{1}{2}$ inches long. Is her calculation correct? If not, how long should the model of the garage be?

DECIMALS AND PERCENTS

This lesson addresses Benchmarks MA.A.1.3.1, MA.A.1.3.2, MA.A.1.3.3, MA.A.3.3.1, and MA.A.3.3.3 of the Sunshine State Standards.

The Challenge

A sales clerk earns a commission of 2% on sales less than $75, and 3% on sales of $75 or more. In one hour, the clerk had sales of $48, $72, $125, and $220. How much did she earn in commission during that hour?

Learning the Ropes

Math in History

Although rational and irrational numbers have been used for thousands of years, decimal representations of these numbers have been used for only a little more than 400 years. The first use of decimal notation to show fractional quantities is credited to Simon Stevin (1548–1620), a Dutch mathematician. The idea of extending the base-10 system to include the place values with fractional representations like $\frac{1}{10}$, $\frac{1}{100}$, and $\frac{1}{1,000}$ had been under development for about a century. It was Stevin, however, who first set down the rules for using decimal numbers in calculations, in 1584.

Calculations with decimal numbers are accomplished much as they are with whole numbers, except that you also must consider how to treat the decimal point.

Adding and Subtracting Decimals. To add or subtract decimal numbers, first align all the numbers so that the decimal point is in the same position for each number. Zeros may be added so that all the numbers have the same number of places to the right of the decimal. Perform the operation, and insert the decimal point in the answer in the same position as in the other numbers in the problem.

EXAMPLE $4.2 + 5.698 + 2.35 + 8$

$$
\begin{array}{r}
4.200 \\
5.698 \\
2.350 \\
+\ 8.000 \\
\hline
20.248
\end{array}
$$

- Align decimal points
- Insert zeros to right of decimal
- Align decimal point in answer

Multiplying Decimals. To multiply two decimal numbers, simply multiply as if no decimal point were present. After finding the product, count the total number of places to the right of the decimal points in the factors. The sum represents the number of decimal places in the final answer.

EXAMPLE 8.56×3.2

$$
\begin{array}{r}
8.56 \quad \leftarrow \boxed{2 \text{ decimal places}} \\
\times\ 3.2 \quad \leftarrow \boxed{1 \text{ decimal place}} \\
\hline
1712 \\
2568 \\
\hline
27.392 \quad \leftarrow \boxed{3 \text{ decimal places}}
\end{array}
$$

- Carry out the multiplication
- Number of decimal places in answer (3) is sum of number of decimal places in factors (2 + 1)

Dividing Decimals. To divide one decimal by another, first determine if there are values to the right of the decimal point in the divisor. If there are, then eliminate the decimal point in the divisor by moving it as many places to the right as necessary. You must also move the decimal point in the dividend (the number you are dividing into) the same number of places. Then carry out the division, and insert the decimal point in the answer in the same position as it now occurs in the dividend.

EXAMPLE $4.2\overline{)7.4844}$

$4.2\overline{)7.4844}$

$$\begin{array}{r} 1.782 \\ 42\overline{)74.844} \\ \underline{42} \\ 328 \\ \underline{294} \\ 344 \\ \underline{336} \\ 84 \end{array}$$

- Move decimal point in divisor to the right as many places as necessary to make it a whole number
- Move decimal point in dividend to the right the same number of places
- Carry out the division
- Align the decimal point in the quotient with the decimal point in the dividend

Percents. Numbers that have two decimal places (two digits after the decimal point) can be written as fractions with denominators of 100.

EXAMPLES $0.02 = \dfrac{2}{100}$ $0.37 = \dfrac{37}{100}$ $4.58 = \dfrac{458}{100}$

Fractions with denominators of 100 are often expressed as **percents.** The percent sign (%) means "divided by 100," so any fraction with a denominator of 100 can be written as the numerator followed by the percent sign.

EXAMPLES $0.02 = \dfrac{2}{100} = 2\%$ $0.37 = \dfrac{37}{100} = 37\%$ $4.58 = \dfrac{458}{100} = 458\%$

$\dfrac{1}{20} = \dfrac{5}{100} = 5\%$ $\dfrac{25}{10} = \dfrac{250}{100} = 250\%$ $0.01 = \dfrac{1}{100} = 1\%$

Converting between Decimals and Percents. Sometimes you do calculations using decimals, and then you need to convert your answer into a percent. To find the percent equivalent of a decimal number, just move the decimal point two places to the right, and then write the percent symbol.

EXAMPLES $0.23 \longrightarrow 23\%$ $1.10 \longrightarrow 110\%$

You may need to convert percents into decimals in order to do calculations. Simply remove the percent symbol and move the decimal point two places to the left.

EXAMPLES $7\% \longrightarrow 0.07$ $82\% \longrightarrow 0.82$

When you see a phrase like "30% of," it means the same as "0.30 times." To do your calculations, change the percent into a decimal and multiply.

EXAMPLES   23% of 485 is the same as 0.23×485

                       5% of 16 is the same as 0.05×16

Converting between Fractions and Percents. If a fraction has a denominator that is a factor of 100, it is easy to convert that fraction into an equivalent fraction with a denominator of 100, and then to convert that fraction into a percent.

EXAMPLES $\dfrac{13}{20} = \dfrac{13 \times 5}{20 \times 5} = \dfrac{65}{100} = 0.65 = 65\%$ $\dfrac{3}{25} = \dfrac{3 \times 4}{25 \times 4} = \dfrac{12}{100} = 0.12 = 12\%$

If the fraction is not easily changed into one with a denominator of 100, divide the numerator by the denominator to make a decimal, and then change to percent. Doing the division with a calculator simplifies the work.

The table below shows common fractions and their corresponding percents.

Fraction	$\dfrac{1}{8}$	$\dfrac{1}{5}$	$\dfrac{1}{4}$	$\dfrac{1}{3}$	$\dfrac{3}{8}$	$\dfrac{2}{5}$	$\dfrac{1}{2}$	$\dfrac{3}{5}$	$\dfrac{5}{8}$	$\dfrac{2}{3}$	$\dfrac{3}{4}$	$\dfrac{4}{5}$	$\dfrac{7}{8}$
Percent	12.5%	20%	25%	33.3%	37.5%	40%	50%	60%	62.5%	66.7%	75%	80%	87.5%

Use of Percents. Percents are often used to indicate a portion of a whole or a change in size. For example, you might say that 65% of the voters (65 out of every 100) voted for Mr. Vargas for mayor. If Mr. Vargas promises to decrease spending by 15%, it means that out of every $100 now being spent, he will spend $15 less.

   You will often want to know the resulting amount when a quantity is increased or decreased by some percent. For example, suppose you wanted to know how much a $9.00 book would cost if it were on sale for 20% off (a decrease of 20%). First determine the change in price by taking 20% of $9.00. Remember that you need to change the percent into a decimal and multiply by the original amount (20% of $9.00 = 0.20 × $9.00 = $1.80). Then subtract the decrease ($1.80) from the original price ($9.00) to find the sale price: $9.00 − $1.80 = $7.20.

Use the same procedure to find the increase in a quantity. Suppose that you had a package of cookies that normally weighs 16 ounces. If you saw a new package of the same cookies offering 25% more at the same price, how much would it weigh? To determine the weight of the new package, find 25% of 16 ounces (0.25 × 16 = 4). Then add the increase to the original, or **base,** weight (16 ounces + 4 ounces = 20 ounces).

Suppose that you went to a store and you saw that the price of a pair of shoes had been marked down from $48 to $36. What percent have the shoes been discounted? To find out, first find the difference between the original price and the discounted price: $48 − $36 = $12. Then divide the difference by the original price and multiply the answer by 100 to calculate the percent change:

$$\frac{\$12}{\$48} = 0.25$$

$$0.25 \times 100 = 25 \qquad 0.25 = 25\%$$

The percent change between the original price and the discounted price is 25%.

Meeting the Challenge

To answer the Challenge, you must add the commissions that the sales clerk earned on her four sales.

STEP 1: To find the commissions, take the correct percent of each sale—2% of sales less than $75 and 3% of sales greater than or equal to $75. Remember that you need to convert the percents to decimals, and that "2% of" means "0.02 ×."

2% of $48 = 0.02 × $48 = $0.96
2% of $72 = 0.02 × $72 = $1.44
3% of $125 = 0.03 × $125 = $3.75
3% of $220 = 0.03 × $220 = $6.60

STEP 2: Now add the commissions on each sale to find the total.
$0.96 + $1.44 + $3.75 + $6.60 = $12.75

The answer to the Challenge is that the clerk made a total of $12.75 on the four sales.

Another Way There are two ways to determine the result when there is a percent change in a base quantity. As you learned in this lesson, you can find out how big the change is and then add it to or subtract it from the original quantity. To find the answer in a single step, you can simply take the percent of the original that the final result will be. Suppose that you are going to buy an item for $50 and pay a 5% sales tax. The total amount you will pay will be 105% (100% + 5%) of the base price (105% of $50 = 1.05 × $50 = $52.50).

Try It Yourself

A. Perform the operations indicated, and write your answers on the lines provided.

1. $42.81 + 8.134 =$ _____

2. $36.74 - 12.522 =$ _____

3. $1.1 \times 0.03 =$ _____

4. $17 \div 0.2 =$ _____

B. Perform the following conversions, and write your answers on the lines provided.

1. $1.72 =$ _____ %

2. $0.03 =$ _____ %

3. $160\% =$ _____

4. $7\% =$ _____

C. Fill in the circle next to the correct answer to each multiple-choice question.

1. To pass a proficiency test, you must answer 70% of the 250 questions correctly. What is the minimum passing score?

Ⓐ 105　　　　Ⓑ 175　　　　Ⓒ 180　　　　Ⓓ 210

2. A candy and nut shop makes a popular mix that includes peanuts and cashew nuts. If the mix includes 3 parts peanuts to 2 parts cashews, what percent of the mixture is peanuts?

Ⓐ 30%　　　　Ⓑ 33%　　　　Ⓒ 50%　　　　Ⓓ 60%

D. Complete the three parts below. Show all your work. Use additional paper if necessary.

You are shopping at a store called TV World. Your state's sales tax is 5%.

Part A How much sales tax would you have to pay if you bought a television for $595?

Part B What would be your total cost, including tax, for a VCR listed at $295?

Part C How much would you pay in total for the VCR if the store were having a 25%-off sale? Assume that you would have to pay tax on the discounted price. Round your answer to the nearest penny.

Name_____ Class _____ Date _____

Try It Yourself

A. Fill in the circle next to the correct answer to each multiple-choice question.

1. A store is selling shirts at 20% off the regular price. What is the sale price of a shirt that originally sold for $35.00?

   Ⓐ $7.00   Ⓑ $15.00   Ⓒ $28.00   Ⓓ $34.30

2. At a sale, Gina was comparing two dresses. The blue dress was originally priced at $120 but was on sale for 15% off. The black dress originally cost $135 but was on sale for 20% off. Which of the following is NOT a true statement?

   Ⓐ After the markdowns, the blue dress was still less expensive than the black dress.
   Ⓑ Even with the reduction in price, the black dress was still selling for a higher price than the original price of the blue dress.
   Ⓒ If both dresses were on sale for 15% off, then the savings on the black dress would be larger than the savings on the blue dress.
   Ⓓ The black dress had been reduced by a larger amount than had the blue dress.

3. Which of the following represents the biggest number?

   Ⓐ 25% of 90   Ⓑ 90% of 30   Ⓒ 0.2% of 10,000   Ⓓ 10% of 345

4. The population of Lindenville was 4,500 in 1990. By the time of the 2000 census, the population had grown to 150% of its 1990 level. What was the population in 2000?

   Ⓐ 675,000   Ⓑ 30,000   Ⓒ 11,250   Ⓓ 6,750

B. Complete the two parts below. Show all your work.

Miguel, Kenny, and Ali operate a booth at the school yard sale. Part of the proceeds (40%) from each booth goes to the school library.

Part A If they take in $160, how much will they be able to keep after paying the money for the library? Explain how you found your answer.

Part B If $4,000 is raised for the school library, what is the total amount of money taken in by all the booths at the yard sale? Explain how you found your answer.

EXPONENTS AND RADICALS

This lesson addresses Benchmarks MA.A.1.3.1, MA.A.1.3.2, MA.A.1.3.3, MA.A.1.3.4, and MA.A.2.3.1 of the Sunshine State Standards.

The Challenge

Albert Einstein's theory of relativity says that mass can be changed into energy, as expressed by the famous equation $E = mc^2$, where E stands for energy, m stands for mass, and c stands for the speed of light. The constant c is equal to 300,000 kilometers per second. What is c^2?

Molecules are measured in very tiny units called angstroms. One angstrom (Å) is equal to 10^{-10} meters. How would you write this number using decimals?

If you know the area of a circle, you can calculate its radius with this formula: $\sqrt{\frac{A}{\pi}} = r$. What does the symbol $\sqrt{}$ mean?

Learning the Ropes

Exponents. An **exponent** is the little number that appears above another number, called the **base number.** It tells you how many times to use the base number as a factor—that is, the **power** to which the base number should be raised. In the example to the right, the base number is 5 and the exponent is 4. The exponent tells you to use the number 5 four times as a factor, that is, $5 \times 5 \times 5 \times 5$.

5^4 ← exponent
↖ base number

A number raised to the second power is said to be **squared.** For example, five to the second power is five squared. It is equal to 25 because $5^2 = 5 \times 5 = 25$. Similarly, a number raised to the third power is said to be **cubed.** For example, four cubed is equal to $4^3 = 4 \times 4 \times 4 = 64$.

If a number is raised to a negative power, it is the **reciprocal** of the number raised to the same positive power. For example, $3^{-2} = \frac{1}{3^2} = \frac{1}{9}$. The places to the right of the decimal point are negative powers of 10.

Radicals. A **radical,** also called a **root,** is the **inverse,** or opposite, operation of raising a number to a power. A radical is written like this: $\sqrt[3]{8}$. The number 8 is called the **radicand,** and the number 3 is called the **index.** The index of a radical tells you how many identical factors are multiplied to give the radicand. For example, $\sqrt[3]{8}$ tells you to find the number that can be multiplied three times to give 8. Since $2 \times 2 \times 2 = 8$, $\sqrt[3]{8} = 2$. This example is a **cube root**—the cube root of 8.

Math in History
The **wind-chill index** tells how cold it feels when the wind is blowing. The wind chill in degrees Fahrenheit is equal to $35.74 + 0.6215T - 35.75v^{0.16} + 0.4275Tv^{0.16}$, where v is the wind speed in miles per hour, and T is the temperature in degrees Fahrenheit. Notice the use of exponents in the calculation. The National Weather Service updates the wind-chill formula from time to time as scientists conduct more research.

If you see a radical without an index, it is a **square root.** The square root is a number that can be multiplied by itself to produce the number under the radical. For example, the square root of 9 is 3 because $3 \times 3 = 9$.

To find the square root of a number, you can split the number into its factors. Then take the square roots of the factors and multiply them together.

EXAMPLE $\quad \sqrt{32} = \sqrt{16 \times 2} = \sqrt{16} \times \sqrt{2} = 4\sqrt{2}$

The table to the right shows how to write some numbers as powers of 10. What is true about the number if its exponent is greater than 0? less than 0? equal to 0?

Notice that any number (other than 0) with an exponent of 0 is equal to 1. The expression 0^0 is undefined.

	$10^0 = 1$	
$10^1 = \quad 10$	$10^{-1} = 0.1$	$= \frac{1}{10}$
$10^2 = \quad 100$	$10^{-2} = 0.01$	$= \frac{1}{100}$
$10^3 = \quad 1,000$	$10^{-3} = 0.001$	$= \frac{1}{1,000}$
$10^4 = 10,000$	$10^{-4} = 0.0001$	$= \frac{1}{10,000}$

Meeting the Challenge

To answer the Challenge, you must know what the exponents do to the numbers.

STEP 1: The exponent in c^2 tells you to multiply $c \times c$.

$c = 300,000 \quad c^2 = 300,000 \times 300,000 = 90,000,000,000$

STEP 2: A negative exponent with a base number of 10 means that the number is less than 1. In this case, it is a very, very tiny number! There are 10 billion angstroms in 1 meter!

$1 \text{ Å} = 10^{-10} \text{ meters} = 0.0000000001 \text{ meters}$

STEP 3: The formula for the area of a circle is $A = \pi r^2$. To find the radius if you know the area, you need to take the square root of $\frac{A}{\pi}$. The symbol $\sqrt{}$ means "the square root."

Another Way To help you picture squares, cubes, square roots, and cube roots, think of geometric squares and cubes.

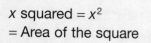

x squared $= x^2$ = Area of the square	x cubed $= x^3$ = Volume of the cube	$\sqrt{A} \times \sqrt{A}$ = Area of the square	$\sqrt[3]{V} \times \sqrt[3]{V} \times \sqrt[3]{V}$ = Volume of the cube
The square of a number x is the area of a square whose sides have a length of x.	The cube of a number x is the volume of a cube whose sides have a length of x.	If A is the area of the square, the sides are equal to the square root of A, $\sqrt{A}$.	If V is the volume of the cube, then each side is equal to the cube root of V, $\sqrt[3]{V}$.

Try It Yourself

A. Fill in the circle next to the correct answer to each multiple-choice question.

1. The Flanagans' house is on a square piece of land whose area is 1 acre. An acre is equal to 43,560 square feet. About how many feet long is each side of the Flanagans' property?

   Ⓐ 200 ft   Ⓑ 1,000 ft   Ⓒ 10,000 ft   Ⓓ 20,000 ft

2. Which number is equal to 2^{-3}?

   Ⓐ $\frac{1}{8}$ Ⓑ -8 Ⓒ $-\frac{1}{8}$ Ⓓ 8

3. What is the cube root of 216?

   Ⓐ 2   Ⓑ 4   Ⓒ 6   Ⓓ 8

4. Hilary is trying to understand why any number to the zero power is equal to 1. Which of the following expressions is equal to 1?

   Ⓐ $5^3 \times 5^{-3}$ Ⓑ $5^3 - 5^{-3}$ Ⓒ $5^3 - 5^3$ Ⓓ $5^3 \div 5^{-3}$

5. Evaluate the following expression: $10^3 \div 10^2 =$

   Ⓐ 0   Ⓑ 1   Ⓒ 10   Ⓓ 10,000

6. How long is the side of a square whose area is 64 square centimeters?

   Ⓐ 4 cm   Ⓑ 8 cm   Ⓒ 16 cm   Ⓓ 32 cm

7. How long is the side of a cube whose volume is 24?

   Ⓐ $\sqrt{24}$ Ⓑ $\sqrt[3]{24}$ Ⓒ 24^2 Ⓓ 24^3

B. Complete the two parts below. Show all your work.

In the set of whole numbers, a **perfect square** is the square of a whole number. Some examples of perfect squares are 1, 4, and 9.

Part A Multiply the following pairs of perfect squares.

$4 \times 9 =$ _____ $9 \times 16 =$ _____

$4 \times 16 =$ _____ $9 \times 25 =$ _____

$4 \times 25 =$ _____ $16 \times 25 =$ _____

Part B Describe what you observe about the products of perfect squares.

Unit 1: Number Sense, Concepts, and Operations

Name________________________ Class __________ Date __________

Try It Yourself

1.6 Exponents and Radicals
Assessment Practice

A. Evaluate the following expressions involving exponents and radicals. Write your answer at the top of the grid and fill in the numbered circles.

1. $8^3 =$

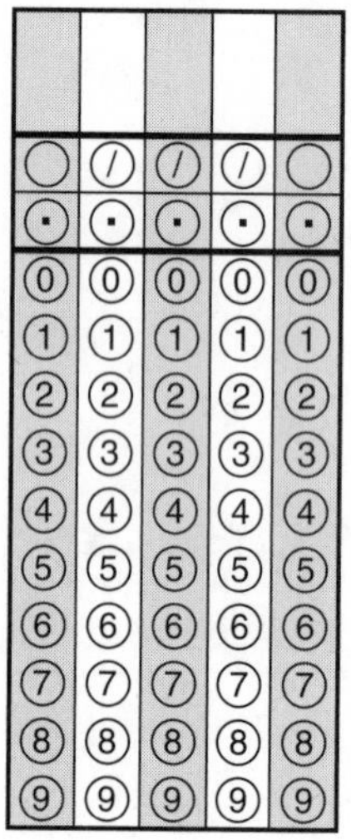

2. $3^5 =$

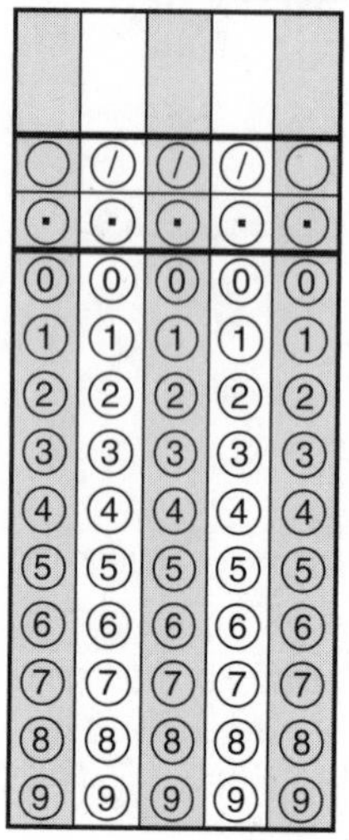

3. $\sqrt{25} =$

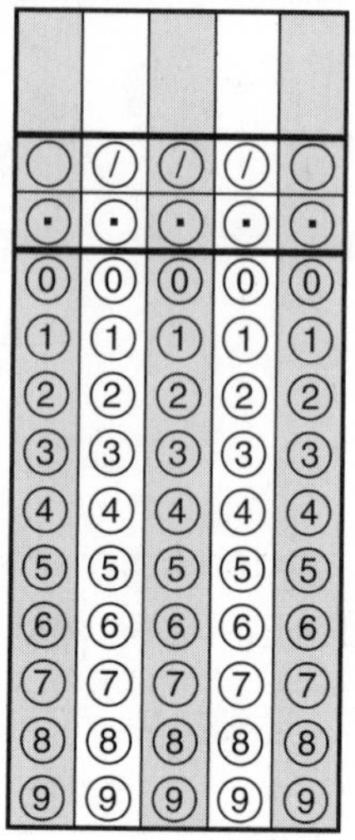

4. $\sqrt[3]{125} =$

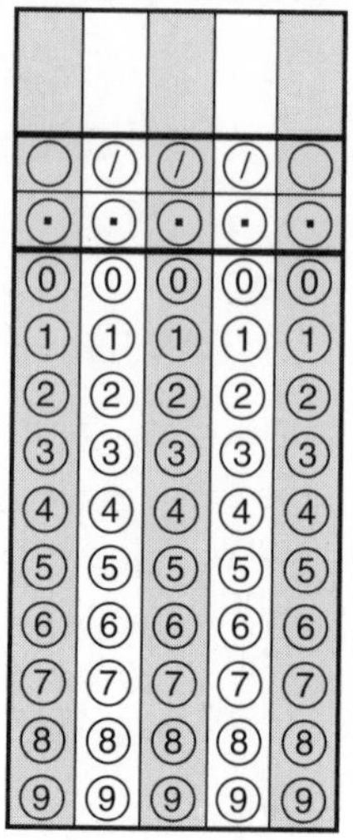

B. Complete the two parts below. Show all your work.

Part A Prove that the following equation is always true: $B^m \times B^n = B^{m+n}$.
(Hint: Remember that the exponent tells you how many times to use B as a factor. Think about how you would write out the expressions on each side.)

Part B Prove that the following equation is always true: $B^m \div B^n = B^{m-n}$.
(Hint: Remember that $B^m \div B^n = \frac{B^m}{B^n}$. Think about how you would write out the numerator and the denominator.)

SCIENTIFIC NOTATION

This lesson addresses Benchmarks MA.A.1.3.1, MA.A.1.3.2, MA.A.1.3.3, and MA.A.2.3.1 of the Sunshine State Standards.

Math in History

In the eighteenth century, the German astronomer Johann Bode made known a simple and beautiful formula for finding the distances of the planets from the sun in AUs, or astronomical units. (One AU is about 1.5×10^8 kilometers.) This formula, known as Bode's Law, says to add 4 to each number in the sequence 0, 3, 6, 12, 24, 48, 96, 192. Then divide each new number by 10 to get the distances in AUs of the planets from the sun. This formula works for all the planets known in the eighteenth century (all but Neptune and Pluto). It even helped astronomers to find the asteroids, because Bode's Law predicted that there should be a planet between Mars and Jupiter.

The Challenge

The boundary between the solar system and interstellar space—called the heliopause—is estimated to occur at a distance of about 100 astronomical units (AUs) from the sun. One AU is equal to about 150 million kilometers and is based on the distance between Earth and the sun. What is the distance from the sun to the heliopause, in kilometers?

The diameter of a period at the end of a sentence is 0.7 millimeter (mm). If 1,000 bacteria can fit end to end across the diameter of a period, how long is each bacterium? Write your answers in scientific notation.

Learning the Ropes

Scientific notation is a way of writing very large and very small numbers to make them easier to work with. Instead of writing out very long numbers with many places, you can use exponents to show the places.

To write a number in scientific notation, you multiply a number between 1 and 10 by a power of 10. For example, suppose you want to write the number 200,000,000 in scientific notation. This number is equal to $2 \times 100,000,000$, or 2×10^8. It is much easier to write 2×10^8 than to write out all the zeros, and it is also easier to keep track of the places.

You can make your number more precise by adding places to the right of the decimal point. For example, the number 214,000,000 can be written as 2.14×10^8.

When converting a decimal number into scientific notation:

1. Move the decimal point so that you get a number between 1 and 10.
2. Count the number of places you move the decimal point.
3. The number of moves the decimal point makes becomes the exponent for your power of 10.
4. If the moves are to the left, the exponent is positive.
5. If the moves are to the right, the exponent is negative.

EXAMPLES $214,000,000 = 2.14 \times 100,000,000 = 2.14 \times 10^8$

$0.00032 = 3.2 \times 0.0001 = 3.2 \times 10^{-4}$

Unit 1: Number Sense, Concepts, and Operations

Study the boxes below to learn how to do operations with exponents.

MULTIPLICATION WITH EXPONENTS
$10 \times 100 = 10^1 \times 10^2 = 10^3 = 1{,}000$
$100 \times 1{,}000 = 10^2 \times 10^3 = 10^5 = 100{,}000$
$10^a \times 10^b = 10^{a+b}$
EXAMPLE $2 \times 10^3 \times 3 \times 10^4 = 6 \times 10^7$

DIVISION WITH EXPONENTS
$100 \div 10 = 10^2 \div 10^1 = 10^1 = 10$
$10{,}000 \div 100 = 10^4 \div 10^2 = 10^2 = 100$
$10^a \div 10^b = 10^{a-b}$
EXAMPLE $8 \times 10^8 \div 2 \times 10^3 = 4 \times 10^5$

Meeting the Challenge

To answer the Challenge, use scientific notation to express the figures and do the calculations.

STEP 1: To answer the first question, write the number of kilometers in 1 AU in scientific notation. Write the number 100 in scientific notation as well.

150 million km = 150,000,000 km = 1.5×10^8 km $100 = 1 \times 10^2$

STEP 2: Multiply the number of kilometers in 1 AU (1.5×10^8) by the number of AUs to the heliopause (10^2). When you multiply two powers of 10 together, add their exponents.

1.5×10^8 km $\times 10^2 = 1.5 \times 10^{10}$ km

STEP 3: To answer the second question, express the length of the diameter in scientific notation. Since you are moving the decimal point to the right, your exponent will be negative. Write the number 1,000 in scientific notation as well.

0.7 mm = 7×10^{-1} mm $1{,}000 = 1 \times 10^3$

STEP 4: To find the length of one bacterium, divide the length of the diameter (7×10^{-1} mm) by the number of bacteria that can fit across it (10^3). When you divide by a power of 10, you subtract its exponent.

7×10^{-1} mm $\div 10^3 = 7 \times 10^{(-1-3)} = 7 \times 10^{-4}$

The answer to the first Challenge question is that the heliopause is about 1.5×10^{10} km (15,000,000,000 or 15 billion km) from the sun. The answer to the second question is that the length of one bacterium is about 7×10^{-4} millimeters (0.0007 mm).

Math in Use: Science   **Microbiology** is the study of living things too small to be seen with the naked eye. **Cosmology** is the study of the universe as a whole. For obvious reasons, microbiologists and cosmologists often use scientific notation. The list below shows approximate dimensions of some small and large objects.

10^{-7} meters	diameter of a virus	10^6 meters	length of California
10^{-5} meters	diameter of a white blood cell	10^9 meters	distance between Earth and the moon
10^{-3} meters	diameter of an eye of a bee	10^{21} meters	length of the Milky Way

Name_____ Class _____ Date _____

Try It Yourself

A. Fill in the circle next to the correct answer to each multiple-choice question.

1. How is 10 billion written in scientific notation?
   Ⓐ 10,000,000,000   Ⓑ 10×10^9 Ⓒ 1×10^{10} Ⓓ 1×10^{-10}

2. The moon is about 2.4×10^5 miles from Earth. What does 2.4×10^5 look like when written in ordinary notation?
   Ⓐ 0.0000024   Ⓑ 0.000024   Ⓒ 240,000   Ⓓ 24,000,000

3. Some E. Coli bacteria are about 2.4×10^{-3} centimeters across. What does 2.4×10^{-3} look like when written in ordinary notation?
   Ⓐ 24,000   Ⓑ 2,400   Ⓒ 0.0024   Ⓓ 0.00024

B. Convert the following numbers to scientific notation.

1. 0.23 _____   3. 0.0009 _____

2. 1,598 _____   4. 1,620,000 _____

C. Convert the following numbers to ordinary notation.

1. 5.36×10^{-4} _____   3. 2.00×10^{-3} _____

2. 6.79×10^6 _____   4. 1.56×10^{-6} _____

D. Write your answer at the top of the grid and fill in the numbered circles.

1. Creatures known as trilobites became extinct at the end of the Paleozoic Era, which was about 2.48×10^8 years ago. How many million years ago was this?

2. There are 36 million seconds in 10,000 hours. To what power should the 10 be raised to express 36 million in scientific notation?

Unit 1: Number Sense, Concepts, and Operations   83

Name_____ Class _____ Date _____

Try It Yourself

A. Fill in the circle next to the correct answer to each multiple-choice question.

1. The speed of light is about 300 million meters per second. What is this number in scientific notation?

   Ⓐ 3×10^6 Ⓑ 300×10^6 Ⓒ 3×10^8 Ⓓ 3×10^9

2. The largest planet in the solar system is Jupiter, with a diameter of about 143,000,000 meters. What is this number in scientific notation?

   Ⓐ 1.43×10^{-8} Ⓑ 143×10^6 Ⓒ 14.3×10^7 Ⓓ 1.43×10^8

3. An electron weighs 9×10^{-31} kilograms. If this number were written out, how many zeros would appear after the decimal point and before the 9?

   Ⓐ none   Ⓑ 1   Ⓒ 30   Ⓓ 31

4. Bats can hear sounds with frequencies up to 1.2×10^5 hertz (hz). What is this number in ordinary notation?

   Ⓐ 1,200,000 hz   Ⓑ 120,000 hz   Ⓒ 0.00012 hz   Ⓓ 0.000012 hz

B. Complete the three parts below. Show all your work.

Neptune, the eighth planet in our solar system, is 30 astronomical units (AUs) from the sun. One AU is equal to about 93 million miles.

Part A Write the number 30 and the number 93 million in scientific notation.

Part B Using your answers to the previous question, write a number sentence that tells how many miles are in 30 AUs.

Part C Find the distance in miles from Neptune to the sun. Write your answer in scientific notation.

COMPARING AND ORDERING REAL NUMBERS

This lesson addresses Benchmark MA.A.1.3.2 of the Sunshine State Standards.

Math in History
Before the time of the Greek mathematician Pythagoras, people generally believed that all numbers were rational—that they could be expressed as ratios of whole numbers. More than 2,500 years ago, Pythagoras discovered that the length of the hypotenuse of a right triangle equals the square root of the sum of the squares of the other two sides. With this formula, the first irrational number, $\sqrt{2}$, was identified. If both legs of a right triangle are 1 unit, then the hypotenuse is the square root of ($1^2 + 1^2$), or $\sqrt{2}$. There is no way to express $\sqrt{2}$ as the ratio of two whole numbers, so it is not a rational number but an "irrational" number.

The Challenge

Two students calculated the answer to the following problem: Find the value of $\sqrt{3(7+1)+5^2+4+2^3}$. Bart wrote the answer as $\sqrt{61}$, while Elizabeth used a calculator and came up with 7.81. Which student's answer is greater?

Learning the Ropes

Comparing and ordering numbers is an important skill that is useful in mathematics and other areas of life. When you **compare** two numbers, you decide which one is greater or which one is smaller. To put a set of numbers in **ascending order,** arrange them from lowest (least) to highest (greatest). **Descending order** is an arrangement from highest to lowest.

Ordering Decimals. When you compare or order **decimals,** it is often helpful to write the decimals in a vertical row, using the decimal point to align them. Then begin at the left to compare them. If the digits in the left-hand place are the same, compare the digits in the next place to the right. Continue until you can determine which decimal is greater.

EXAMPLE   Rewrite this chart so that the bolts listed below are arranged with their diameters in ascending order of size.

DIAMETERS OF BOLTS					
Part Number	2-A	4-T	6-H	3-C	6-B
Diameter	1.2 cm	6.75 mm	1.05 cm	1.55 mm	8.2 mm

Notice that some of the sizes are given in centimeters (cm) and some are in millimeters (mm). First, you need to change the centimeter measures to millimeters by multiplying each centimeter measure by 10.

Math in Use: Approximation An irrational number can be expressed as a nonrepeating, nonterminating decimal. The value of such a number is not exact but can be approximated to any convenient number of decimal places. Engineers, architects, astronomers, and other specialists regularly use approximations of irrational numbers in their work. Computers have made calculating these approximations much easier than when manual calculations were needed. The value of π, for example, has been computed to more than 2 billion decimal places!

Once the measures are all in millimeters, you can line them up vertically, as shown in the first list to the right. Compare the digits in the ones and tens places. Then put the numbers in ascending order (smallest to largest), as shown in the second list (far right).

2-A	12.0 mm
4-T	6.75 mm
6-H	10.5 mm
3-C	1.55 mm
6-B	8.2 mm

3-C	1.55 mm
4-T	6.75 mm
6-B	8.2 mm
6-H	10.5 mm
2-A	12.0 mm

Ordering Decimals, Fractions, and Percents. To compare decimals, fractions, and percents, first change all the numbers so that they are in the same form. Usually, decimals are the most convenient form.

EXAMPLE Six students carried out a probability experiment in which each student tossed 4 coins 100 times. The chart below shows how often each person got 2 heads and 2 tails out of 100 tosses. Arrange the results in descending order (largest to smallest).

COIN-TOSS RESULTS: 2 HEADS AND 2 TAILS						
Student	Abe	Ben	Kate	Del	Eve	Fred
Portion of Coin Tosses	0.37	38%	$\frac{39}{100}$	42%	0.34	$\frac{9}{25}$

Change the percents to decimals.

$$38\% = 0.38 \qquad 42\% = 0.42$$

Change the fractions to decimals.

$$\frac{39}{100} = 0.39 \qquad \frac{9}{25} = 0.36$$

You can now compare decimals to order the numbers from highest to lowest.

COIN-TOSS RESULTS: 2 HEADS AND 2 TAILS						
Student	Del	Kate	Ben	Abe	Fred	Eve
Portion of Coin Tosses	0.42	0.39	0.38	0.37	0.36	0.34

Ordering Rational Numbers. A **rational number** is any number that can be expressed in the form $\frac{a}{b}$, where a is any integer, and b is any integer other than zero. Any rational number can be graphed as a specific point on a number line. You can use a number line to order a set of rational numbers. If one rational number lies to the right of another, it is greater than the other.

EXAMPLE   The chart below shows the low temperatures for five days in a cold January week. Which day had the lowest temperature?

Day	Mon.	Tues.	Weds.	Thurs.	Fri.
Temperature (°F)	$1\frac{1}{2}°$	$-12.5°$	$-4.8°$	$5°$	$11°$

When the temperatures are ordered on a number line, Tuesday's temperature is the farthest to the left, so it was the coldest day. Notice that -12.5 is colder than -4.8 because it is farther below zero.

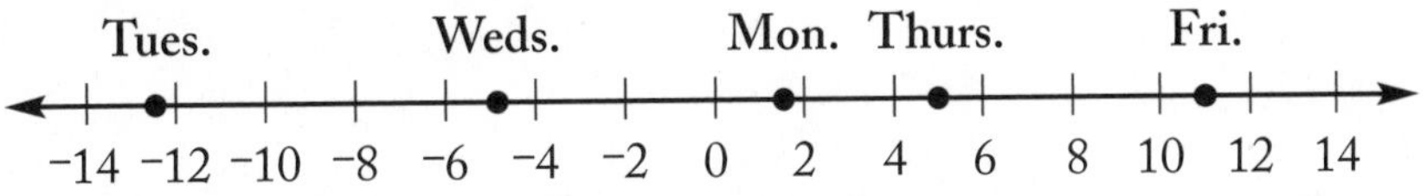

Ordering Irrational Numbers. An **irrational number** is one that cannot be expressed as a ratio of two integers. Familiar irrational numbers include π (the ratio of the distance around any circle to the distance across the circle) and the square roots of nonperfect squares.

Numbers such as $\sqrt{2}$ and $\sqrt{3}$ occur frequently in math problems. They cannot be expressed exactly as common fractions or repeating decimals. You can use a calculator or a table such as the partial table shown below to find an approximate value for the square root of each number, n.

n	$\sqrt{n}$	n	$\sqrt{n}$
1	1.000	11	3.317
2	1.414	12	3.464
3	1.732	13	3.606
4	2.000	14	3.742
5	2.236	15	3.873
6	2.449	16	4.000
7	2.646	17	4.123
8	2.828	18	4.243
9	3.000	19	4.359
10	3.162	20	4.472

Comparing Rational and Irrational Numbers. To compare rational and irrational numbers, you can find the decimal approximations for the irrational numbers and the decimal equivalents for the rational numbers.

EXAMPLE   Order 325%, $\sqrt{10}$, $\sqrt{11}$, and 3.1 from least to greatest.

3.1	$\sqrt{10}$	325%	$\sqrt{11}$
3.10	3.162...	3.25	3.317...

You can also square the numbers and compare the squares.

EXAMPLE   Which is greater, $\sqrt{11}$ or 3.21?

$$\sqrt{11}^2 = \sqrt{11} \times \sqrt{11} = 11$$
$$(3.21)^2 = 3.21 \times 3.21 = 10.3041$$
$$11 > 10.3041, \text{ so } \sqrt{11} > 3.21$$

Meeting the Challenge

To answer the Challenge, you must compare a decimal and a square root. You can either square both numbers or use a calculator to find a decimal approximation for the square root.

STEP 1:   Square the results found by each student.
$$\sqrt{61}^2 = \sqrt{61} \times \sqrt{61} = 61$$
$$(7.81)^2 = 7.81 \times 7.81 = 60.9961$$

STEP 2:   Compare the squares.

61 > 60.996

Therefore, $\sqrt{61} > 7.81$.

STEP 3:   To check your answer, find the square root of 61 on a calculator.
$$\sqrt{61} \approx 7.81025$$

Since 7.81025 is greater than 7.81, you can conclude that $\sqrt{61}$ is greater than 7.81.

The answer to the Challenge is that the square root of 61 (Bart's answer) is the greater number.

Another Way   When comparing or ordering decimals, you can add zeros after the last decimal place to make the digits easier to compare. For example, in the problem about the bolts at the beginning of this lesson, the measurements could be rewritten as shown to the right.

1.55	1.55
6.75	6.75
8.2	8.20
10.5	10.50
12	12.00

Name________________________ Class ________ Date ________

Try It Yourself

1.8 Comparing and Ordering Real Numbers
Practice Exercises

A. Fill in the circle next to the correct answer to each multiple-choice question.

1. Irene and Kevin measured the mass of some chemicals on different scales. Which mass is the smallest?

   Ⓐ 10.4 grams Ⓑ 10.098 grams Ⓒ 10.115 grams Ⓓ 10.42 grams

2. Ms. VanHoff offers her students extra points on their math test. They can choose to get 10 points, $\sqrt[3]{500}$ points, $\sqrt{90}$ points, or 1^{15} points. Sheila wants as many extra points as she can get. What should she choose?

   Ⓐ 10 points Ⓑ $\sqrt[3]{500}$ points Ⓒ $\sqrt{90}$ points Ⓓ 1^{15} points

3. Which list shows the numbers in ascending order (from smallest to greatest)?

   Ⓐ $5, \sqrt{21}, \sqrt{32}, 6$ Ⓑ $\sqrt{21}, 5, \sqrt{32}, 6$ Ⓒ $\sqrt{21}, \sqrt{32}, 5, 6$ Ⓓ $5, 6, \sqrt{21}, \sqrt{32}$

B. Write your answers on the lines provided below.

1. Name a decimal whose value falls between 0.5% and 0.05.

   ____

2. The chart shows the low temperatures recorded for five different towns on a cold night in January. In which town was the overnight low the highest (warmest)?

   ____

LOW TEMPERATURES ON JANUARY 10	
Bergtown	−4° F
Chattertown	−8° F
Porth Knoll	−12° F
Fridgeton	−1° F
Snowboro	−6° F

C. Complete the activity below. Show all your work.

Draw a number line from 0 to 10. Put the following numbers in order on the number line:

$2\pi, \sqrt{37}, 6.25, 3$

Name________________________ Class __________ Date __________

Try It Yourself

1.8 Comparing and Ordering Real Numbers Assessment Practice

A. Fill in the circle next to the correct answer to each multiple-choice question.

1. Which number has the least value?

Ⓐ 0.65 Ⓑ 0.56 Ⓒ 0.056 Ⓓ 0.605

2. Which number has the greatest value?

Ⓐ 42% Ⓑ 0.402 Ⓒ 4% Ⓓ 0.24

3. Which list shows the numbers in descending order?

Ⓐ $4, 5, \sqrt{17}, \sqrt{22}$ Ⓑ $5, 4, \sqrt{22}, \sqrt{17}$ Ⓒ $5, \sqrt{22}, \sqrt{17}, 4$ Ⓓ $\sqrt{22}, \sqrt{17}, 5, 4$

4. Valerie chooses a number x with one decimal place such that $\sqrt{20} \leq x \leq \sqrt{24}$. Ken has to guess her number. What is a possible value for x?

Ⓐ 4.1 Ⓑ 4.3 Ⓒ 4.7 Ⓓ 5.1

5. Which list shows the numbers in ascending order (from smallest to greatest)?

Ⓐ $\sqrt{83}, 3\pi, 9.56, 7\sqrt{2}$

Ⓑ $3\pi, \sqrt{83}, 7\sqrt{2}, 9.56$

Ⓒ $\sqrt{83}, 3\pi, 7\sqrt{2}, 9.56$

Ⓓ $3\pi, \sqrt{83}, 9.56, 7\sqrt{2}$

B. Complete the two parts below.

A nurse recorded the change in a patient's body temperature over five days. The results are shown in the chart below.

Day	Mon.	Tues.	Weds.	Thurs.	Fri.
Change in Temperature (°F)	+2°	+1°	0°	−3°	−1°

Part A On which day did the patient's temperature decrease the most? Explain your answer.

Part B Suppose that the patient's temperature was 100 degrees on Sunday. The chart shows that his temperature rose 2 degrees on Monday, another 1 degree on Tuesday, etc. What was his temperature by Friday? Show how you found your answer.

PROPERTIES AND IDENTITIES

This lesson addresses Benchmark MA.A.3.3.1 of the Sunshine State Standards.

The Challenge

Scott took $40 to the mall. He spent $12 for a CD and $5 for a pair of socks. For each of his two nephews, he bought a baseball cap for $7 and a pencil for $1. He bought a notebook for $3 at a "Buy One, Get One Free" sale and received a second notebook for free. He also received a refund of $12 for a T-shirt he returned. How much money did Scott have when he left the mall? Name and describe the properties of real numbers that are involved in solving this problem.

Math in History
Although humans have been using basic laws of arithmetic for thousands of years, it wasn't until relatively recently that the associative, distributive, and commutative properties were set down in writing. French artillery expert François-Joseph Servois (1767–1847) and Irish mathematician William Rowan Hamilton (1805–1865) first formulated these rules after developments in advanced algebra surprisingly showed that some of the properties did not hold true in certain rare cases.

Learning the Ropes

You probably knew several rules about numbers long before you learned the names of those rules. For example, you probably understood that adding zero to a number does not change the number. (Zero is called the **identity element** for addition.) It is possible to solve problems involving real numbers because the real numbers always behave the same way in certain situations. These predictable behaviors, or rules, are known as **properties.** This lesson will identify these properties by name and describe what they tell us about how numbers work. The table below and on the next page shows properties of real numbers.

Property	Examples
Commutative (Order) Property of Addition Changing the order of the addends does not change the sum.	$a + b = b + a$ $3.2 + 0.4 = 0.4 + 3.2$
Commutative (Order) Property of Multiplication Changing the order of the factors does not change the product.	$ab = ba$ $5 \times {}^-4 = {}^-4 \times 5$

Property	Examples
Associative (Grouping) Property of Addition Changing the grouping of three or more addends does not change the sum.	$(a + b) + c = a + (b + c)$ $(6 + 2) + 7 = 6 + (2 + 7)$
Associative (Grouping) Property of Multiplication Changing the grouping of three or more factors does not change the product.	$(a \times b) \times c = a \times (b \times c)$ $(\frac{1}{2} \times \frac{2}{3}) \times \frac{3}{4} = \frac{1}{2} \times (\frac{2}{3} \times \frac{3}{4})$
Distributive Property of Multiplication over Addition Multiplying the sum of two numbers by a third number is the same as multiplying each of the two numbers by that third number and then adding the products.	$a \times (b + c) = (a \times b) + (a \times c)$ $^-3 \times (6 + 4) = (^-3 \times 6) + (^-3 \times 4)$
Identity Element for Addition Adding zero to any number does not change the number.	$a + 0 = a \qquad 0.397 + 0 = 0.397$ $0 + a = a \qquad 0 + 0.397 = 0.397$
Identity Element for Multiplication Multiplying any number by 1 does not change the number.	$a \times 1 = a \qquad ^-251 \times 1 = ^-251$ $1 \times a = a \qquad 1 \times ^-251 = ^-251$
Zero Property of Multiplication The product of any number and 0 is 0.	$a \times 0 = 0 \qquad \frac{4}{9} \times 0 = 0$ $0 \times a = 0 \qquad 0 \times \frac{4}{9} = 0$
Transitive Property of Equality Two quantities are equal if both of them are equal to a third quantity.	If $a = b$ and $b = c$, then $a = c$. $\qquad 10 \times 10 = 5 \times 20$ and $5 \times 20 = 4 \times 25$, so $10 \times 10 = 4 \times 25$
Additive Inverse Property The sum of any number and its opposite is 0.	$a + {^-a} = 0 \qquad 7.9 + {^-7.9} = 0$
Multiplicative Inverse Property The product of any number and its reciprocal is 1.	$a \times \frac{1}{a} = \frac{a}{a} = 1 \quad 5 \times \frac{1}{5} = \frac{5}{5} = 1$
Closure Property The real numbers are closed under addition, subtraction, multiplication, and division because the sum, difference, product, or quotient of two real numbers is a real number. In other words, performing these operations with real numbers will yield only real numbers.	If a and b are real numbers, then $c, d, e,$ and f are real numbers. $\qquad a + b = c$ $\qquad a - b = d$ $\qquad a \times b = e$ $\qquad a \div b = f$

The operations that you use to calculate with real numbers also have properties. For example, **inverse operations** are operations that undo each other. The table below shows pairs of inverse operations.

Inverse Operations	Examples
Addition and Subtraction	$a + b = c$ and $c - b = a$ $4 + 5 = 9$ and $9 - 5 = 4$
Multiplication and Division	$a \times b = c$ and $c \div b = a$ $3 \times {}^-7 = {}^-21$ and ${}^-21 \div {}^-7 = 3$
Powers and Roots	$a \times a = a^2$ and $\sqrt{a^2} = a$ $7 \times 7 = 49$ and $\sqrt{49} = 7$

When you subtract a number, you are adding its inverse—the corresponding negative number.

EXAMPLE $\quad 9 - 5 = 9 + {}^-5$

Notice that when you change a subtraction problem to addition of the inverse, you can use the commutative property of addition.

EXAMPLE $\quad 9 - 5$ is *not* equal to $5 - 9$, but $9 + {}^-5$ *is* equal to ${}^-5 + 9$

Similarly, when you divide by a number, you are multiplying by the inverse, or reciprocal.

EXAMPLE $\quad 15 \div 3 = 15 \times \frac{1}{3}$

Once you have a multiplication problem, you can apply the commutative property of multiplication.

EXAMPLE $\quad 15 \div 3$ is *not* equal to $3 \div 15$, but $15 \times \frac{1}{3}$ *is* equal to $\frac{1}{3} \times 15$

Since $7 \times 7 = 49$, the square root of 49 is 7. However, ${}^-7 \times {}^-7$ is also equal to 49. Therefore, ${}^-7$ is also a square root of 49. As you know, the symbol $\sqrt{}$ is used to represent a square root.

EXAMPLES $\quad \sqrt{16} = 4, {}^-4 \qquad 4 \times 4 = 16 \qquad {}^-4 \times {}^-4 = 16$

$\qquad\qquad \sqrt{81} = 9, {}^-9 \qquad 9 \times 9 = 81 \qquad {}^-9 \times {}^-9 = 81$

$\qquad\qquad \sqrt{100} = 10, {}^-10 \qquad 10 \times 10 = 100 \qquad {}^-10 \times {}^-10 = 100$

Can you find the two square roots of 225?

Unit 1: Number Sense, Concepts, and Operations

Meeting the Challenge

To answer the Challenge, you must name and describe the properties of real numbers that are involved in the calculations required to solve the problem. There are different ways to look at this situation; the steps below show one approach.

STEP 1: Write a number sentence to represent the situation. Since addition and subtraction are inverse operations, each of Scott's purchases can be shown either by subtracting the amount from his original $40 or by adding the negative amount.

original amount	CD	socks	2 caps	2 pencils	first notebook	second notebook	refund	

$$40 + {}^-12 + {}^-5 + (2 \times {}^-7) + (2 \times {}^-1) + {}^-3 - 0 + 12 = \text{the amount left}$$

STEP 2: Notice the number properties you could apply to solve the problem. Scott bought 2 caps and 2 pencils. The distributive property says that the expression for the purchase of these items can be written as either $(2 \times {}^-7) + (2 \times {}^-1)$ or $2({}^-7 + {}^-1)$. The first expression shows that he bought 2 caps for $7 each $(2 \times {}^-7)$ plus 2 pencils for $1 each $(2 \times {}^-1)$. The second expression shows that he bought a cap and a pencil $({}^-7 + {}^-1)$ for each of 2 boys. You can use either expression.

$$(2 \times {}^-7) + (2 \times {}^-1) = 2({}^-7 + {}^-1) = (2 \times {}^-8) = {}^-16$$

STEP 3: The commutative property of addition allows you to switch the order of the addends. If you do this by putting $+ 12$ next to $+ {}^-12$, you will see that you can cancel these two numbers because the additive inverse property says that this sum is equal to 0. Whenever you can cancel two inverses, you simplify your work because you do not have to perform either operation.

$$40 + {}^-12 + {}^-5 + {}^-16 + {}^-3 - 0 + 12 = 40 + \cancel{{}^-12} + \cancel{12} + {}^-5 + {}^-16 + {}^-3 - 0$$

STEP 4: The second notebook is free ($0). The identity element for addition is 0, so this term can also be canceled, since adding (or subtracting) 0 does not change a number.

STEP 5: Now the number sentence can be solved to find how much money Scott had left. You started with a number sentence that expressed how much money Scott started with and what he did with the money. Each time you performed the operations correctly, you created a new expression that was equal to the previous one. The transitive property tells you that the final result, $16, is equal to the quantity in the original number sentence, so Scott had $16 left.

Another Way Instead of subtracting the price of each item Scott bought, you can add the prices of all his purchases and subtract the sum from his original $40:

$$12 + 5 + 2(7 + 1) + 3 = 12 + 5 + 16 + 3 = 36 \qquad 40 - 36 = 4$$

You know that the clerk could add up Scott's purchases in any order or with any groupings and still get the same total. These facts illustrate the commutative and associative properties of addition.

Commutative

$$12 + 5 + 16 + 3$$
$$= 5 + 12 + 3 + 16$$

Associative

$$(12 + 5) + (16 + 3)$$
$$= 12 + (5 + 16) + 3$$

Try It Yourself

A. Fill in the circle next to the correct answer to each multiple-choice question.

1. Which property is demonstrated by the equation $4 \times (9 \times 2) = (4 \times 9) \times 2$?
   - Ⓐ commutative property of multiplication
   - Ⓑ identity element for multiplication
   - Ⓒ associative property of multiplication
   - Ⓓ distributive property of multiplication over addition

2. Which property is demonstrated by the equation $(7.2 + 3) + 0.9 = (3 + 7.2) + 0.9$?
   - Ⓐ commutative property of addition
   - Ⓑ distributive property
   - Ⓒ associative property of addition
   - Ⓓ identity element for addition

3. Which equation is an example of the zero property of multiplication?
   - Ⓐ $2,000 + 0 = 2,000$
   - Ⓒ $0 \times 2,000 = 0$
   - Ⓑ $2,000 \times 0 = 0 \times 2,000$
   - Ⓓ $2,000 - 2,000 \times 1 = 0$

4. Which equation is an example of the identity element for addition?
   - Ⓐ $(^-3 + 0) + 2 = ^-3 + 2$
   - Ⓒ $^-3 \times 0 = 0$
   - Ⓑ $^-3 \times 1 = ^-3$
   - Ⓓ $3 + 1 = 4$

B. Complete the activity below. Show all your work.

Are subtraction and division commutative and associative? In other words, do the *orders* and *groupings* of numbers in subtraction and division problems affect the answers? Explain your answer and give examples.

Try It Yourself

A. Fill in the circle next to the correct answer to each multiple-choice question.

1. Which property is demonstrated by the equation $\frac{3}{5} \times \frac{1}{4} = \frac{1}{4} \times \frac{3}{5}$?

   Ⓐ associative property of multiplication

   Ⓑ closure property of multiplication

   Ⓒ distributive property of multiplication over addition

   Ⓓ commutative property of multiplication

2. Which property is demonstrated by the equation $-5 + (0 + 3) = (-5 + 0) + 3$?

   Ⓐ zero property of addition

   Ⓑ commutative property of addition

   Ⓒ identity element for addition

   Ⓓ associative property of addition

3. Which equation is an example of the additive inverse property?

   Ⓐ $6 + 0 = 6$ Ⓒ $6 + (-6) = (-6) + 6$

   Ⓑ $6 + (-6) = 0$ Ⓓ $6 + \frac{1}{6} = 6\frac{1}{6}$

4. Which equation is an example of the identity element for multiplication?

   Ⓐ $1 \times \frac{2}{5} = \frac{2}{5}$ Ⓒ $-1 \times \frac{2}{5} = -\frac{2}{5}$

   Ⓑ $0 \times \frac{2}{5} = 0$ Ⓓ $\frac{2}{5} \times \frac{5}{2} = 1$

B. Complete the two parts below. Show all your work.

If a set of numbers is **closed** for a particular operation, then performing that operation on any two numbers in the set will give another number in the set.

Part A Consider the set of numbers that are integer powers of 10, such as 10^2, 10^0, and 10^{-9}. Is this set closed for multiplication? Explain your answer and give examples.

Part B Is this same set closed for addition? Explain your answer and give examples.

PERFORMING OPERATIONS

This lesson addresses Benchmarks MA.A.3.3.2 and MA.A.3.3.3 of the Sunshine State Standards.

Math in History
Negative numbers are used extensively in modern times. For example, we are used to seeing temperatures expressed as negative numbers, as in –10°F. By the sixth century A.D., mathematicians in India and China had figured out the basic rules for operations with negative numbers. However, as late as 1796, William Fredn, in his book *The Principles of Algebra,* wrote that a number "submits to being taken away from another number greater than itself, but to attempt to take it away from a number less than itself is ridiculous."

The Challenge

There are at least four possible solutions to the following expression, depending on the order in which the mathematical operations are performed. Which solution is correct?

Expression: $3^3 - {}^-2 \times 5 + \sqrt{16} \div (7.5 \times 10^{-1} + \frac{1}{4})$

Possible Solutions: A) 41 B) 45 C) 149 D) 261

Learning the Ropes

A **mathematical operation** is any process that involves a change in a quantity, like adding, dividing, cubing, or taking a square root. You have already studied many different ways to express quantities and work with them. In this lesson, you will review some rules for performing operations on real numbers in different forms.

Converting to Decimals. When you are comparing numbers or performing operations on a set of numbers, it is helpful to change your numbers into the form that will be easiest to work with in that situation. Comparing numbers is easy if they are all in decimal form. Converting a number to a decimal is quick and easy on a calculator:

- If the number is a fraction, divide the fraction on your calculator. EXAMPLE $\frac{2}{5} = 2 \div 5 = 0.4$

- If the number is a percent, convert it to a decimal by dividing the percent by 100. EXAMPLE $38\% = 38 \div 100 = 0.38$

- If the number is the percent of a particular number, multiply. EXAMPLE 50% of $\$35.00 = 0.50 \times 35.00 = \$17.50$

- If the number is a radical, find the root. EXAMPLE $\sqrt{6} \approx 2.449$

- If the number is in scientific notation, write it out as a decimal, moving the decimal point as needed. EXAMPLE $3.46 \times 10^{-2} = 0.0346$

Try converting these numbers into decimals. Which keys on a calculator should you press, and in what order, to find each answer?

$\frac{5}{8}$ $\sqrt{2,601}$ 450%

6% 20% of 90 $\frac{11}{12}$

Operating with Positive and Negative Numbers. Here is a review of guidelines for performing operations with positive and negative numbers:

1. When you are adding, multiplying, or dividing all positive numbers, the result will be positive. When you subtract one positive number from another, the result will be positive as long as the smaller number is subtracted from the larger number.

2. Adding a negative number is the same as subtracting a positive number. When adding all negative numbers, the result will be negative. Subtracting a negative number is the same as adding a positive number.

3. When you are adding, if you have both negative and positive numbers, add the positive numbers as a group; then add the negative numbers as a group. Find the difference between the two sums. The result will have the sign of the larger sum.

4. The following tables show the rules for multiplication and division of positive and negative integers.

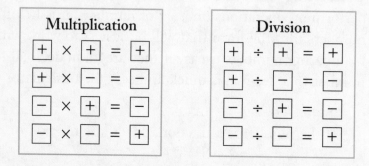

Multiplication	Division
+ × + = +	+ ÷ + = +
+ × − = −	+ ÷ − = −
− × + = −	− ÷ + = −
− × − = +	− ÷ − = +

5. When multiplying an even number of negative numbers (no matter how many positive numbers there are in the equation), the result will be positive.

6. When multiplying an odd number of negative numbers (no matter how many positive numbers there are in the equation), the result will be negative.

7. In division, if either the dividend *or* the divisor is a negative number, the quotient will be negative.

8. In division, if both the dividend *and* the divisor are positive, or if both are negative, the quotient will be positive.

Inverse Operations. Understanding the relationships between **inverse operations,** or opposite operations, can help you solve problems. Addition and subtraction are inverse operations; applying these operations causes movement in opposite directions on the number line. Multiplication and division are also inverse operations. Another pair of inverse operations is squaring a number and taking the square root.

You can use inverse operations to check your answers to problems. For example, suppose you find that the square root of 43 + 38 is equal to 9. To check your answer, find the square of 9 ($9^2 = 81$), and then subtract 38 ($81 - 38 = 43$). Applying the inverse operations takes you back to the number you started with, so your answer is correct.

Order of Operations. Performing mathematical operations in the correct order is critical to arriving at the correct answer. Answers can be quite different depending on the order in which the operations are performed. To ensure that everyone who solves a given expression gets the same answer, there are rules for the order of operations. Here is an expression being simplified according to the rules of the order of operations:

$$4^2 \div 2 + (7 - 1) - 3$$

P	1. **Parentheses:** Always do the operations enclosed in parentheses first.	1. $4^2 \div 2 + (7 - 1) - 3$ $4^2 \div 2 + 6 - 3$
E	2. **Exponents and Radicals:** Then simplify the exponents and radicals.	2. $4^2 \div 2 + 6 - 3$ $16 \div 2 + 6 - 3$
M D	3. **Multiplication and Division:** Next, multiply and divide in order from left to right.	3. $16 \div 2 + 6 - 3$ $8 + 6 - 3$
A S	4. **Addition and Subtraction:** Finally, perform addition and subtraction in order from left to right.	4. $8 + 6 - 3$ $14 - 3 = 11$

Another Way   When adding integers, one way to get the signs right is to consider their absolute values.

When the signs of the integers are the same, as in $^-3 + {}^-6$, add the absolute values of the integers. Then use the sign of the addends.

$|^-3| + |^-6| = 3 + 6 = 9$ The sign of both addends is negative, so change 9 to $^-9$.

When the signs of the integers are different, as in $^-6 + 3$, find the difference of their absolute values. Then use the sign of the addend with the greater absolute value.

$|^-6| - |3| = 6 - 3 = 3$ The sign of the number with the greater absolute value is negative, so change 3 to $^-3$.

Meeting the Challenge

To answer the Challenge, you should convert the numbers into decimals and carry out the operations in the correct order. Try to understand each step before moving on to the next.

STEP 1: This expression will be easier to solve if all the terms are in decimal form. Start by changing the scientific notation and the fraction into decimals.

$$3^3 - {}^-2 \times 5 + \sqrt{16} \div (7.5 \times 10^{-1} + \tfrac{1}{4})$$
$$7.5 \times 10^{-1} = 0.75$$
$$\tfrac{1}{4} = 1 \div 4 = 0.25$$

The expression now reads: $3^3 - {}^-2 \times 5 + \sqrt{16} \div (0.75 + 0.25)$

STEP 2: Now you can start performing the operations, beginning with the operation inside the parentheses.

$$3^3 - {}^-2 \times 5 + \sqrt{16} \div (0.75 + 0.25)$$
$$(0.75 + 0.25) = 1$$

The expression now reads: $3^3 - {}^-2 \times 5 + \sqrt{16} \div 1$

STEP 3: Next, calculate the exponent and the radical.

$$3^3 - {}^-2 \times 5 + \sqrt{16} \div 1$$
$$3^3 = 3 \times 3 \times 3 = 27$$
$$\sqrt{16} = 4$$

The expression now reads: $27 - {}^-2 \times 5 + 4 \div 1$

STEP 4: Next, multiply and divide from left to right.

$$27 - {}^-2 \times 5 + 4 \div 1$$
$${}^-2 \times 5 = {}^-10$$
$$4 \div 1 = 4$$

The expression now reads: $27 - {}^-10 + 4$

STEP 5: Finally, add and subtract from left to right. To subtract a negative number, add its absolute value.

$$27 - {}^-10 + 4 = 27 + 10 + 4 = 41$$

The solution to the Challenge is choice A: 41.

Name_____ Class _____ Date _____

Try It Yourself

A. Carry out each operation below. Write your answer at the top of the grid and fill in the numbered circles.

1. $^-45 \times ^-3 =$

2. $2^3 + 3 \times 4 - (5 + 1) =$

3. $56 - ^-13 =$

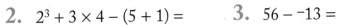

B. Complete the two parts below. Show all your work.

Maria works in a department store where her purchases are deducted from her paycheck at the end of the month. On Tuesday, she bought a pair of shoes, and on Wednesday, she bought a sweater. On Friday, her mother asked her to buy 3 towels. In the chart to the right are the prices of the items she purchased. Maria's monthly paycheck is $288.00.

Item	Price
Shoes	$28.46
Sweater	$15.98
Towels	3 for $17.35 each

Part A What was the total cost of Maria's purchases?

Part B How much money did Maria have left after her charges were deducted from her paycheck?

Unit 1: Number Sense, Concepts, and Operations

Try It Yourself

A. Fill in the circle next to the correct answer to each multiple-choice question.

1. Gerhard chose two numbers between −1 and 0 and multiplied them together. What can you say about the product, p?

   Ⓐ $p < -1$ Ⓑ $-1 < p < 0$ Ⓒ $0 < p < 1$ Ⓓ $p > 1$

2. Suppose that $x > 0$ and $y < 0$. Which of the following statements will **always** be true?

   Ⓐ $x + y > 0$ Ⓑ $x - y > 0$ Ⓒ $x \times y > 0$ Ⓓ $x \div y > 0$

3. Eva and Elliot are playing a card game. On each turn they draw 5 cards. They have to arrange their cards and perform all four operations on them. Which of the following orders gives the biggest score for the cards 1, 2, 3, 4, and 5?

   Ⓐ $5 \times 4 + 3 - 2 \div 1$ Ⓒ $(3 + 4) \times 5 \div (2 - 1)$

   Ⓑ $(4 + 5) \times 3 \div 1 - 2$ Ⓓ $4 \div (2 - 1) \div 5 + 3$

4. James and Elise found different values for this expression: $4^2 - (3 - 2) + 7 \times 8$. Which one is correct?

   Ⓐ 67   Ⓑ 71   Ⓒ 144   Ⓓ 176

B. Complete the two parts below. Show all your work.

The conversion from Celsius (°C) temperature to Fahrenheit (°F) temperature is as follows:

Temperature in °F = (Temperature in °C $\times \frac{9}{5}$) + 32.

To convert from Fahrenheit to Celsius, simply do the opposite:

Temperature in °C = (Temperature in °F − 32) $\times \frac{5}{9}$.

Part A Use the equations above to complete the chart to the right.

Part B At what temperature is the number of degrees Celsius equal to the number of degrees Fahrenheit?

Celsius	Fahrenheit
−55°C	
−40°C	
	14°F
	32°F
	95°F

FORMING ESTIMATES

This lesson addresses Benchmark MA.A.4.3.1 of the Sunshine State Standards.

Math in History

In 1959, the Nobel prize-winning physicist Richard Feynman gave a speech called "There's Plenty of Room at the Bottom." In this speech, he estimated the number of individual book titles in the world at about 24 million. He then explained how the information in all of these books could, in principle, be written in a cube of material one two-hundredth of an inch wide! Feynman's speech inspired a new field of science called nanotechnology, which involves building tiny machines out of individual atoms and molecules.

The Challenge

Ebony is at a restaurant, trying to decide what to order. She has narrowed her meal choices down to three, and she also wants to order iced tea, which costs $2.00. The chef's salad costs $6.95, the chicken tacos cost $7.95, and the steak costs $8.95. She knows that she should also leave 20% of the total meal price to cover the tax and tip. If Ebony has $12.00 to spend, which of these meals can she afford?

Learning the Ropes

When you **estimate,** you simplify problems to make quick calculations of answers that are close to the exact answers. Good estimation skills can help you to spot mathematical mistakes. They can also help you to make decisions quickly when there is no time to go through a complete problem-solving process.

How you estimate depends largely on the type of problem that you are facing. When you need to find out if you have enough money to pay for several items, it is wise to overestimate the total cost by rounding the price of each item up. If your rounded estimate is less than the money you have, then you know you have enough money. On the other hand, suppose you have to reach a minimum goal; for example, you might need to sell a certain number of tickets by a certain date. If you underestimate your ticket sales as you track your daily progress and your low estimate reaches your goal, you can be sure that you will actually achieve your goal.

Here are some general tips for estimating an answer:

1. **Round** the numbers involved. For example, estimate the answer to 4.268×53. The numbers can be rounded to $4 \times 50 = 200$. Therefore, 4.268×53 will be a number slightly larger than 200.

2. **Break** the problem into simpler parts. For example, if you need to figure out the discounted price for an item, first figure out approximately how much should be subtracted. Then do the subtracting.

Math in Use: Geology   Because it is impossible to pinpoint an exact date in the geologic record, geologic time periods are given in approximate, estimated intervals. For example, the dinosaurs roamed the Earth during the Mesozoic Era. The Mesozoic Era began approximately 240 million years ago and ended approximately 63 million years ago. The end of an era is generally marked by the extinction of a vast number of species. The extinction probably did not take place in one year or even in 100 years, but when compared to the rest of geologic time, extinctions tend to cluster. This is another reason why the end of an era can be roughly described but not pinpointed in time.

3. **Think** about the answer. Use common sense.

   EXAMPLE   You are asked to figure out how many people live in an apartment building. You know that there are 24 apartments and that each one has only 2 bedrooms. Common sense tells you that there is at least 1 person per apartment and probably an average of roughly 3 people per apartment. A good estimate of the number of people would be about 75 (or approximately 3 people per apartment).

4. **Substitute** numbers that are close in size but easier to work with.

   EXAMPLE $651 \div 7$ is approximately equal to $630 \div 7$. Seven divides evenly (9 times) into 63, so the estimated answer would be "about 90."

Meeting the Challenge

To answer the Challenge, you need to use estimating strategies to find the approximate cost of the meal, drink, tax, and tip.

STEP 1: Round the cost of each meal to the nearest dollar, then add $2 for the iced tea to each meal's price.

Chef's salad:	$6.95 rounds to $7	+ $2 =	$9
Chicken tacos:	$7.95 rounds to $8	+ $2 =	$10
Steak:	$8.95 rounds to $9	+ $2 =	$11

STEP 2: Determine the 20% tax and tip for each meal. A simple way to find 20% is to take 10% (by moving the decimal point one place to the left) and double it. Then add the tax and tip to the cost of the meal and drink.

	Meal + Drink	10%	20% (10% × 2)	Meal + Drink + Tax/Tip
Chef's salad:	$9	$0.90	$1.80	$10.80
Chicken tacos:	$10	$1.00	$2.00	$12.00
Steak:	$11	$1.10	$2.20	$13.20

The answer to the Challenge is that Ebony can afford either the chef's salad or the chicken tacos because the total for each meal is equal to or less than $12.00. She doesn't have enough money to order both the iced tea and the steak and still cover the tip and taxes.

Name_____ Class _____ Date _____

Try It Yourself

A. Fill in the circle next to the correct answer to each multiple-choice question.

1. Maggie's local music store sells CDs for $12.99 each. They are having a sale that gives a 25% discount to anyone who spends $50 or more. Which of the following is the best estimate of how much Maggie could save on 4 CDs with the discount?

   Ⓐ 50¢   Ⓑ $2   Ⓒ $10   Ⓓ $20

2. Nicholas wants to paint his room. His walls are 7 feet high and 12 feet long. He has 4 walls. If a gallon of paint will cover an area of about 350 square feet, which is the best estimate of how many gallons Nicholas will need to give his walls 2 coats of paint?

   Ⓐ 1 gal   Ⓑ 2 gal   Ⓒ 3 gal   Ⓓ 4 gal

3. Harvey's car gets about 20 miles per gallon of gasoline. Which of the following is the best estimate of how many gallons of gasoline the car will need in order to go 954 miles?

   Ⓐ 5 gal   Ⓑ 25 gal   Ⓒ 40 gal   Ⓓ 50 gal

4. Julie is buying cookies for a class party. There will be about 60 people at the party and she wants to make sure that each person can have at least 3 cookies. If there are 40 cookies in a package, how many packages should she buy?

   Ⓐ 2 packages   Ⓑ 3 packages   Ⓒ 4 packages   Ⓓ 5 packages

B. Complete the two parts below. Show all your work.

For a party, Beatrice wants to serve punch that includes the following ingredients:

   3 quarts lemon sherbet   juice from 6 lemons
   3 quarts club soda   fresh strawberries

Part A ESTIMATE how large a punch bowl (in gallons) she will need. Explain your reasoning.

Part B ESTIMATE how many 4-ounce servings she will get from the recipe.

Name_____ Class _____ Date _____

Try It Yourself

A. Complete each activity below. Show your work.

1. Mary Beth and her family are planning to take a trip. In order to make reservations at a hotel, they must pay a deposit of 20% of the total cost of their seven-night stay. ESTIMATE the amount they need to pay in advance if the hotel charges $148.00 per night.

2. ESTIMATE the size cooking pot (in quarts) that Cho would need to make the following recipe for chili. Keep in mind that 4 cups = 1 quart.

   2 lbs ground beef, browned   4 cups tomato puree
   2 cups onions   3 cups beef stock
   4 cups kidney beans   cayenne pepper and cumin

3. Milton and Fred are traveling with their parents. They are going from Lakeland, Florida, to Atlanta, Georgia, a distance of 454 miles. If they travel at about 50 miles per hour, ESTIMATE how long it will take the family to get to Atlanta.

B. Complete the two parts below. Show all your work. Use additional paper if necessary.

Read the two problems below. Explain how you would round the numbers in each problem in order to find a useful estimate.

Part A The maximum weight an elevator can carry is 1,000 pounds. There are 5 people on the elevator so far. Their weights are 175 pounds, 88 pounds, 205 pounds, 167 pounds, and 110 pounds. Can one more person who weighs 150 pounds safely get on the elevator?

Part B Mr. Brock's car gets about 24 miles to the gallon. His tank holds 19 gallons. He fills up before leaving for a 520-mile trip. Can he make it all the way on one tank?

EXTENDED-RESPONSE QUESTION PRACTICE

1. Each of the numbers below belongs to the set of real numbers. Each number also belongs to one or more of the following sets:

   A. natural numbers
   B. whole numbers
   C. integers
   D. fractions

   E. prime numbers
   F. composite numbers
   G. rational numbers
   H. irrational numbers

Unit 1

Part A For each number below, use the letters above to name all the sets to which the number belongs. The first one has been done for you.

-3 ____C, G____ $|{-2.6}|$ _____ $\frac{6}{5}$ _____

$\sqrt{16}$ _____ $\sqrt{5}$ _____ $-\sqrt{21}$ _____

1.5^3 _____ -0.05 _____ 2.005 _____

$-\frac{5}{4}$ _____ 67% _____ 7×10^{-2} _____

Part B On your own paper, draw a number line from -5 to 5. Place each number above in the correct position on the number line. Put a dot at the point where the number goes, and write the number above that point.

Part C The closure property tells you that if you add, subtract, multiply, or divide any two real numbers, the result will be a real number. In other words, the set of real numbers is **closed** for these operations. Tell whether or not the set of integers is closed for subtraction. Tell whether or not the set of rational numbers is closed for division. Explain your answer.

✔ If you have trouble with this problem, review the following lessons:
   1.1, "Discovering Numbers"
   1.2, "Absolute Value"
   1.3, "Prime and Composite Numbers"
   1.4, "Fractions, Ratios, and Proportions"
   1.5, "Decimals and Percents"
   1.6, "Exponents and Radicals"
   1.7, "Scientific Notation"
   1.9, "Properties and Identities"

Unit 1

2. Your boss promises to increase your wages by 3% every month for the next 6 months if you continue to work hard. Right now you are earning $10 per hour.

Part A If you keep up the good work, how much per hour will you be earning 6 months from now? Explain how you found your answer.

Part B You work 20 hours per week. If your wages continue to increase by 3% each month, what will your weekly wages be 6 months from now? Show your work.

Part C On holidays you earn "time-and-a-half," which means that you get 50% more than your regular wages. If you work 5 hours on a holiday at time-and-a-half and 15 hours at $10 per hour the rest of the week, how much will you earn that week? Show your work.

Part D Suppose you were to get a 6% increase every month for the next 6 months. What would your hourly wage be after 6 months? Show your work.

✔ If you have trouble with this problem, review the following lessons:
1.5, "Decimals and Percents"
1.10, "Performing Operations"

VARIABLES, EXPRESSIONS, AND EQUATIONS

This lesson addresses Benchmarks MA.D.1.3.1 and MA.D.2.3.1 of the Sunshine State Standards.

Math in History
The word *algebra* comes from two Arabic words in the title of a book by a ninth-century Arab mathematician, al-Khwarizmi, but the origins of algebra go back to at least the seventeenth century B.C. In 1858, in a shop in the Nile village of Luxor, Henry Rhind, a Scottish collector of ancient relics and art-work, bought a scroll dated around 1650 B.C. This document, called the Rhind Papyrus in his honor, contains many mathematical problems showing that the ancient Egyptians were already trying to use algebraic equations to find the value of an unknown.

The Challenge

Abigail, Blake, Carina, Dominick, and Elzbieta participate in a walk to raise money for the children's wing of a hospital. Let x stand for the number of miles that Abigail walks. Blake walks 2 miles more than Abigail. Carina walks half as many miles as Blake. Dominick walks 3 miles less than Abigail. Elzbieta walks 6 miles more than Dominick. Write the number of miles each participant walks as an algebraic expression in terms of x.

Learning the Ropes

As you know, **arithmetic** is the science (some would say "the art") of doing computations—adding, subtracting, multiplying, and dividing. **Algebra** is a kind of generalized arithmetic that uses letters to stand for numbers. Consider the following statements:

$$1 - 0 = 1 \qquad 785.6 - 0 = 785.6 \qquad \sqrt{2} - 0 = \sqrt{2}$$

These statements are all examples of a more general principle: If you take any number and subtract 0 from it, you end up with the same number. Algebra allows you to express this more general idea. By letting a letter, a, stand for any number, you can express the idea generally:

For any number a: $\qquad a - 0 = a$

Variables and Constants. The letters used in algebra most often stand for variable or constant quantities. **Variables** are symbols for unknown quantities or for quantities that change, like the amount of money that the federal government spends per year. **Constants** are symbols for any fixed value or for quantities that do not change, like the number of dimes in a dollar. The chart on the next page shows some variables and constants.

Let x represent the year of a person's birth and y represent the year of a person's retirement. A person's age at retirement is equal to $y - x$.	In this example, x and y are both variables because they stand for quantities that change, depending on the person we are talking about.
The constant c represents the speed of light in a vacuum.	The letter c is a constant because it represents a number that does not change (186,000 mi/sec or 300,000 km/sec).
For any number b, $b \times 1 = b$.	The letter b is a variable because it can take on any fixed value.

As a matter of convention, mathematicians tend to use letters from the end of the alphabet, such as x, y, and z, to stand for variables. They tend to use letters from the beginning of the alphabet, such as a, b, and c, to stand for constants. This is not a hard-and-fast rule, however; sometimes people choose letters simply because they are meaningful. For example, the formula for the area of a rectangle can be stated as $A = lw$, where A stands for area, l stands for length, and w stands for width. Capital letters are commonly used for variables that stand for area, circumference, perimeter, surface area, and volume.

Expressions, Equations, and Terms. In algebra, one or more numbers, variables, constants, and operation signs (such as + or −) without an equals sign make up an **expression.**

EXAMPLES x

$2n + 4n$

mc^2

$x(y + z)$

A statement that contains an equals sign, and thus says that two expressions are equal, is called an **equation.**

EXAMPLES $x = 2y + 1$

$2n + 4n = 6n$

$E = mc^2$

$x(y + z) = xy + xz$

Typically, in algebraic expressions, several items are added or subtracted. In the expression $2y + 1$, for example, there are two items. The individual items are called **terms.**

Another Way Remember that variables can stand for numbers that you do not yet know, or **unknowns.** Think of variables as temporary placeholders that you can use until you figure out what they stand for. You can think of terms as words that make up expressions (phrases or clauses) that can be used in equations (sentences).

Creating Algebraic Expressions. Algebra is extremely useful because it allows people to translate everyday problems into expressions that can be manipulated mathematically. For example, how much is dinner plus a 20% tip in a restaurant? If p represents the price of dinner, the total cost, including the tip, can be expressed as

$$p + 0.20p$$

If a class of students is to be divided into teams for baseball, with 9 players on a team, you can let s represent the total number of students and express the number of teams as

$$\frac{s}{9}$$

When translating word problems into expressions, look for key words like *fewer* or *times* that indicate what operation you should use.

EXAMPLES	8 more than Barry	$b + 8$
	7 fewer than Philippe	$p - 7$
	3 times as many as Claudio	$3 \times c$, or $3c$
	half as many as Daryl	$d \div 2$, or $\dfrac{d}{2}$

Meeting the Challenge

To answer the Challenge, you must set up expressions to show each of the quantities in the problem.

STEP 1: The problem tells you to let x represent the number of miles Abigail walks. Write an expression for the number of miles Blake walks compared to Abigail. He walks 2 miles more than Abigail.

Blake's distance = $x + 2$

STEP 2: Using the expression from Step 1 for Blake's distance, write the expression for Carina's distance, which is one-half of Blake's.

Carina's distance = $\frac{1}{2}(x + 2)$

STEP 3: Write Dominick's distance in terms of Abigail's. He walks 3 miles less than she does.

Dominick's distance = $x - 3$

STEP 4: Using the expression from Step 3 for Dominick's distance, write the expression for how far Elzbieta walks, which is 6 miles more than Dominick.

Elzbieta's distance = $(x - 3) + 6$

If x represents how far Abigail walked, then the other participants' distances can be written as the following algebraic expressions:

Blake's distance	$x + 2$
Carina's distance	$\frac{1}{2}(x + 2)$
Dominick's distance	$x - 3$
Elzbieta's distance	$(x - 3) + 6$

112   AIM Higher! FCAT Mathematics

Try It Yourself

A. Fill in the circle next to the correct answer to each multiple-choice question.

1. The perimeter of a regular octagon is P. Which expression represents the length of one side of the octagon?

   Ⓐ $P + 8$ Ⓑ $P \div 8$ Ⓒ $8P$ Ⓓ $P - 8$

2. Mr. Battacherya invests his money in an account that pays 5% interest at the end of 1 year. If m stands for the money that he invests, which expression describes how much he will have after 1 year?

   Ⓐ $5m$ Ⓑ $0.05m$ Ⓒ $m + 5m$ Ⓓ $m + 0.05m$

3. Felicia has 3 times as many stamps in her collection as Christa does. She has half as many stamps as Gabe does. Using each person's initial as a variable, which set of equations represents the information in this problem?

   Ⓐ $f = 3c$ $g = 2f$ Ⓑ $c = 3f$ $g = 2f$ Ⓒ $f = 3c$ $f = 2g$ Ⓓ $f = 3c$ $g = \frac{1}{2}f$

4. Alexis is now twice as old as Javier will be in 3 years. If a represents Alexis's age now, and j represents Javier's age now, which equation correctly relates their ages?

   Ⓐ $a = 2(j + 3)$ Ⓑ $a + 3 = 2j$ Ⓒ $a + 3 = 2(j + 3)$ Ⓓ $a = 2j + 3$

B. Complete the two parts below. Show all your work.

Ms. Mitner wants each student in her math class to have a protractor and a compass. She would also like to have 6 meter sticks for her students to share, and 1 graphing calculator for every 4 students. Let the following letters represent the variables in this problem:

p = cost of 1 protractor m = cost of 1 meter stick
c = cost of 1 compass g = cost of 1 graphing calculator
s = number of students in the class

Part A Write an expression to show the total cost of each of the different items.

cost of protractors: cost of meter sticks:

cost of compasses: cost of graphing calculators:

Part B Write an expression to show the total cost of all the items for the math class.

Try It Yourself

A. Fill in the circle next to the correct answer to each multiple-choice question.

1. There are c cars in a parking garage, with the same number of cars on each of 5 levels. How many cars are on 1 level?

   (A) $5c$ (B) $c + 5$ (C) $c - 5$ (D) $c \div 5$

2. Warren runs m miles on Monday. For each of the next 2 days, he runs twice as far as the day before. Which expression shows how many miles he runs altogether?

   (A) $m + 2m + 2m$ (B) $m + 2m + 4m$ (C) $2m + 4m + 8m$ (D) $m + (2 + m) + (4 + m)$

3. There are some horses and some chickens in a barn. If h represents the number of horses and c represents the number of chickens, which expression shows how many legs are in the barn?

   (A) $h + c$ (B) $4h + 2c$ (C) $2h + 4c$ (D) $4(h + c)$

4. James and Katrina are playing a basketball game in which they get 1 point for each lay-up and 2 points for each foul shot. If they make a shot from 20 feet, their score at that point of the game is tripled. Katrina makes l lay-ups and f foul shots, and then she makes a basket from 20 feet. Which expression represents her score?

   (A) $(l + 2f) \times 3$ (B) $2(l + f) \times 3$ (C) $(l + 2f) + 3$ (D) $(2l + f) \times 3$

B. Complete the two parts below. Show all your work.

Dr. Li went to the store to buy gifts for his patients. He bought some pins for $6 each, some dolls for $10 each, and some notebooks for $2 each.

Part A Write an expression showing how many dollars Dr. Li spent on all the pins, dolls, and notebooks. Explain what each of your variables stands for.

Part B Suppose Dr. Li bought enough items to be able to get them all at half-price. Write a new expression showing how much all the items would cost at half-price.

SIMPLIFYING ALGEBRAIC EXPRESSIONS

This lesson addresses Benchmarks MA.D.1.3.1 and MA.D.2.3.1 of the Sunshine State Standards.

The Challenge

Simplify the expression below:

$$\frac{3a^3 + 5a^3 - 2a^3}{a + 7a - 5a}$$

Learning the Ropes

Math in History

One of the nation's worst forest fires occurred in 1871 in Peshtigo, Wisconsin. About 4 million acres burned in a devastating fire that lasted a week. Today, forest rangers climb tall towers to keep a lookout for fires. How tall do the towers have to be? An approximate formula for figuring this out is $\frac{d^2}{2r} = h$, where d is the distance the ranger will be able to see, r is the radius of Earth (about 4,000 miles), and h is the height of the tower.

As you learned in Lesson 2.1, algebraic expressions use symbols, called variables, to stand for numbers. A **variable** is a letter that represents a set of one or more numbers. A variable can stand for a negative or positive number, a fraction, or a decimal. You can add, subtract, multiply, and divide with variables just as you do with numbers.

Algebraic expressions are made up of terms. Possible **terms** in an expression include real numbers (like 5.2 or $\frac{3}{7}$), variables (like x or y), and products of real numbers and variables (like $7xy$ or $4m^3$). The **coefficient** of a term is the number that is multiplied by the variable (like the 7 in $7xy$ or the 4 in $4m^3$). An **expression** is created by combining terms using mathematical operations.

To make an expression easier to work with, you can simplify it. When you **simplify,** you apply number properties to an expression and reorganize it so that it becomes smaller and more manageable. There are several ways to simplify algebraic expressions.

One way is to add and subtract **like terms,** those that have the same variable and the same exponent. For example, $5x^2$ and $3x^2$ are like terms because they have the same variable (x) and the same exponent (^{2}). To add like terms, simply add the coefficients and keep the variable and exponent the same. For example, $5x^2 + 3x^2 = 8x^2$. The same principle works for subtraction: $5x^2 - 3x^2 = 2x^2$.

To get your like terms together, you may have to use the commutative property of addition to rearrange the terms in the expression.

EXAMPLES $\quad 3r^2 + 2r + r^2 + 4r = 3r^2 + r^2 + 2r + 4r = 4r^2 + 6r$

$\quad\quad\quad\quad v^2 + 4v - 3v^2 - 2v = v^2 - 3v^2 + 4v - 2v = {}^-2v^2 + 2v$

If you have different variables, like x, y, and z, be sure to rearrange the expression so that terms with like variables are together.

EXAMPLES $4x + y - 3x + 5y = 4x - 3x + y + 5y = x + 6y$

$7f + 3g - 4 - 2f = 7f - 2f + 3g - 4 = 5f + 3g - 4$

Another way to simplify is by **canceling** like variables in the numerator and denominator of an expression. You know that any number divided by itself is equal to 1. This is true of variables as well, so any time you see a variable as a factor in both the numerator and denominator of a fraction, you can cross out both variables. Study the examples below.

EXAMPLES $\dfrac{8\cancel{t}}{\cancel{t}} = \dfrac{8 \times 1}{1} = 8$ $\dfrac{3\cancel{v^2}}{2\cancel{v^2}} = \dfrac{3 \times 1}{2 \times 1} = \dfrac{3}{2}$ $\dfrac{2y^2\cancel{x}}{10\cancel{x}} = \dfrac{2y^2 \times 1}{10 \times 1} = \dfrac{y^2}{5}$

As you can see from the last example above, you can also simplify fractions in expressions. All these methods of simplifying can make an expression much easier to read and your computations much easier to carry out.

Meeting the Challenge

To answer the Challenge, you must write the most simplified version of the algebraic expression.

STEP 1: First, combine the like terms in the numerator and in the denominator.

$$\frac{3a^3 + 5a^3 - 2a^3}{a + 7a - 5a} = \frac{6a^3}{3a}$$

STEP 2: Next, cancel the like variable in the numerator and denominator.

$$\frac{6a^3}{3a} = \frac{6a^{\cancel{3}}}{3\cancel{a}} = \frac{6a^2}{3}$$

STEP 3: Finally, simplify the fraction.

$$\frac{6a^2}{3} = 2a^2$$

The whole expression $\dfrac{3a^3 + 5a^3 - 2a^3}{a + 7a - 5a}$ is equal to nothing more than $2a^2$.

Another Way   To understand why adding or subtracting like terms works, recall the distributive property of multiplication over addition. This rule says that multiplying a number (x) by the sum of two addends ($a + b$) is equal to the sum of the number multiplied by each addend ($ax + bx$).

$(a + b)x = (ax + bx)$

When a and b are the coefficients and x is the variable, the quantity on the right of the equation above shows two terms with the same variable, and the quantity on the left is the sum of the coefficients times the variable.

Name______________________ Class __________ Date __________

Try It Yourself

2.2 Simplifying Algebraic Expressions Practice Exercises

A. Fill in the circle next to the correct answer to each multiple-choice question.

1. What is the most simplified form of the expression $2x^2 + 3x - 2x$?

   Ⓐ $3x$　　Ⓑ $2x^2 + x$　　Ⓒ $3x^2$　　Ⓓ $5x^2 - 2x$

2. Jen gave Gonzalo this riddle: Think of a number, x. Square the number. Multiply by 3. Divide by x. Subtract x. What is the result?

   Ⓐ 3　　Ⓑ $2x$　　Ⓒ x^2　　Ⓓ $3x$

3. Then Gonzalo gave Jen a riddle: Think of a number, n. Multiply by 3. Square your answer. Subtract n^2. Divide by 2. What is the result?

   Ⓐ 4　　Ⓑ n　　Ⓒ n^2　　Ⓓ $4n^2$

4. What is the most simplified form of the expression $\dfrac{7a^2 + 5a^2}{a + 2a}$?

   Ⓐ $4a$　　Ⓑ $4a^2$　　Ⓒ 6　　Ⓓ $6a$

5. What is the most simplified form of the expression $\dfrac{t^2 - 2t^2 + 3t^2}{4t - 2t - t}$?

   Ⓐ $2t^2$　　Ⓑ $2t$　　Ⓒ $3t$　　Ⓓ $6t$

B. Complete the two parts below. Show all your work. Use additional paper if necessary.

Part A Akane wanted to find the most simplified form of the expression shown below. Show her each step you would take to simplify the expression. Explain what you are doing in each step.

$$\frac{8a - 3a - a - 2a + 6a - 7 + 11}{3a - a + 2a + 2}$$

Part B To check the simplified expression, substitute the number 3 for the variable a in the original expression. **Evaluate** the expression (find its value). If your answer does not match what you found when you simplified the expression with the variable, go back and find out where you made a mistake.

Try It Yourself

A. Fill in the circle next to the correct answer to each multiple-choice question.

1. Shelby had b baseball cards. Ron had 5 times as many cards as Shelby. Shelby gave all her cards to Ron. Then Ron gave half of the cards to Pam. How many did Pam get?

   Ⓐ $(5 + b) \div 2$ Ⓑ $3b$ Ⓒ $2b$ Ⓓ $3 + b$

2. What is the most simplified form of the expression $2a + b - 13 - a + 21$?

   Ⓐ $a + b + 34$ Ⓑ $a + b + 8$ Ⓒ $3a + b - 34$ Ⓓ $3a + b - 8$

3. Philip ran around the outside of a rectangular park. He wanted to estimate how far he had run. He knew that the park was about 4 times as long as it was wide. If he measured the width to be about f feet, how far did he run?

   Ⓐ $10f$ Ⓑ $8f$ Ⓒ $5f$ Ⓓ $4f$

4. Mrs. Reese put this expression on the board: $\dfrac{10a^2 - 5a^2 + 10a^2}{4a - 2a + a}$.

   She asked her students to find the value of the expression when $a = 1$, $a = 3$, $a = 5$, $a = 7$, and $a = 9$. Steven decided to simplify the expression before putting in the values of a. What is the most simplified form of the expression?

   Ⓐ $3a$ Ⓑ $5a$ Ⓒ $\dfrac{15a^2}{3a^3}$ Ⓓ $5a^2$

B. Complete the three parts below. Show all your work.

Natasha has a coin collection. The variables below represent the following quantities:

p = number of pennies Natasha has d = number of dimes Natasha has

n = number of nickels Natasha has q = number of quarters Natasha has

Part A Write an expression that shows how many coins Natasha has.

Part B Write an expression that shows the total face value of Natasha's coins (in cents).

Part C Suppose that Natasha has an equal number of each kind of coin. If she has c coins of each kind, what is the most simplified expression giving the total face value of her collection?

SOLVING EQUATIONS WITH ONE VARIABLE

This lesson addresses Benchmark MA.D.2.3.1 of the Sunshine State Standards.

The Challenge

Tim had $110 in savings. Then he received $40 for his birthday and earned $65 babysitting. He bought 2 CDs with some of the money. He also spent $21 on a new shirt. Then he bought one more CD at another store. He now has $152. If CDs cost the same at the two stores, how much did Tim spend for each CD?

Learning the Ropes

Many algebraic equations contain a single variable. The variable may appear in more than one term in the equation.

Problem	Variable	Equation
You used a coupon to buy a movie ticket and received a 20% discount. You paid $8.40 for the ticket. What is the usual ticket price?	Let t represent the usual price.	$t - 0.20t = \$8.40$ $0.80t = \$8.40$ $t = \$10.50$
A veterinarian gave 24 rabies shots on Monday and Tuesday. He gave twice as many on Tuesday as on Monday. How many did he give on Monday?	Let s represent the number of shots given on Monday.	$s + 2s = 24$ $3s = 24$ $s = 8$

How do you solve such equations? The secret is to remember that an equation is like a balance scale. The quantities on either side of the equals sign balance each other because they are the same. Because this is so, you can do anything you want to one side of the equation as long as you do the same thing to the other side.

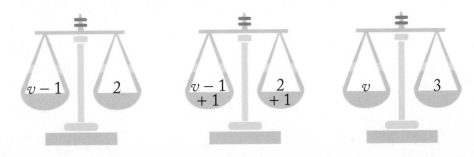

Math in History

A Greek named Diophantus is some-times called "The Father of Algebra." We don't know exactly when he lived—sometime between A.D. 100 and 400—but we do know how long he lived, because someone wrote a riddle about his life that can be solved using algebra. The riddle says that his youth lasted one-sixth of his life. After one-seventh more, he got married. After another one-twelfth of his life, he grew a beard. Five years later, he had a son. The son lived half as long as his father, and Diophantus died 4 years after his son. All this adds up to the years of his life. If x represents the number of years he lived, can you solve for x?

By manipulating both sides of the equation, you can get the unknown variable by itself on one side. Once the variable is alone on one side of the equation, the equation is solved, and you know the value of the variable. The process of getting the variable by itself is called **isolating the variable.**

Whenever you want to move a term from one side of the equation to the other, simply subtract that term from both sides. Since addition and subtraction are inversely related, subtracting a number is the same as adding its opposite.

EXAMPLES

$k - 7 = 11$
$k - 7 + 7 = 11 + 7$ Subtract $^-7$ from both sides (same as adding 7).
$k = 11 + 7$
$k = 18$

$3p + 4 = 4p$
$3p + 4 - 3p = 4p - 3p$ Subtract $3p$ from both sides.
$4 = 4p - 3p$
$4 = p$

You can also multiply or divide both sides of an equation by the same quantity and the two sides will still be equal. Since multiplication and division are inversely related, dividing by a number is the same as multiplying by its reciprocal.

EXAMPLES

$\dfrac{3b}{2} = 6$

$\dfrac{3b}{2} \times 2 = 6 \times 2$ Multiply both sides by 2.

$3b = 12$

$\dfrac{3b}{3} = \dfrac{12}{3}$ Divide both sides by 3.

$b = 4$

$\dfrac{45}{f} = 15$

$\dfrac{45}{f} \times f = 15 \times f$ Multiply both sides by f.

$45 = 15f$

$\dfrac{45}{15} = \dfrac{15}{15}f$ Divide both sides by 15.

$3 = f$

If you are left with an equation that says that a number is equal to the square of a variable, you can take the square root of both sides of the equation.

EXAMPLES

$2x^2 = 18$

$\dfrac{2x^2}{2} = \dfrac{18}{2}$

$x^2 = \dfrac{18}{2} = 9$

$\sqrt{x^2} = \sqrt{9}$ Take the square root of both sides.

$x = 3 \text{ or } ^-3$

$b^2 + 2b^2 = 15$

$3b^2 = 15$

$\dfrac{3b^2}{3} = \dfrac{15}{3} = 5$

$\sqrt{b^2} = \sqrt{5}$ Take the square root of both sides.

$b = \sqrt{5} \text{ or } ^-\sqrt{5}$

Sometimes you will need to use the distributive property to **expand** an expression before you can isolate the variable.

EXAMPLES $(-2)(3 + x) = 6$

$-6 - 2x = 6$

| Expand, using the distributive property |

$3(3 + y) = 24$

$9 + 3y = 24$

| Expand, using the distributive property |

The box below summarizes the steps you should take to isolate a variable.

ISOLATING A VARIABLE IN AN ALGEBRAIC EQUATION	
• Use the commutative property to rearrange the terms on each side of the equation so that like terms are together.	$4x^2 - 14 - x^2 + 5 = x^2 - 1$ $4x^2 - x^2 - 14 + 5 = x^2 - 1$
• Add and subtract like terms.	$4x^2 - x^2 - 14 + 5 = x^2 - 1$ $3x^2 - 9 = x^2 - 1$
• Get all the terms with the variable on one side of the equation. You can cancel a term from one side of an equation by subtracting that term from both sides. (To subtract a negative number, add a positive number.)	$3x^2 - 9 = x^2 - 1$ $3x^2 - 9 + 9 = x^2 - 1 + 9$ $3x^2 = x^2 + 8$ $3x^2 - x^2 = x^2 + 8 - x^2$ $2x^2 = 8$
• Multiply or divide both sides of the equation by the same quantity to leave the variable standing alone. Reduce any fractions.	$2x^2 = 8$ $\dfrac{2x^2}{2} = \dfrac{8}{2}$ $x^2 = 4$
• If necessary, take the square root of both sides.	$x^2 = 4$ $\sqrt{x^2} = \sqrt{4}$ $x = 2$ or -2

Another Way Once you become more confident about the process of isolating the variable, you can do many of the steps in your head. For example, you can mentally subtract $3x$ from both sides of the equation $7x = 32 + 3x$. If you want to write it in a shorthand way, change $7x$ on the left side to $4x$, and cross out $3x$ on the right side, leaving $4x = 32$. Then it is easy to divide both sides by 4, leaving $x = 8$.

$$\overset{4}{7x} = 32 + 3\cancel{x} \qquad x = 8$$

Meeting the Challenge

To answer the Challenge, you must write an algebraic equation that represents the information in the problem. Then isolate the variable and solve the equation to find the value of the unknown.

STEP 1: Write an algebraic equation that shows how much money Tim gained and spent. Add the amounts that he received to the amount he started with. Subtract the amounts he spent. Use the variable p to represent the unknown—the price of each CD.

Tim started with $110 and gained $40 and $65: $110 + 40 + 65$

He bought 2 CDs: $110 + 40 + 65 - 2p$

He spent $21 on a shirt: $110 + 40 + 65 - 2p - 21$

Then he bought another CD: $110 + 40 + 65 - 2p - 21 - p$

The amount he has now is equal to $152: $110 + 40 + 65 - 2p - 21 - p = 152$

STEP 2: Rearrange the terms on the left side of the equation so that the numbers are together and the variables are together.

$$\boxed{110 + 40 + 65 - 21}\ \boxed{- 2p - p} = 152$$

STEP 3: Perform the operations indicated on the numbers and on the variables.

$$194 - 3p = 152$$

STEP 4: Subtract 194 from both sides to isolate the variable on one side.

$$194 - 194 - 3p = 152 - 194$$
$$^-3p = {}^-42$$

STEP 5: Multiply both sides by $^-1$.

$$^-3p \times {}^-1 = {}^-42 \times {}^-1$$
$$3p = 42$$

STEP 6: Divide both sides by 3.

$$\frac{3p}{3} = \frac{42}{3}$$
$$p = 14$$

STEP 7: Check your answer by plugging it into your original equation to see if Tim did, in fact, end up with $152.

$$110 + 40 + 65 - (2 \times 14) - 21 - 14 = \$152$$

The answer to the Challenge is that Tim paid $14 for each CD.

Name_____ Class _____ Date _____

Try It Yourself

A. Find the value of x in each of the following equations. Write your answer at the top of each grid and fill in the numbered circles.

1. $5x + 12 = 52$

2. $3x - 23 = 34$

3. $90 \div 3x = 15$

B. Complete the activities below. Show all your work.

1. There are 12 ninth-grade homerooms at Ridgefield High School. There will be 55 fewer students starting ninth grade than there were last year. Last year, the ninth-grade class had 307 students. How many students per homeroom will there be this year?

2. Marta is making a quilt. At the foot of the quilt is the following design.

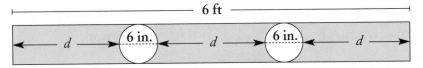

6 ft

d — 6 in. — d — 6 in. — d

The quilt is 6 feet wide, and the circles are each 6 inches in diameter. If d represents the distance between the circles and the distance from either edge to a circle, what is d, in inches?

Unit 2: Algebraic Thinking **123**

Try It Yourself

A. Fill in the circle next to the correct answer to each multiple-choice question.

1. Grady had d dollars in his wallet. He spent $4 and had $29 left. Which equation could you solve to find out how much money he started with?

   Ⓐ $d - 4 = 29$ Ⓑ $d + 4 = 29$ Ⓒ $d = 29 - 4$ Ⓓ $d + 29 = 4$

2. Solve the following equation for x: $8 - 5x + 4 + 2x = 18$

   Ⓐ -2 Ⓑ 2 Ⓒ 4 Ⓓ 6

3. At first, there were n people on a bus. Then 6 more got on. At the next stop, half the people got off, leaving 11 people. How many people (n) were on the bus at first?

   Ⓐ 8 Ⓑ 11 Ⓒ 16 Ⓓ 22

4. Solve the following equation for t: $4t - 8 = 32$

   Ⓐ 4 Ⓑ 6 Ⓒ 8 Ⓓ 10

5. Roland had p points in a card game. On his next turn, he quintupled (multiplied by 5) his points. Then he lost 14 points and ended up with 36. How many points (p) did he have at first?

   Ⓐ 5 Ⓑ 10 Ⓒ 125 Ⓓ 250

B. Complete the two parts below. Show all your work.

The batting average for a baseball player is calculated by dividing the number of hits a player has by the number of times the player has officially been at bat.

Part A In June and July, Slugger McGee had a batting average of 0.275. If he was at bat 240 times, how many hits did he have? Write an equation to solve this problem, and then find the solution.

Part B If Slugger McGee goes up to bat 30 more times and makes 11 hits, what will his new batting average be? Write an expression that shows his new batting average, and then solve it to find his new average. Round to the nearest thousandth.

SOLVING EQUATIONS WITH TWO VARIABLES

This lesson addresses Benchmarks MA.D.2.3.1 and MA.D.2.3.2 of the Sunshine State Standards.

The Challenge

Given these two equations, what are the values of s and t?

$$3s + t = 18 \qquad s + t = 10$$

Learning the Ropes

Math in History
The Hindu mathematician Brahmagupta, who lived around A.D. 630, described methods for solving equations containing more than one variable. He also used negative numbers and zero, long before these concepts reached Europe. Another Hindu, Bhaskara, who lived in the twelfth century A.D., introduced the idea of using letters as variables to stand for unknowns.

You have already solved algebraic equations with one variable. You simplify the equation, then isolate the variable and determine its value. What if there are two different variables? How can you find their values?

To determine unique values of *two* different variables, you need *two* algebraic equations. To find the value of one variable, such as the x variable, you must make an equation that contains only x variables. You can do this by using one equation to express y in terms of x, and then putting that value for y back into the other equation.

EXAMPLE What are the values of x and y if $3x + y = 144$ and $x + y = 50$?

First, use the equation $x + y = 50$ to get the variable y on one side of the equals sign by itself. To isolate y, subtract x from both sides of the equation: $x + y - x = 50 - x$; $y = 50 - x$.

Since the value of y is $50 - x$, you can substitute this expression for y in the first equation and solve for x.

$$3x + y = 144$$

Substitute $50 - x$ for y.	$3x + (50 - x) = 144$
Combine the like variables, $3x - x$.	$2x + 50 = 144$
Subtract 50 from both sides.	$2x = 94$
Divide both sides by 2.	$\dfrac{2x}{2} = \dfrac{94}{2}$
Simplify the fractions.	$x = 47$

Now that you know the value of x, you can find the value of y by replacing x with the number 47 in either equation.

$$3x + y = 144 \qquad \text{or} \qquad y = 50 - x$$
$$3(47) + y = 144 \qquad\qquad\qquad y = 50 - 47$$
$$141 + y = 144 \qquad\qquad\qquad\quad y = 3$$
$$y = 3$$

Meeting the Challenge

To answer the Challenge, you must find the values of *s* and *t*.

STEP 1: First, choose either equation and isolate one of the variables on one side of the equals sign. If you start with the second equation, you can isolate the *t* on one side by subtracting *s* from both sides.

$$s + t - s = 10 - s$$
$$t = 10 - s$$

STEP 2: Substitute the expression $10 - s$ for *t* in the first equation.

$$3s + t = 18$$
$$3s + (10 - s) = 18$$

STEP 3: Simplify the equation and solve for *s*.

$$3s + 10 - s = 18$$
$$2s + 10 = 18$$
$$2s + 10 - 10 = 18 - 10$$
$$2s = 18 - 10 = 8$$
$$s = 4$$

STEP 4: Plug the value of *s* back into either of the equations and solve for *t*.

$$3s + t = 18 \qquad \text{or} \qquad s + t = 10$$
$$3(4) + t = 18 \qquad\qquad\quad 4 + t = 10$$
$$12 + t = 18 \qquad\qquad\qquad\quad t = 6$$
$$t = 6$$

The answer to the Challenge is that the value of *s* is 4, and the value of *t* is 6.

Remember that you will always need two equations to solve for two variables; you will always need three equations to solve for three variables, and so on.

Another Way Another way to solve two equations for two variables is by subtracting one equation from the other. Look again at the Challenge problem. The first equation tells you that $3s + t = 18$. You can subtract the same quantity from both sides of this equation and the two sides will still be equal. Since the second equation tells you that $s + t = 10$, you can subtract $s + t$ from the left side of the first equation and 10 from the right. The subtraction problem will look like this:

$$\begin{array}{r} 3s + t = 18 \\ - \quad s + t = 10 \\ \hline 2s \quad\;\; = 8 \end{array}$$

Now you can solve for *s* and substitute that value into either equation to find *t*.

Name_____ Class _____ Date _____

Try It Yourself

A. Complete the activities below. Show all your work.

1. Arnold is a years old. His sister Barb is b years old. The sum of their ages is 15 years. In 3 years, she will be twice as old as Arnold will be. Write two equations that express this information. (Hint: Remember that in 3 years, both Arnold and Barb will be 3 years older!)

2. Vivian read v books over the summer. Chip read 3 times as many books (c). Together, they read 16 books. Solve the two equations below to find out how many books each one read.

$$c = 3v \qquad v + c = 16$$

3. Kim bought some hot dogs and hamburgers for a picnic. Each package of hot dogs cost \$3. Each package of hamburgers cost \$5. Altogether, she bought 10 packages and spent \$42. Solve the two equations below to find out how many package of each she bought.

d = number of packages of hot dogs \qquad $d + h = 10$
h = number of packages of hamburgers \qquad $\$3d + \$5h = \$42$

B. Complete the two parts below. Show all your work.

Robin and Kai went to swim team practice. Robin and Kai swam a total of 1800 meters. The distance Robin swam subtracted from twice the distance Kai swam is equal to 600.

Part A Write two equations showing the distance Robin and Kai swam. Tell what your variables stand for.

Part B What distance did Robin swim? What distance did Kai swim?

Try It Yourself

A. Complete each grid. Write your answer at the top and fill in the numbered circles.

1. Stephanie ate s plums, and Clyde ate twice as many. Together, they ate 6 plums. Solve the equations below to find out how many plums Clyde ate.

   $s + c = 6$
   $c = 2s$

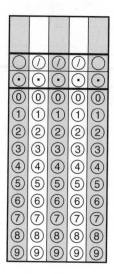

2. What is the value of v in these equations?

   $8v + w = 70$
   $v + w = 56?$

B. Fill in the circle next to the correct answer to each multiple-choice question.

1. What is the value of q in the equations $2q - r = 11$ and $q + r = 7$?
   - Ⓐ 1
   - Ⓑ 3
   - Ⓒ 4
   - Ⓓ 6

2. Alfredo and his sister collect coins. Together they have 336 coins. Alfredo has 3 times as many coins as his sister. How many coins does Alfredo have?
   - Ⓐ 252
   - Ⓑ 224
   - Ⓒ 112
   - Ⓓ 84

C. Complete the two parts below. Show all your work. Use additional paper if necessary.

Gina has a balance scale and is trying to figure out how much a package weighs. The package perfectly balances a 2-pound bag of sugar plus a book. If she puts the package and the book together, they balance a 5-pound bag of flour.

Let p = the weight of the package and b = the weight of the book.

Part A Write two equations that express the information in this problem. Explain what each equation represents.

Part B Solve the equations to find the weight of the package. Explain each step in your solution.

SOLVING INEQUALITIES

This lesson addresses Benchmarks MA.D.1.3.1 and MA.D.2.3.1 of the Sunshine State Standards.

The Challenge

The load limit for the back of Phil's pickup truck is 2,000 pounds. It is already carrying 5 barrels weighing 250 pounds each. He wants to add some crates that weigh 50 pounds each. How many crates can he add without exceeding the weight limit?

Learning the Ropes

An **inequality** is a number sentence that uses one of four signs: *greater than* (>), *less than* (<), *greater than or equal to* (≥), or *less than or equal to* (≤).

As you become more involved in algebra, you will encounter inequalities that use variables. You can solve these problems the same way you solve algebraic equations. Try the following problem:

EXAMPLE For what values of z is this inequality true? $3z > 15$

You can solve this inequality as if the greater than sign were an equals sign.

$$\frac{3z}{3} > \frac{15}{3} \qquad z > \frac{15}{3} \qquad z > 5$$

In order for the inequality $3z > 15$ to be true, z must be greater than 5. If z were less than 5, the inequality would not be true. Also, if z were equal to 5, the inequality would not be true because $3z$ would be *equal to* 15, not greater than 15. You can show this inequality on a number line as follows:

<-- -2 -1 0 1 2 3 4 5 6 7 8 9 10 -->

The open circle at 5 shows that z is not equal to 5. The ray to the right of 5 shows that z is greater than 5.

Now try another problem:

EXAMPLE For what values of x is this inequality true? $-2x \le 24$

This inequality is different because it contains a negative number in front of a variable, $-2x$. Whenever you have to multiply or divide both sides of an inequality by a negative number, you must at the same time switch the direction of the inequality sign. A greater than sign (>) becomes a less than sign (<), and vice versa. A greater than or equal to sign (≥) becomes a less than or equal to sign (≤), and vice versa.

Math in History

Inequalities play an important role in engineering and can often be a matter of life and death. For example, on May 31, 1881, one of the worst technological disasters in United States history occurred. Members of the South Fork Fishing and Hunting Club owned a dam 14 miles upriver from Johnstown, Pennsylvania. The dam held back a mile-long private lake. As long as pressure on the dam was less than or equal to a certain level of force, the dam was safe. Unfortunately, after a heavy rain, the dam burst, and over 2,200 people in Johnstown drowned.

Divide both sides by ⁻2 and switch the direction of the inequality sign.	$^-2x \leq 24$ $$\frac{^-2x}{^-2} \geq \frac{24}{^-2}$$
Simplify the fractions.	$x \geq ^-12$

As you can see, solving inequalities with variables is similar to solving equations with variables. Just remember to isolate the variable. If there is a negative number in front of the variable, divide both sides by the negative number and flip the sign.

Meeting the Challenge

To answer the Challenge, you need to write and solve an inequality showing that the total weight on the truck is less than or equal to the maximum weight allowed.

STEP 1: Write an algebraic expression that shows how much weight the truck would be carrying with 5 barrels and some number of crates, represented by the variable c. There are 5 barrels weighing 250 pounds each (250×5) and c crates weighing 50 pounds each ($50c$).

$$(250 \times 5) + 50c = 1,250 + 50c$$

STEP 2: Since this weight must not exceed the weight limit of the truck (2,000 pounds), write an inequality showing that this weight is less than or equal to the limit.

$$1,250 + 50c \leq 2,000$$

STEP 3: Solve the inequality by performing the same operations on both sides to isolate the variable.

$$1,250 + 50c \leq 2,000$$

Subtract 1,250 from both sides.	$50c \leq 750$
Divide both sides by 50.	$c \leq 15$

The solution of the inequality, $c \leq 15$, shows that the number of crates, c, must be less than or equal to 15. The answer to the Challenge is that Phil can carry up to 15 crates in his truck, along with the 5 barrels, without exceeding the load limit of the truck.

Another Way Perhaps the trickiest part of working with inequalities is reversing the sign when you multiply or divide by a negative number. To understand why it is necessary to switch the sign, consider a very simple inequality, $^-x < 0$. What integers will make the inequality true? Any positive number for x will make it true because ^-x will be a negative number, which is less than 0. If x were a negative number, ^-x would be positive and the inequality would *not* be true. Therefore, the inequality $^-x < 0$ is the same as $x > 0$. What you are really doing to $^-x < 0$ is multiplying both sides by $^-1$ and reversing the inequality sign.

Try It Yourself

A. Complete the activities below.

1. Desmond has more than twice as many CDs as Juanita. Write an inequality to compare the number of CDs owned by Desmond and Juanita. Use the variable d to represent the number of CDs Desmond has and j to represent the number of CDs Juanita has.

2. Pei peels a apples. His sister peels three times as many, plus 4 more. Together, Pei and his sister peel fewer than 48 apples. Write an inequality showing the number of apples Pei and his sister peel. Simplify your answer.

3. Sharice makes k key chains to give out at her birthday party. Her mother makes 3 less than one quarter as many key chains as Sharice. Sharice's brother Derek makes n necklaces. The number of necklaces Derek makes is fewer than the number of key chains Sharice and her mother make. Write an inequality comparing the number of key chains and necklaces the family makes altogether. Simplify your answer.

B. Complete the three parts below. Show all your work.

Part A Write an inequality showing that 8 times one variable, x, subtracted from another variable, y, is greater than or equal to 76.

Part B If the sum of x and y is 13, what must the values of x be in order for the previous inequality to be true? Explain how you found your answer.

Part C On your own paper, show the answer to the previous question on a number line.

Try It Yourself

A. Fill in the circle next to the correct answer to each multiple-choice question.

1. For what values of x is this inequality true? $-x - 5 > 8\frac{1}{2}$

   Ⓐ $x > 3\frac{1}{2}$ Ⓑ $x < 3\frac{1}{2}$ Ⓒ $x < -13\frac{1}{2}$ Ⓓ $x < 13\frac{1}{2}$

2. Kevin is on a diet that lets him eat a maximum of 2,000 calories per day. He had b calories for breakfast, l calories for lunch, and d calories for dinner. He wants to know if he can eat a snack with s calories and still stay on his diet. Which of the following inequalities shows the values of s that would be allowed by his diet?

   Ⓐ $s \le 2,000 + b + l + d$ Ⓒ $s \le (b + l + d) - 2,000$

   Ⓑ $s \le 2,000 - (b + l + d)$ Ⓓ $s \le 2,000 - (b - l - d)$

3. For what values of p is this inequality true? $2p + 3 \le 9 - p$

   Ⓐ $p \le -2$ Ⓑ $2 \ge p$ Ⓒ $p \le 3$ Ⓓ $-3 \ge p$

4. Which graph represents the solution to the following inequality? $x + 2 < 6$

   Ⓐ

   Ⓑ

   Ⓒ

   Ⓓ

B. Complete the three parts below. Show all your work. Use your own paper.

The elevator at the local bookstore can carry only 1,000 pounds or less. There are 7 people on the elevator already, and their combined weight is 872 pounds. Suppose that one more person wants to get on the elevator. If the total weight of all the passengers cannot exceed the limit of 1,000 pounds, how much can that person weigh ?

Part A Write an inequality that expresses the information in this problem. Tell what your variable stands for.

Part B Solve the inequality to find the values for the unknown.

Part C Show your solution on a number line.

SETS, RELATIONS, FUNCTIONS, AND SEQUENCES

This lesson addresses Benchmark MA.D.1.3.1 of the Sunshine State Standards.

The Challenge

A jeweler sells diamond rings at the prices given in the table to the right. What function tells the price of the ring [*f(w)*] based on the weight of the diamond (*w*)? What price would you predict that the jeweler would charge for a 6-carat diamond ring?

weight in carats (*w*)	price *f(w)*
1	$1,000
2	$4,000
3	$9,000
4	$16,000
5	$25,000
6	?

Learning the Ropes

Sets. A **set** is any group of one or more elements. The set of whole numbers contains an infinite number of elements:

$$\{0, 1, 2, 3, \ldots\}$$

The set of whole numbers less than one (<1) contains one element:

$$\{0\}$$

Notice that the elements of a set are enclosed in brackets: { }.

Relations. A **relation** is a matching up of elements from one set with elements from another set. For example, consider the set *S* of all the social security numbers of people living in the United States and the set *T* of all the telephone numbers of these people. These sets can be matched up to create pairs of numbers consisting of a person's social security number followed by his or her telephone number:

social security no., telephone no.
(304-60-9970, 978-555-3687)

Such a pair of numbers is called an **ordered pair** or a **coordinate pair.**

Notice that people with different social security numbers could have the same telephone number, so there could be ordered pairs like these:

(018-56-2215, 978-555-3687)
(215-42-9632, 978-555-3687)

Math in History

The founder of modern set theory was Georg Cantor, a German mathematician who lived from 1845 to 1918. Cantor was especially interested in the strange, paradoxical concept of infinity. It was Cantor who first recognized that the set of all the natural numbers {1, 2, 3, . . . } and the set of all the even natural numbers {2, 4, 6, . . . } are the same size because they can be matched up in a one-to-one correspondence. Our intuition would tell us that the set of even integers would be half the size of the set of integers, but that is wrong. This is one of the many paradoxes of infinite sets!

A geometric **fractal** is a pattern that repeats in ever-smaller versions of itself. An example of a fractal is the Sierpinski Triangle. It starts with a triangle formed by the midpoints of the sides of a larger triangle. The pattern keeps repeating with smaller and smaller triangles formed by the midpoints of the triangles in the previous step. Computers can create fractal images by plotting graphic functions on the screen over and over.

Furthermore, one person could have more than one telephone number. As you can see, relations can match up any number of items from one set with any number of items from another set. Relations can be one to one, one to many, many to one, or many to many.

Mathematicians give special names to the items that are matched up by a relation. The first set is called the **domain.** The individual elements in the domain are all values of the **independent variable.** The second set is called the **range.** The elements in the range are all values of the **dependent variable.** In the example just given, the domain is the set of social security numbers. The range is the set of telephone numbers. The number 304-60-9970 is a value of the independent variable. The number that it is matched with, 978-555-3687, is a value of the dependent variable because its value depends upon that of the independent variable.

Here is another example. Consider the domain "people with social security numbers" and the range "fingerprint patterns." This is an example of a one-to-one relation because every element in the domain (each person) is paired with only one element from the range (a unique fingerprint pattern).

Functions. A **function** is a special kind of relation that matches each element from the first set with exactly one element from the second set. For example, consider the set N of the natural numbers and the set E of the even natural numbers. Both of these sets are infinite:

$$\{1,\ 2,\ 3,\ 4,\dots\}$$
$$\uparrow\ \uparrow\ \uparrow\ \uparrow$$
$$\downarrow\ \downarrow\ \downarrow\ \downarrow$$
$$\{2,\ 4,\ 6,\ 8,\dots\}$$

As you can see, the elements of these sets can be paired to create coordinate pairs like these:

$$(1, 2)\ (2, 4)\ (3, 6)$$

In each case, the second number in the pair is twice the first number. Mathematically, we can say that, if the first number is x, then the second number is equal to $2x$.

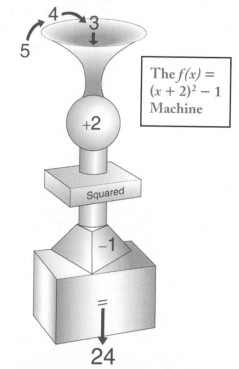

The $f(x) = (x + 2)^2 - 1$ Machine

You can think of a function as a machine that takes an input number, performs certain operations on it, and outputs another number.

If one number in a pair is dependent on the value of the other, we call the mathematical relationship a function and use the symbol $f(x)$, meaning "function of x," to stand for it. The value of $f(x)$ is dependent upon the value of x. In the previous example, $f(x) = 2x$. This equation is read "f of x equals two x." It simply means that if you plug a number into the equation as a substitute for the variable x, you will get another number that is two times x as a result. For example, if you substitute the number 5 for x, you will get 2×5, or 10, for $f(x)$.

Suppose that for a trip from the airport, a taxi driver charges a flat rate of $5.00, plus $2.00 per passenger. If x is the number of passengers, then the cab fare, $f(x)$, is given by this formula:

$$f(x) = \$5.00 + \$2.00x$$

Representing Functions: Tables and Graphs. You have seen that functions can be represented by equations. Functions can also be represented in tables or graphs. Consider the function $f(x) = \$5.00 + \$2.00x$. If you plug in a set of numbers for the variable x, you get a different set of numbers for the function $f(x)$. For example, if $x = 1$, then $f(x) = \$7.00$. If $x = 2$, then $f(x) = \$9.00$. By substituting various possible values for x, you can generate a series of ordered pairs in the form $(x, f(x))$:

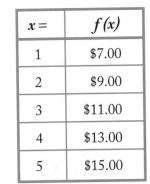

$x =$	$f(x)$
1	$7.00
2	$9.00
3	$11.00
4	$13.00
5	$15.00

(1, $7.00)   (2, $9.00)   (3, $11.00)   (4, $13.00)   (5, $15.00)

These numbers can easily be displayed in a table.

Another way to display this information is to create a **graph** of it. Make a **grid** with two number lines that are perpendicular to one another and other lines that are parallel to them. Label the horizontal number line x and the vertical line $f(x)$. Then **plot** (mark) the points on the graph for each of the ordered pairs created by the function. You can also graph functions on a graphing calculator.

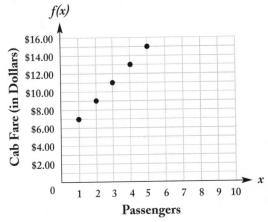

Sequences. A **sequence** is an ordered set of numbers, each of which is generated by performing an operation on one or more numbers preceding it. An example is the famous Fibonacci sequence, named after an Italian mathematician of the twelfth century:

1, 1, 2, 3, 5, 8, 13,…

Each number in this sequence is the sum of the two numbers preceding it.

Sequences of numbers can be generated by functions. For example, consider this function:

$$f(x) = \tfrac{1}{2}x$$

If you start with $x = 1$, you get $f(x) = \tfrac{1}{2}$. If you substitute the result back into the function, so that $x = \tfrac{1}{2}$, you get $f(x) = \tfrac{1}{4}$. Thus, you can generate the following sequence:

$\tfrac{1}{2}, \tfrac{1}{4}, \tfrac{1}{8},\ldots$

Patterns. A **pattern** is an arrangement of numbers, events, or shapes in a particular order. The arrangement of dots in these arrays shows the pattern of triangular numbers.

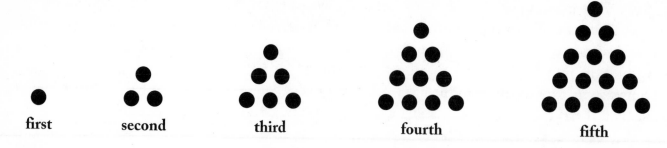

| first | second | third | fourth | fifth |

A table can help you to discover and continue the pattern. The table below shows the first five triangular numbers.

1	2	3	4	5
1	3	6	10	15

Notice that the pattern of dots for the third triangular number is $1 + 2 + 3$. The pattern of dots for the fourth triangular number is $1 + 2 + 3 + 4$. To find the twelfth triangular number, you would follow the same pattern:

$1 + 2 + 3 + 4 + 5 + 6 + 7 + 8 + 9 + 10 + 11 + 12 = 78$

The pattern that you would follow to find the nth triangular number is $1 + 2 + 3 + 4 + \ldots + n$. The algebraic expression that represents the nth triangular number is $\frac{n(n+1)}{2}$.

Meeting the Challenge

To answer the Challenge, you can use the trial-and-error method to determine the function that is used to generate $f(w)$ from w.

Step 1: Consider the second example in the chart. If you square the 2, you get 4. If you take that number times $1,000, you get $f(w)$, which is $4,000.

Step 2: Try your equation with the other number pairs in the chart:

$f(w) = \$1,000w^2$

If $w = 1$, then $f(w) = \$1,000 \times 1^2 = \$1,000 \times 1 = \$1,000$.

If $w = 3$, then $f(w) = \$1,000 \times 3^2 = \$1,000 \times 9 = \$9,000$.

If $w = 4$, then $f(w) = \$1,000 \times 4^2 = \$1,000 \times 16 = \$16,000$.

Step 3: Substitute the last variable, 6, into the function.

If $w = 6$, then $f(w) = \$1,000 \times 6^2 = \$1,000 \times 36 = \$36,000$.

The answer to the Challenge is that a 6-carat ring would sell for $36,000.

Try It Yourself

A. Fill in the circle next to the correct answer to each multiple-choice question.

1. Which of the following represents the set of all the odd natural numbers?

   Ⓐ $\{1, 3, 5, \ldots\}$ Ⓑ $\{0, 1, 3, \ldots\}$ Ⓒ $\{1, 3, 5, \ldots, 999\}$ Ⓓ $\{1, 2, 3, \ldots\}$

2. Which of the following ordered pairs is generated by the function $f(x) = x^2 - 1$?

   Ⓐ $(2, 5)$ Ⓑ $(12, 144)$ Ⓒ $(9, 73)$ Ⓓ $(3, 8)$

3. Mario has a large sheet cake. He cuts it in thirds one way and then in thirds the other way. The following sequence shows what fraction of the cake each piece is: $1, \frac{1}{3}, \frac{1}{9}, \ldots$ If he cuts each piece in thirds again, what will be the next number in the sequence?

   Ⓐ $\frac{1}{15}$ Ⓑ $\frac{1}{21}$ Ⓒ $\frac{1}{27}$ Ⓓ $\frac{1}{30}$

4. Which of the following functions yields the ordered pair $(4, 17)$?

   Ⓐ $f(x) = 5x - 3$ Ⓑ $f(x) = x - 13$ Ⓒ $f(x) = 3x + 7$ Ⓓ $f(x) = 2x - 30$

B. Complete the two parts below. Show all your work.

Use your knowledge of relations and functions to answer the following questions.

Part A Guests arrive at a banquet to raise money for the school drama club. Each of the guests is assigned a seat numbered from 1 to 128. Each guest buys one or more raffle tickets, numbered from 00639 to 01842. Is the pairing of the seat numbers with the numbers of the raffle tickets an example of a function or a relation? Explain your answer.

Part B Water bills for residents of the town of Barrow are calculated using the following formula:

$f(g) = 0.023g$, where g = the number of gallons of water used

Fill in the following table to show the dollar amount of a water bill—$f(g)$—as a function of the number of gallons used—g. On your own paper, show your work, and explain why this formula is a function.

g	100 gal	200 gal	300 gal	400 gal	500 gal	600 gal
$f(g)$						

Try It Yourself

A. Fill in the circle next to the correct answer to each multiple-choice question.

1. Ignoring air resistance, the speed of a falling object is given by the function $f(t) = 32t$, where t is the time (in seconds) for which the object has been falling, and $f(t)$ is the speed (in feet per second). If a rock has been falling for 20 seconds, what is its speed?

   Ⓐ $f(t) = 64$ ft/sec   Ⓑ $f(t) = 640$ ft/sec   Ⓒ $f(t) = 32$ ft/sec   Ⓓ $f(t) = 6.4$ ft/sec

2. If the domain is animals and the range is number of legs, what is the value of the dependent variable if the independent variable is an octopus?

   Ⓐ 2   Ⓑ 4   Ⓒ 5   Ⓓ 8

3. If $x =$ the length of one side of a square city block, what function gives the distance around the whole block, $f(x)$?

   Ⓐ $f(x) = 2x$ Ⓑ $f(x) = 4x$ Ⓒ $f(x) = x^2$ Ⓓ $f(x) = 2x^2$

B. Complete the two parts below. Show all your work.

An electrical contractor gets paid $100 a day plus $20 for each light fixture that she installs.

Part A Write a function to describe how much the contractor gets paid for a day's work. Let x represent the number of light fixtures she installs and $f(x)$ represent the amount she is paid.

Part B Fill in the table and plot the ordered pairs on the graph below.

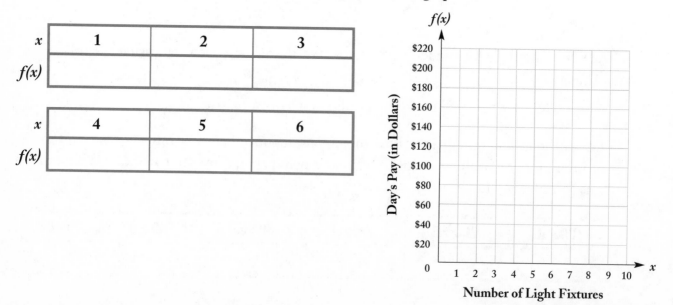

x	1	2	3
$f(x)$			

x	4	5	6
$f(x)$			

GRAPHING LINEAR EQUATIONS

This lesson addresses Benchmarks MA.C.3.3.2, MA.D.1.3.2, MA.D.2.3.1, and MA.D.2.3.2 of the Sunshine State Standards.

The Challenge

Graph $y = \frac{1}{2}x - 1$ on the coordinate grid to the right.

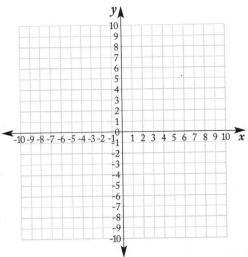

Learning the Ropes

You have already learned how to plot individual points on a graph. Now you will learn how to graph equations. To graph an equation, you find ordered pairs that work in the equation and plot them on a coordinate grid. A **coordinate grid** is a network of evenly spaced, numbered horizontal and vertical lines (the **x-axis** and **y-axis**) like the one above.

EXAMPLE Graph $y = 2x + 3$ on a coordinate grid.

First, substitute any number for x. Then solve the equation to find the value of y. The values of x and y make the ordered pair that you plot on the graph.

$$y = 2x + 3$$

Let $x = 2$.
$y = 2(2) + 3$
$y = 4 + 3 = 7$
$(2, 7)$

Let $x = {}^-5$.
$y = 2({}^-5) + 3$
$y = {}^-10 + 3 = {}^-7$
$({}^-5, {}^-7)$

After finding two ordered pairs, you can plot them on the graph. The ordered pairs that work in, or **satisfy,** the equation $y = 2x + 3$ all lie on a single line. You can draw a straight line that passes through all the points that satisfy the equation. An equation with a graph that is a line is called a **linear equation.** This line passes through three of the four **quadrants,** or sections, of the coordinate grid.

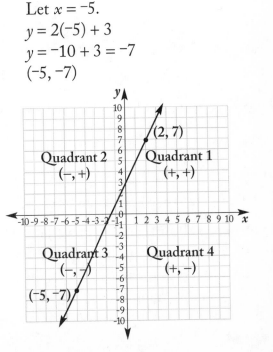

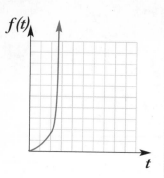

$f(t)$

t

Math in Use: Physics As scientists learned how to plot on graphs what they observed and measured, their ability to see and understand relationships in nature increased greatly. Putting the results of their experiments on graphs helped them to see patterns and create formulas to describe how the universe works. For example, the movement of a falling object can be plotted on a graph. The equation that describes a free fall is $f(t) = 16t^2$, where t is the time, and $f(t)$ is the distance the object falls. As you can see on the graph to the left, the graph of this equation is curved, not linear. Discoveries like this opened vast new possibilities for exploring the world and using its resources.

Any equation of the form $y = mx + b$ will have a line as its graph. If the variables in an equation are squared, cubed, or raised to any powers other than 0 or 1, then the graph of the equation will be **nonlinear,** that is, not a straight line. A **quadratic function,** for example, has a variable raised to the second power. It has the standard form $y = ax^2 + bx + c$. The graph of a quadratic function is a **parabola,** a curve like the one to the right. The graphs of nonlinear equations can be very complex and intricate curves, such as hearts, loops, or petal shapes.

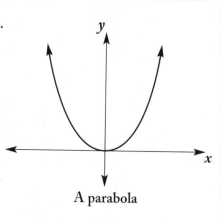

A parabola

Meeting the Challenge

To answer the Challenge, you must graph the equation on a coordinate grid by finding values for x and y.

Step 1: To find a point on the graph, substitute any value for x in the equation and solve for y. For example, let $x = {}^-6$.

$y = \frac{1}{2}x - 1$ $y = {}^-3 - 1$

$y = \frac{1}{2}({}^-6) - 1$ $y = {}^-4$

The point $({}^-6, {}^-4)$ is on the line.

Step 2: To find another point on the graph, substitute another value for x in the equation and solve for y. Let $x = 8$.

$y = \frac{1}{2}x - 1$ $y = 4 - 1 = 3$

$y = \frac{1}{2}(8) - 1$ $y = 3$

The point $(8, 3)$ is on the line.

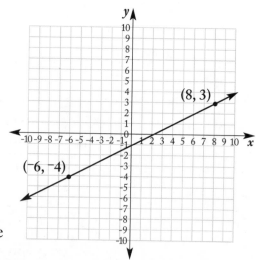

Step 3: Plot the points on the graph and draw a straight line that passes through both points. Since this equation is of the form $y = mx + b$, all the points on the line connecting your two points will satisfy the equation. You can also graph linear equations on a graphing calculator. (For information about using a graphing calculator to graph linear equations, see Appendix D.)

Name_____ Class _____ Date _____

Try It Yourself

A. Fill in the circle next to the correct answer to each multiple-choice question.

1. Hayley drew a line through the points (0, 1) and (3, 4). Which of the following points is also on that line?

   Ⓐ (0, 4)　　　Ⓑ (1, 0)　　　Ⓒ (2, 3)　　　Ⓓ (4, 3)

2. In the equation $y = 2x + 3x - 5$, what is the x-coordinate if the y-coordinate is equal to 20?

   Ⓐ −4　　　Ⓑ 3　　　Ⓒ 4　　　Ⓓ 5

3. Carmen graphed the line $y = -3x + 2$. Which of the following points is on her line?

   Ⓐ (1, 3)　　　Ⓑ (3, 5)　　　Ⓒ (−1, 5)　　　Ⓓ (1, 5)

B. Complete the two parts below. Show all your work.

For each of the following equations, fill in the table with two coordinate pairs that satisfy the equation. Then graph the equations on the grids provided.

Part A $y = 3x + 2$

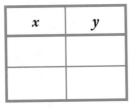

x	y

Part B $y = -2x - 4$

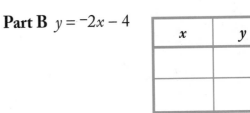

x	y

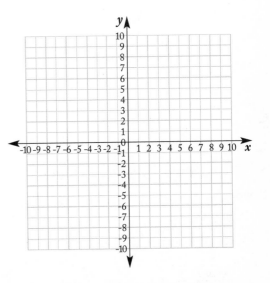

Try It Yourself

A. Fill in the circle next to the correct answer to each multiple-choice question.

1. Vanessa made a graph showing the length of one side of an equilateral triangle on the x-axis and its perimeter on the y-axis. What is the equation for her graph?

   Ⓐ $x = 3y$ Ⓑ $x = y^3$ Ⓒ $y = 3x$ Ⓓ $y = x^3$

2. Devon graphed the line $y = 4x + 3$. Where does the line cross the y-axis? (Hint: A point is on the y-axis if its x-coordinate is 0.)

   Ⓐ $(0, 3)$ Ⓑ $(0, 4)$ Ⓒ $(4, 0)$ Ⓓ $(3, 0)$

3. Guillermo made a graph of the line $y = 4x - 7$. Which of these points is on his line?

   Ⓐ $(-2, -2)$ Ⓑ $(21, 3)$ Ⓒ $(8, 6)$ Ⓓ $(2, 1)$

B. Complete the three parts below. Show all your work.

Part A Graph and label the lines given by the equations below:

   Line A $y = 2x$

   Line B $y = -2x$

   Line C $y = 2x - 3$

   Line D $y = 2x + 3$

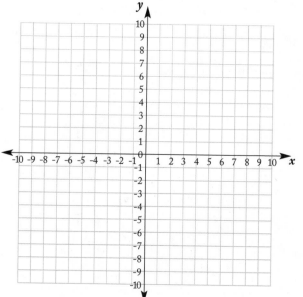

Part B How does the graph of $y = -2x$ (line B) differ from the graph of $y = 2x$ (line A)?

Part C Identify the point at which each line crosses the y-axis.

   Line A _____   Line C _____

   Line B _____   Line D _____

INTERPRETING GRAPHS

This lesson addresses Benchmarks MA.C.3.3.2, MA.D.1.3.2, MA.D.2.3.1, and MA.D.2.3.2 of the Sunshine State Standards.

The Challenge

Troy and his family are driving through Iowa during a snowstorm. He starts keeping track of how far they travel by recording the highway mile-marker number every few minutes for an hour. Plot his numbers on the graph and write an equation to represent the line. What is the slope of the line? What does the *y*-intercept represent?

Time (minutes)	Mile Marker
4	7
10	10
18	14
32	21
46	28
60	35

Math in History

René Descartes, (1596–1650, is generally considered the father of analytic geometry. However, the distinction might well have gone to another great mathematician, Pierre de Fermat (1601–1665), who developed the subject independently in a work called *Introduction to Plane and Solid Loci,* written sometime before 1636 but not published in Fermat's lifetime. Fermat discovered, among other things, that every first-degree equation (equation that has no variables with exponents other than 0 or 1) represents a straight line.

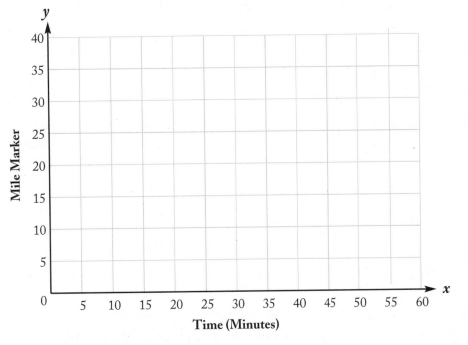

Learning the Ropes

You have learned that a linear equation is an equation whose graph is a line. You have also learned how to graph linear equations. In this lesson, you will learn how to write a linear equation by analyzing a line on a graph. You will also learn how to interpret what the line represents.

There are two important parts of a linear equation. One is the *y*-intercept. The **y-intercept** is the point where the line crosses the *y*-axis. The other important part of a linear equation is the **slope,** or the steepness of the line.

Writing Equations to Represent Lines. Suppose you want to write an equation that represents the line on the graph to the right. To find the y-intercept, look for the point where the line crosses the y-axis. The line crosses the y-axis at $(0, 2)$, so the y-intercept is 2.

To calculate the slope, pick two points that lie on the line. Then find the ratio of the difference between the y values and the difference between the x values of the two points. The formula below shows how to arrive at the slope, given two points, (x_1, y_1) and (x_2, y_2).

$$\text{slope} = \frac{y_1 - y_2}{x_1 - x_2}$$

To calculate the slope of the line in this example, we can use the points $(2, 8)$ and $(1, 5)$.

$$(x_1, y_1) = (2, 8) \qquad (x_2, y_2) = (1, 5)$$

$$\text{slope} = \frac{8 - 5}{2 - 1} = \frac{3}{1} = 3$$

The slope of the line is 3.

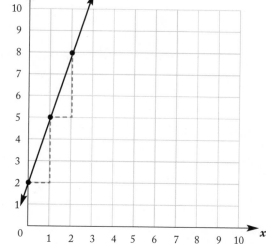

Slope: For every 1 space to the right on the x-axis, one must move 3 spaces up on the y-axis to find a point on the line. The slope is thus $\frac{3}{1}$, or 3.

After you find the y-intercept and the slope, you can write a linear equation that represents the line. You can model your equation after the **slope-intercept form,** $y = mx + b$, where m represents the slope and b represents the y-intercept.

$y = mx + b$
$m = 3$
$b = 2$
$y = 3x + 2$

The equation that represents the line is $y = 3x + 2$. You can check your equation by substituting values of x and solving for y. The points that you calculate should lie along the line.

Here is another example to try.

EXAMPLE Write the equation represented by the line on the graph to the right.

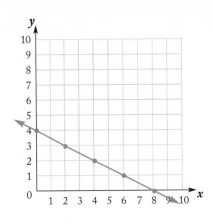

First, find the y-intercept. The line crosses the y-axis at $(0, 4)$, so the y-intercept is 4. Then, find the slope. In this example, we use the points $(2, 3)$ and $(6, 1)$.

$$(x_1, y_1) = (2, 3) \qquad (x_2, y_2) = (6, 1)$$

$$\text{slope} = \frac{3-1}{2-6} = \frac{2}{-4} = \frac{-1}{2}$$

The slope of the line is $-\frac{1}{2}$.

The equation of the line is $y = -\frac{1}{2}x + 4$. Notice that the slope is negative. Compare the line in the first graph, which has a positive slope, with the one in the example above. A line with a positive slope goes up from the left side of the graph to the right side. A line with a negative slope goes down from left to right, as shown in the graph on this page.

Understanding Slope. To understand what slope means, think of walking up or down a hill. Suppose that every time you go up 1 foot in altitude, you are going 8 feet forward. The steepness of the path with that slope would look like the first diagram to the right (slope = 1 foot up to 8 feet forward = $\frac{1}{8}$). If you went forward only 4 feet each time you went up 1 foot, your path would be steeper (slope = $\frac{1}{4}$). If you had to climb 8 feet up to go another foot forward, your route would be very steep (slope = 8). What would the route be like if you went 1 foot forward without going up at all? What would the route be like if its slope were negative?

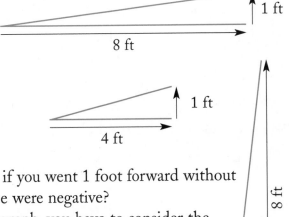

To tell exactly what the slope means for a particular graph, you have to consider the quantities that are expressed on your x- and y-axes. You know that the slope is a ratio: the change in the y-coordinate divided by the change in the x-coordinate. If you have distance (in miles) on your y-axis and time (in hours) on your x-axis, the slope is distance divided by time, or in this case, miles per hour. If your graph shows the flow of water through a pipe, it might give gallons on the y-axis and seconds on the x-axis. The slope would show the rate of flow in gallons per second.

Another Way To find the slope without using subtraction, count the number of spaces you must go up or down from one point to reach a second point on the line. Then count the number of spaces you must go right to get to the second point. You can express these two numbers as a ratio that represents the slope. Remember the formula **slope = rise ÷ run**, where **rise** is the number of spaces up (positive) or down (negative), and **run** is the number of spaces to the right.

Meeting the Challenge

To answer the Challenge, you must plot the time and mileage on the graph, and then write a linear equation that represents the line on the graph.

Step 1: Using the time in minutes as your x-coordinate and the number on the mile marker as your y-coordinate, plot the ordered pairs from the chart on the graph. Connect the points with a straight line.

Step 2: Find the y-intercept. The line crosses the y-axis at $(0, 5)$, so the y-intercept is 5.

Step 3: Calculate the slope. You can use the points $(18, 14)$ and $(4, 7)$.

$$\text{slope} = \frac{14-7}{18-4} = \frac{7}{14} = \frac{1}{2}$$

Step 4: Write a linear equation, following the formula $y = mx + b$. The slope (m) is $\frac{1}{2}$, and the y-intercept (b) is 5.

$$y = \tfrac{1}{2}x + 5$$

Step 5: To interpret the meaning of the slope, think of the variables on your axes. The y-axis shows the distance traveled between mile markers, and the x-axis shows the time that it takes to travel between mile markers. If you divide the distance between any two mile markers ($y_1 - y_2$) by the time it takes to travel between them ($x_1 - x_2$), you find the speed at which you travel between those two mile markers. In this case, the distance is given in miles and the time in minutes, so if the slope is $\frac{1}{2}$, it means that you traveled $\frac{1}{2}$ mile per minute, which is the same as 30 miles in 60 minutes (1 hour) = 30 mph.

Step 6: The y-intercept tells you the value of y when x is 0. In this case, 0 minutes is the time when Troy started recording their travel. Assuming they were traveling at a constant speed the whole time, the y-intercept (5) would show the number of the mile marker when Troy started.

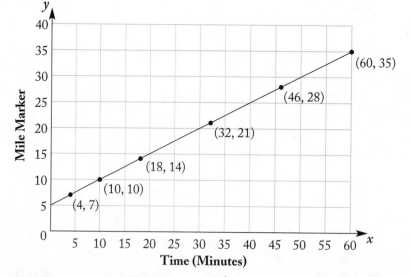

The answer to the Challenge is that the equation $y = \frac{1}{2}x + 5$ represents the line on the graph. The slope ($\frac{1}{2}$) shows the speed in miles per minute, and the y-intercept (5) shows the mile marker at which he began recording.

146   AIM Higher! FCAT Mathematics

Try It Yourself

A. Use the graph to the right to answer the multiple-choice questions. Fill in the circle next to the correct answer to each multiple-choice question.

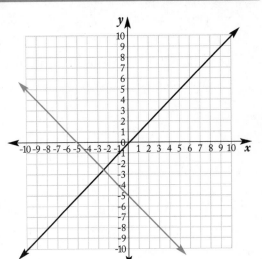

1. Which of the following equations represents the blue line?

   Ⓐ $y = {}^-x - 5$ Ⓑ $y = x - 5$ Ⓒ $y = x + 5$ Ⓓ $y = 5x - 5$

2. Which of the following equations represents the black line?

   Ⓐ $y = {}^-x$ Ⓑ $y = x$ Ⓒ $y = 2x$ Ⓓ $y = \frac{1}{2}x$

3. Which of the following points lies on the blue line?

   Ⓐ $(-5, {}^-5)$ Ⓑ $(0, 0)$ Ⓒ $(-9, 1)$ Ⓓ $(-10, 3)$

B. Complete the two parts below.

Griff went hiking in the mountains. He started at an elevation of 1,000 feet and gained 1,200 feet every hour for 6 hours.

Part A On the grid to the right, draw a line showing Griff's elevation during his hike.

Part B Write an equation to show his time in hours (t) and his elevation in feet (e).

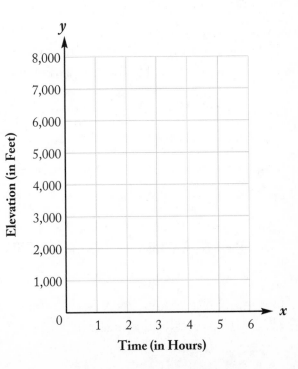

Try It Yourself

A. Fill in the circle next to the correct answer to each multiple-choice question.

1. Alicia started out with $25 and saved $5 every week. Which equation shows how many dollars (d) she would have after w weeks?

   Ⓐ $d = 5w + 25$ Ⓑ $d = 25w + 5$ Ⓒ $w = 5d + 25$ Ⓓ $w = 25d + 5$

2. In the equation $y = 5x + 2$, what is the slope?

   Ⓐ 5   Ⓑ 2   Ⓒ x Ⓓ y

3. Which of the following points lies on the line $y = x + 4$?

   Ⓐ (−1, 4)   Ⓑ (0, 0)   Ⓒ (6, 2)   Ⓓ (10, 14)

4. Which description of the line produced by the equation $y = 3$ is correct?

   Ⓐ It is parallel to the y-axis.   Ⓒ It slopes down from left to right.

   Ⓑ It is parallel to the x-axis.   Ⓓ It slopes up from left to right.

5. The formula for the number of words that an excellent typist can type in a given time is $y = 80x$, where y is the number of words, and x is the number of minutes. How many words can this typist type in 20 minutes?

   Ⓐ 0   Ⓑ 40   Ⓒ 160   Ⓓ 1,600

B. Complete the two parts below. Show all your work.

Ms. Shin drove to visit her grandson. She made a graph showing how far she traveled every hour.

Part A What does the line on the graph represent?

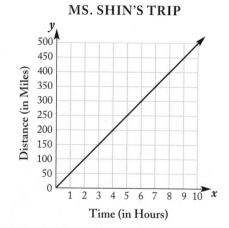

MS. SHIN'S TRIP

Part B At this rate, how many miles would Ms. Shin have driven after 12 hours?

GRAPHING INEQUALITIES

This lesson addresses Benchmarks MA.C.3.3.2, MA.D.1.3.2, MA.D.2.3.1, and MA.D.2.3.2 of the Sunshine State Standards.

The Challenge

Graph the inequality $y > \frac{1}{3}x + 1$ on the coordinate grid to the right.

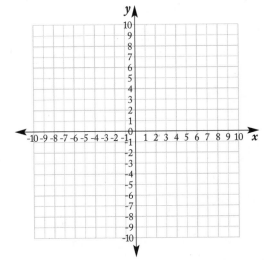

Learning the Ropes

You have already seen how to graph inequalities on a number line (Lesson 2.5, "Solving Inequalities). You can also graph inequalities on a coordinate grid. Graphing inequalities is similar to graphing equations. The graph of a linear inequality is a region in the coordinate plane. The region is bounded by a line called the **boundary line.**

EXAMPLE Graph $y \geq 4x + 2$ on a coordinate grid.

The equation for the boundary line is $y = 4x + 2$. Substitute values for x to find some points on this line.

$$y \geq 4x + 2$$

Let $x = -1$.	Let $x = 0$.
$y = 4(-1) + 2$	$y = 4(0) + 2$
$y = -4 + 2$	$y = 0 + 2$
$y = -2$	$y = 2$
$(-1, -2)$	$(0, 2)$

Next, you must plot the points on the graph. Before you draw a line through the points, however, look at the inequality. If the inequality has a greater than or equal to ($\geq$) sign or a less than or equal to ($\leq$) sign, then you must draw a *solid* line to connect the points. If the inequality has a greater than ($>$) sign or a less than ($<$) sign, then you draw a *dotted* line to connect the points. The type of line tells you whether or not the points that lie on the line satisfy the inequality, or make it true. A solid line shows that the points on the line do satisfy the inequality. A dotted line shows that they do not satisfy the inequality.

Math in History

English mathematician and scientist Thomas Harriott is generally thought to be the first person to have used symbols resembling > and < to represent the inequalities "greater than" and "less than." His work was published in 1631, ten years after his death. The symbols $\geq$ ("greater than or equal to") and $\leq$ ("less than or equal to") were introduced in their present form by French mathematician and scientist Pierre Bouguer in 1734. Other symbols in common use include $\neq$ ("not equal to"), $\not>$ ("not greater than"), and $\not<$ ("not less than").

The boundary line for the graph of $y \geq 4x + 2$ is shown to the right. The line is solid because the inequality is greater than *or equal to* ($\geq$). The points on the line satisfy the condition that y is equal to $4x + 2$.

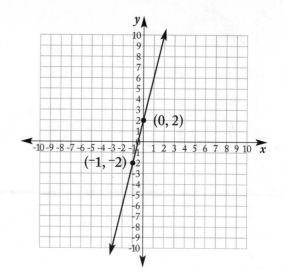

After you draw the boundary line, you need to shade the graph. You shade the area that contains all the points that satisfy the inequality. To find this area, first select a random point near the line. Replace the x- and y-variables in the inequality with the coordinates of the point. If you find that the inequality is true, then you should shade the whole area on the same side as that point. If the inequality is not true, then you should shade the area on the opposite side of the line. The shaded area, along with the solid line, represents the solution set. The **solution set** consists of all the points that satisfy the inequality.

To determine how to shade the graph of $y \geq 4x + 2$, choose a random point, such as ($^-7$, 6).

$$y \geq 4x + 2$$
$$6 \geq 4(^-7) + 2$$
$$6 \geq ^-28 + 2$$
$$6 \geq ^-26$$

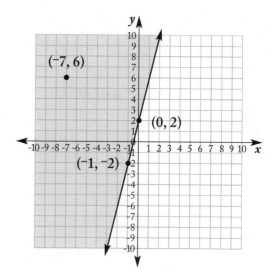

The point ($^-7$, 6) does satisfy the inequality $y \geq 4x + 2$, so you should shade the area that contains ($^-7$, 6). All the points in this shaded area satisfy the inequality. The solid line tells you that all the points along the line also satisfy the inequality.

Now try graphing the same statement with a different inequality sign: $y < 4x + 2$. The graph will have the same boundary line. This time, however, the line should be dotted, since points on the line do *not* satisfy the inequality. (Remember that the points on the line satisfy the condition that y is *equal to* $4x + 2$.) If you test the point ($^-7$, 6), you will find that the inequality is *not* true, so you should shade everything on the opposite side of the line.

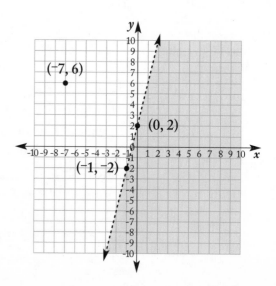

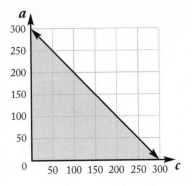

People use inequalities often in business. For example, a museum sells tickets for adults and children under twelve. Altogether, the museum can accommodate 300 people at one time. If the variable a represents the number of adults and c represents the number of children in the museum at any time, the total number of people in the museum must be $a + c \leq 300$. The graph to the left shows this inequality.

You can also graph the solution set of a system that consists of two inequalities whose boundary lines are not parallel. You can then find the region that satisfies *both* inequalities.

EXAMPLE Graph the solution set for these two inequalities: $y \geq x$ and $y \geq {}^-x + 2$.

Each graph below shows the solution for one of the inequalities.

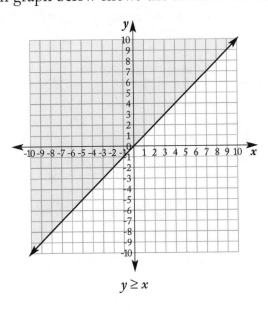

$y \geq x$

$y \geq {}^-x + 2$

In the graph for the solution set of both inequalities, the dark shaded region defines all the points that satisfy both inequalities.

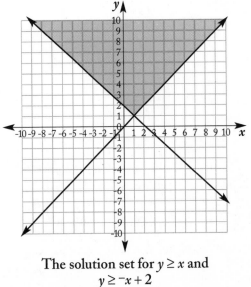

The solution set for $y \geq x$ and
$y \geq {}^-x + 2$

Meeting the Challenge

To answer the Challenge, you must graph the inequality, using the appropriate boundary line and shading the correct portion of the graph.

Step 1: Substitute any value for x into the equation for the boundary line and find the value of y. The equation for the boundary line is $y = \frac{1}{3}x + 1$.

$y = \frac{1}{3}x + 1$ $y = \frac{1}{3}x + 1$

Let $x = {}^-6$.   Let $x = 9$.

$y = \frac{1}{3}({}^-6) + 1$ $y = \frac{1}{3}(9) + 1$

$y = {}^-2 + 1$ $y = 3 + 1$

$y = {}^-1$ $y = 4$

$({}^-6, {}^-1)$ $(9, 4)$

Step 2: Plot the points and draw a line to connect the points. The line should be dotted because points on the line do not satisfy the inequality.

Step 3: Pick a point near the line and substitute the values of the x- and y-coordinates to see which area to shade. In this example, we use the point $(3, 0)$.

$y > \frac{1}{3}x + 1$

$0 > \frac{1}{3}(3) + 1$

$0 > 1 + 1$

$0 > 2$

Step 4: Because the inequality is not true, you must shade the area on the opposite side of the line.

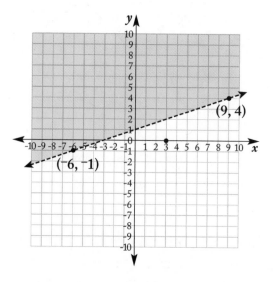

Another Way Remember that if you have an inequality in slope-intercept form, such as $y < mx + b$ or $y > mx + b$, you can graph the boundary line based simply upon the intercept and the slope. First, plot the y-intercept point $(0, b)$. Then express m, the slope, as a fraction. The top, or numerator, of the fraction will give you the rise and the bottom, or denominator, will give you the run, enabling you to start with the y-intercept and plot a second point. Then you will need to determine whether the line should be solid or dotted and which side should be shaded.

Name_____   Class _____   Date _____

Try It Yourself

A. Fill in the circle next to the correct answer to each multiple-choice question.

1. If the value of the y-coordinate is 16, what is one value of the x-coordinate that would make the inequality $y \leq 5x - 3$ true?

   Ⓐ 1   Ⓑ 2   Ⓒ 3   Ⓓ 4

2. Jared has more than 500 baseball and football cards altogether. He has 300 baseball cards. Which inequality shows how many football cards he has? (f = number of football cards)

   Ⓐ $f > 800$ Ⓑ $f < 800$ Ⓒ $f > 200$ Ⓓ $f < 200$

3. Julia charges $8 for each necklace she makes and $5 for each bracelet. She wants to earn at least $100 for new clothes. Which inequality shows how many necklaces and bracelets she needs to make? (n = number of necklaces, b = number of bracelets)

   Ⓐ $8n + 5b \leq 100$ Ⓑ $8n + 5b \geq 100$ Ⓒ $5n + 8b \leq 100$ Ⓓ $5n + 8b \geq 100$

B. Complete the two parts below. Show all your work.

Sonya is going to buy some pens and notebooks for school. The pens cost $2 each. The notebooks cost $3 each. The most she can spend is $18.

Part A Write an inequality to show how many pens (p) and how many notebooks (n) she could buy.

Part B On the grid to the right, graph your inequality. (Hint: How many pens could she buy if she bought 0 notebooks? How many notebooks could she buy if she bought 0 pens?) Remember to use the appropriate type of line and to shade your graph.

Unit 2: Algebraic Thinking **153**

Try It Yourself

A. Fill in the circle next to the correct answer to each multiple-choice question.

1. Kevin is allowed to watch 6 hours of television per week. He wants to watch some 2-hour movies and some $\frac{1}{2}$-hour shows. Which inequality shows how many movies and shows he can watch? (m = number of movies, s = number of $\frac{1}{2}$-hour shows)

   Ⓐ $2m + \frac{1}{2}s \leq 6$ Ⓑ $2m + \frac{1}{2}s \geq 6$ Ⓒ $\frac{1}{2}m + 2s \leq 6$ Ⓓ $\frac{1}{2}m + 2s \geq 6$

2. Which of the following ordered pairs satisfies the inequality $y \geq 5x + 2$?

   Ⓐ $(2, 14)$ Ⓑ $(3, 5)$ Ⓒ $(-1, -4)$ Ⓓ $(0, 1)$

3. Roberta has over $25 in her collection of pennies and nickels. Which inequality shows how many pennies and nickels she could have? (p = number of pennies, n = number of nickels)

   Ⓐ $p + n > 2,500$ Ⓑ $p + 5n > 2,500$ Ⓒ $5p + 5n > 2,500$ Ⓓ $5p + n > 2,500$

B. Complete the two parts below. Show all your work.

Roger wants to make some picture frames of different sizes. He needs 3 feet of wood for each large frame and 2 feet for each smaller frame. He has 30 feet of wood.

Part A Write an inequality to show how many large frames (l) and how many small frames (s) Roger could make with 30 feet of wood or less.

Part B On the grid to the right, graph your inequality. Remember to use the appropriate type of line and to shade your graph.

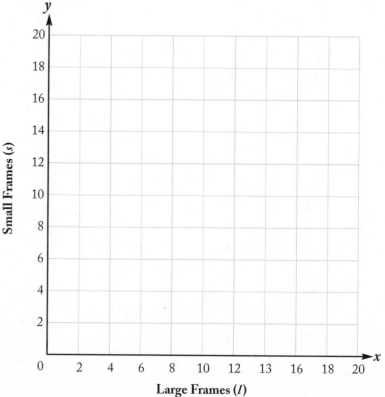

© GREAT SOURCE. COPYING IS PROHIBITED.

EXTENDED-RESPONSE QUESTION PRACTICE

Gabe is saving money to buy a new guitar. His parents gave him some money to start a guitar fund, and each week he adds a certain amount to the fund. After 4 weeks, he has $148 in the fund. After 6 weeks, he has $172.

Part A On the grid provided, draw a graph showing how the money in Gabe's guitar fund is growing. Remember to label the units on the x-axis and the y-axis of your graph.

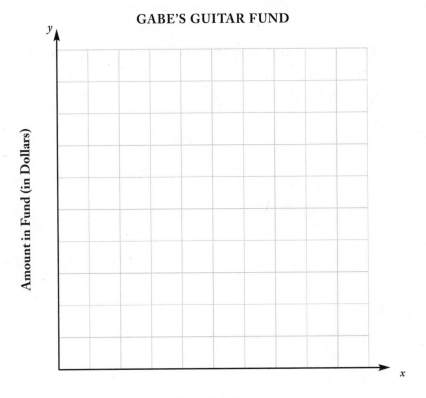

GABE'S GUITAR FUND

Amount in Fund (in Dollars)

Time (in Weeks)

Part B Calculate how much money Gabe puts into his fund each week. Explain how you found your answer.

Unit 2

Part C Tell how much money Gabe's parents gave him to start with. Explain how you found your answer.

Part D Write an equation that shows how much money Gabe has at any time after he starts saving. Let x = the number of weeks he has been saving and y = the amount of money he has.

Part E After how many full weeks will Gabe have enough money in his fund to buy a $190 guitar? Show your work.

 If you have trouble with this problem, review the following lessons:
2.1, "Variables, Expressions, and Equations"
2.3, "Solving Equations with One Variable"
2.7, "Graphing Linear Equations"
2.8, "Interpreting Graphs"

POINTS, LINES, AND ANGLES

This lesson addresses Benchmarks MA.B.1.3.2 and MA.C.3.3.1 of the Sunshine State Standards.

The Challenge

1) Name two angles that are congruent to ∠4 and explain your answers.

2) Name two angles that are supplementary to ∠4 and explain your answers.

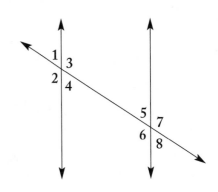

Math in History

People used to believe that, except for local variations like mountains and valleys, the Earth was a flat plane. They believed that if you sailed far enough toward the horizon, you would fall off the edge of the Earth. Then astronomers and mathematicians, using **geometry** (from the Greek words for "Earth measurement"), began to figure out that the Earth is really spherical (ball-shaped). In 1522, a fleet of ships led by Ferdinand Magellan, a Portuguese navigator working for the government of Spain, proved that the Earth was round by sailing all the way around it.

Learning the Ropes

Geometry is the study of points, lines, planes, and figures, including their characteristics, measurements, and relationships to each other. The vocabulary of geometry includes words you already know, but with special definitions:

A **point** has a location but no dimensions. Points are represented by dots and are often labeled with letters, as shown below.

•*A*

A **line** is a set of points that extends forever in both directions. The arrowheads on either end of the line show that it extends infinitely.

A **ray** is a part of a line that begins at a point and extends forever in one direction.

A **segment** is a part of a line that has a beginning and an end.

A **plane** is a flat, two-dimensional surface that extends infinitely.

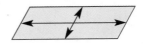

Parallel lines are lines within the same plane that never meet. They are always the same distance apart.

Skew lines are lines that are not in the same plane. Think of two airplanes flying in different directions at different altitudes.

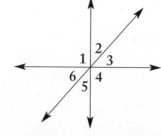

Intersecting lines occur when two lines cross at one point that belongs to both lines. If two lines intersect, there is exactly one plane that contains both of them.

When lines or parts of lines intersect, they form **angles.** The symbol $\angle$ means "angle." If two rays intersect at their common **endpoint** and extend in opposite directions, they form a **straight angle,** which looks just like a straight line. A straight angle measures 180 **degrees** (180°).

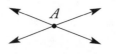

Perpendicular lines are lines whose intersecting angles are **right angles** (measuring 90°). Right angles are denoted by a little box in the corner of the two lines.

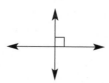

Angles are **complementary** if together they make a right angle. If angles are complementary, their sum is 90°. This would happen if two perpendicular lines were intersected by a third line.

In the drawing to the right, angles 2 and 3 are complementary pairs, as are $\angle 5$ and $\angle 6$.

When two lines intersect, they create four angles. The angles formed have special relationships to each other. Look at the figure to the right. Angles whose sides are opposite rays to one another are called **vertical angles.** Vertical angles are **congruent,** which means that their measures are equal. For example, ∠1 and ∠4 are vertical angles and are congruent to one another. The symbol ≅ shows that two angles are congruent.

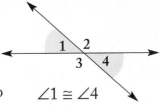

∠1 ≅ ∠4

Angles 1 and 2 have one ray in common, and their other sides form a straight angle. The sum of these two angles is 180°, so the angles are **supplementary.** What other pairs of angles add up to 180°?

This table gives the relationships among the four angles in the drawing above.

	∠1	∠2	∠3	∠4
∠1		supplementary	supplementary	vertical
∠2	supplementary		vertical	supplementary
∠3	supplementary	vertical		supplementary
∠4	vertical	supplementary	supplementary	

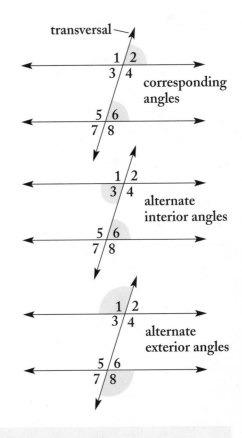

When two parallel lines are crossed by a third line, called a **transversal,** eight angles with special relationships to one another are created. Angles that are in the same position relative to the transversal and the parallel lines are called **corresponding angles.** Corresponding angles are congruent, so ∠1 ≅ ∠5, ∠2 ≅ ∠6, ∠3 ≅ ∠7, and ∠4 ≅ ∠8.

Angles that are between the two parallel lines but on opposite sides of the transversal are **alternate interior angles.** Alternate interior angles are congruent, so ∠3 ≅ ∠6 and ∠4 ≅ ∠5.

Angles that are above and below the two parallel lines but on opposite sides of the transversal are **alternate exterior angles.** Alternate exterior angles are congruent, so ∠1 ≅ ∠8 and ∠2 ≅ ∠7.

Another Way   It is easy to confuse the words *complementary* (C) and *supplementary* (S). Here are two memory tricks to help you remember them:
• C comes before S in the alphabet, just as the number 90 comes before 180.
• C is for corner (a right angle). S is for straight (line).

Unit 3: Geometry and Spatial Sense   159

Meeting the Challenge

To answer the Challenge, you must identify two angles in the drawing that are congruent to ∠4 and two that are supplementary to ∠4, and explain why these angles fit the definitions.

STEP 1: You know that vertical angles are congruent, and in the case of parallel lines cut by a transversal, alternate interior angles are congruent. Angle 1 is vertical to ∠4, and ∠5 is the alternate interior to ∠4, so these angles are congruent. In addition, ∠8 is vertical to ∠5, so it is also congruent to all these angles.

$$∠1 ≅ ∠4 ≅ ∠5 ≅ ∠8$$

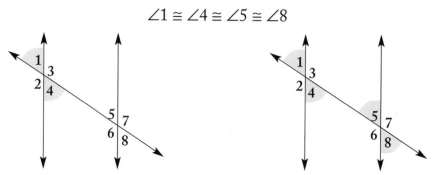

STEP 2: Two angles are supplementary if they form a straight line, or if their measures add up to 180°. Angle 4 is supplementary to both ∠2 and ∠3 because each pair forms a straight line.

$$∠4 + ∠2 = 180°$$ $$∠4 + ∠3 = 180°$$

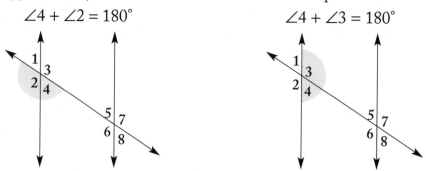

STEP 3: Any angle that is congruent to ∠2 or ∠3 will also form a supplementary pair with ∠4. Since ∠3 and ∠6 are alternate interior angles and are congruent, ∠6 is supplementary to ∠4. Since ∠7 is congruent to ∠6 (vertical angles), it also forms a supplementary pair with ∠4.

$$∠4 + ∠6 = 180°$$ $$∠4 + ∠7 = 180°$$

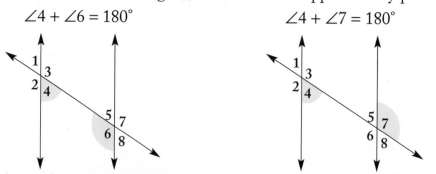

If you apply the rules of geometry, you find that angles 1, 4, 5, and 8 are all congruent. Angle 4 forms a supplementary pair with ∠2, ∠3, ∠6, or ∠7.

Try It Yourself

A. Use the figure below to answer the following questions.

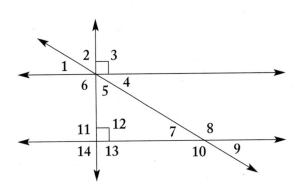

1. Name two complementary angles.

   _____

2. Name two supplementary angles.

   _____

3. Name two vertical angles.

   _____

4. Name two alternate interior angles.

   _____

B. Complete the activity below.

Lines *AB* and *CD* are parallel. The measure of ∠1 is 30°. Remember that a triangle's angles add up to 180°. Find the measure of each angle and explain each of your answers.

Angle	Measure	Explanation
2	_____	_____
		_____
3	_____	_____
		_____
4	_____	_____
		_____
5	_____	_____
		_____
6	_____	_____
		_____

Try It Yourself

A. Fill in the circle next to the correct answer to each multiple-choice question.

1. Think of a flat bridge that crosses over a river. What kind of lines are formed by the bridge and the river?

   Ⓐ parallel   Ⓑ skew   Ⓒ intersecting   Ⓓ perpendicular

2. Usually a person has about 150° of motion in his or her elbow—from 0° (straight) to 150° (fully flexed). Jeremy broke his arm and can only bend it from about 10° to 115°. How many degrees does he need to regain in order to have full range of motion?

   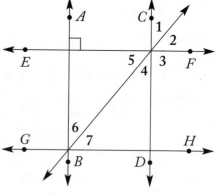

   Ⓐ 140°   Ⓑ 105°   Ⓒ 45°   Ⓓ 35°

B. Complete the activity below.

Lines *AB* and *CD* are parallel. Lines *EF* and *GH* are parallel to each other and perpendicular to lines *AB* and *CD*. The measure of ∠1 is 40°. Find the measure of each angle from ∠2 to ∠7, and explain each of your answers.

Angle	Measure	Explanation
2	_____	_____
3	_____	_____
4	_____	_____
5	_____	_____
6	_____	_____
7	_____	_____

TWO- AND THREE-DIMENSIONAL SHAPES

This lesson addresses Benchmarks MA.C.1.3.1 and MA.C.3.3.1 of the Sunshine State Standards.

The Challenge

What is the sum of the exterior angles of a regular 15-gon? What is the sum of the interior angles of a 15-gon? What is the measure of one interior angle of a regular 15-gon?

How many vertices does a dodecahedron have?

dodecahedron

Learning the Ropes

The word *polygon* means "many-sided." A **polygon** is a closed shape whose sides are all line segments. Many polygons have their own names, such as *triangle, pentagon,* and *octagon.* A polygon with *n* sides can be called an *n*-gon. For example, a polygon with 20 sides is a 20-gon. The sides of an **irregular polygon** are of different lengths. The sides of a **regular polygon** are all the same length, and its angles are equal in size.

An **exterior angle** is an angle that is outside a polygon. In the pentagon to the right, angles 1 through 5 are exterior angles. The sum of the exterior angles of any polygon is 360°. Each exterior angle is adjacent and supplementary to an interior angle. An **interior angle** is an angle formed on the inside of a polygon by two of its sides as they meet to form a **vertex.** In the pentagon shown, angles *A* through *E* are interior angles. A polygon has as many interior angles as it does sides. A **convex** polygon is one in which no interior angle is greater than 180°. A **concave** polygon has at least one interior angle greater than 180°.

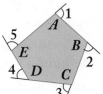

convex polygon
(each interior
angle < 180°)

concave polygon
(angle *A* > 180°)

Triangles are classified by the relative lengths of their sides or by their angles, as shown in the chart on the next page. The sum of the exterior angles of any triangle is 360°, as in all other polygons. The sum of the interior angles in any triangle equals 180°. If two sides of a triangle are of equal length, the angles opposite those sides are equal as well. When two or more sides or angles are marked with the same number of little slashes, it means that those parts are equal in size.

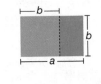

TRIANGLES					
equilateral	**isosceles**	**scalene**	**right**	**acute**	**obtuse**
all 3 sides of equal length	2 sides of equal length	no sides of equal length	1 right angle (90°)	3 acute angles (< 90°)	1 obtuse angle (> 90°)

A **quadrilateral** is a four-sided figure. The sum of the interior angles in a quadrilateral is 360°. Here are some special quadrilaterals:

QUADRILATERALS			
parallelogram	**rhombus**	**trapezoid**	**isosceles trapezoid**
two pairs of parallel equal sides; opposite angles are equal	parallelogram with all sides equal	exactly one pair of parallel sides (bases)	trapezoid with equal nonparallel sides

You can measure the interior angles of a polygon by dividing it into triangles that have a common vertex at a vertex of the polygon. This works for any polygon, whether it's regular or not. How many triangles can be drawn inside a figure with n sides? Experiment with different figures to find the relationship between the number of sides and the number of triangles that can be drawn inside the figure.

Start with an irregular hexagon. Draw segments from one vertex to all the other vertices that don't share a side with it. This divides the hexagon into four triangles.

The sum of the interior angles of each of the triangles is 180°. What is the sum of the interior angles of the whole hexagon? $4 \times 180° = 720°$

You can use this method to find the sum of the interior angles of any polygon. Notice that the number of triangles that can be made inside a polygon using this method is 2 less than the number of sides the polygon has. In other words, if a polygon has n sides, then $n - 2$ triangles can be made inside it this way. The sum of the angles is always the number of triangles times 180°: $(n - 2) \times 180$.

If a polygon is regular, then all its angles are equal. To get the measure of one angle, divide the sum of the interior angles by the number of angles—which is the same as the number of sides. For example, each angle of a regular hexagon is 120°: $720° \div 6 = 120°$.

Another Way Here is a hands-on way to see why the sum of the interior angles of a triangle is 180°. Cut a large triangle of any dimensions out of a piece of paper. Make sure the sides are straight. Fold one corner (A) over to the opposite side so that the fold is parallel to the opposite side (base of the triangle). Fold the other corners (B and C) so that they meet at the same place on the base. The three corners of the triangle together form a straight line, which measures 180°.

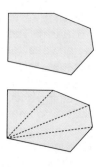

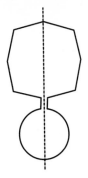

Math in Use: Astronomy Sometime between 200 B.C. and A.D. 500, Native Americans who lived in the area that is now Newark, Ohio, built a symmetrical structure whose floor plan was a circle connected to an octagon. The structure was discovered in 1848, but no one knew what it was used for until the early 1980s, when Ray Hively, a physicist, and Robert Horn, a philosopher, discovered that the axis of symmetry of the structure (see dotted line) is aimed directly at the point on the horizon where the moon rises on the summer solstice (the longest day of the year). This alignment suggests that the structure might have been used as an astronomical observatory or for religious ceremonies celebrating the solstice.

Polyhedrons are **solid figures** (three-dimensional figures) with faces that are polygons. Three types of polyhedron are regular polyhedrons, prisms, and pyramids. The five **regular polyhedrons** are illustrated below. The prefix of each name tells how many faces the figure has. For example, the **tetrahedron** (*tetra* = 4) has four faces, each of which is an equilateral triangle. It is also a triangular pyramid. The **hexahedron,** which is the same as a cube, has six square faces. The **octahedron** has eight triangular faces. Use a dictionary to find out how many faces an **icosahedron** has.

tetrahedron	hexahedron	octahedron	dodecahedron	icosahedron
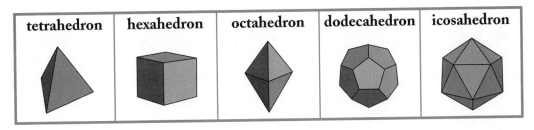

A **prism** is a polyhedron with two congruent parallel **bases** and any number of lateral faces formed by joining the corresponding vertices of the bases. Prisms are named by the shape of the bases. To the right are some examples of prisms.

triangular prism	rectangular prism	pentagonal prism

A **pyramid** is a polyhedron with one face (usually called the base) that is a polygon with any number of sides. All the other faces are triangles that meet at a single point called a **vertex.** Pyramids are named by the shape of the base. To the right are some examples of pyramids.

rectangular pyramid	hexagonal pyramid	octagonal pyramid

Some three-dimensional figures have curved sides. A **sphere** has the shape of a round ball. A **cone** has a circular base and a curved side that comes to a point at the vertex. A **cylinder** has two parallel circular faces. To the right are some figures with curved sides.

sphere	cone	cylinder

Unit 3: Geometry and Spatial Sense   **165**

Meeting the Challenge

To answer the Challenge, follow these steps.

STEP 1: Think of a 15-gon. It is unnecessary (and difficult) to draw one, but one is shown to help you picture it.

STEP 2: As with any polygon, the sum of the exterior angles is 360°.

STEP 3: The measure of one exterior angle of a regular 15-gon is found by using the formula $360 \div n$, where n is the number of sides. Thus, one exterior angle of a regular 15-gon is $\frac{360}{15}$, or 24°.

STEP 4: How many triangles could be drawn inside the 15-gon? There are 13 triangles, 2 less than the number of sides.

STEP 5: To find the sum of the interior angles of the 15-gon, add the measures of all the angles of all the triangles that could fit in the 15-gon. In each of the 13 triangles, the angles add up to 180°, so you can multiply:

13 triangles × 180° per triangle = 2,340°.

The sum of the interior angles of a 15-gon is 2,340°.

STEP 6: To find the measure of one interior angle of a regular 15-gon, divide the sum of all the interior angles by the number of angles.

2,340° ÷ 15 = 156°

STEP 7: Look at the dodecahedron below. You can see six of its twelve pentagonal faces; the other six faces are on the back side. Around the outer edge, you can see ten vertices. Also visible are the five vertices at the points of the pentagon facing you. There are five more vertices at the points of the pentagon on the back side, facing away from you. The total number of vertices is 20.

The answer to the Challenge is that the sum of the exterior angles of a 15-gon is 360°. Each exterior angle of a regular 15-gon measures 24°. The sum of the interior angles of a 15-gon is 2,340°. Each interior angle of a regular 15-gon measures 156°. A dodecahedron has 20 vertices.

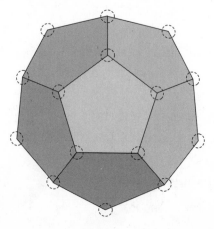

Try It Yourself

A. Fill in the circle next to the correct answer to each multiple-choice question.

1. What is the measure of each acute angle in an isosceles right triangle?
   Ⓐ 30°   Ⓑ 40°   Ⓒ 45°   Ⓓ 60°

2. Which is the best description of the figure to the right?
   Ⓐ regular pentagon   Ⓒ concave pentagon
   Ⓑ convex pentagon   Ⓓ isosceles pentagon

3. A book could be considered which of the following geometric shapes?
   Ⓐ a rectangular prism   Ⓒ a triangular prism
   Ⓑ a rectangular pyramid   Ⓓ a tetrahedron

4. What two polyhedrons form the basic structure of this house?
   Ⓐ a tetrahedron and a hexahedron
   Ⓑ a rectangular prism and a triangular prism
   Ⓒ a triangular prism and an octahedron
   Ⓓ a rectangular pyramid and a rectangular prism

5. If you divide a cube in half along the diagonal, you will get two identical three-dimensional shapes. What are these shapes?
   Ⓐ rectangular prisms.   Ⓒ rectangular pyramids.
   Ⓑ triangular prisms.   Ⓓ tetrahedrons.

B. Complete the activity below.

Look at the five regular polyhedrons on the third page of this lesson. Fill in the chart below to show the characteristics of each polyhedron. Some of the boxes have been filled in for you.

	Shape of Faces	Number of Faces	Number of Vertices	Number of Edges
Tetrahedron				6
Hexahedron			8	
Octahedron	equilateral triangle			
Dodecahedron		12		
Icosahedron				30

Try It Yourself

3.2 Two- and Three-Dimensional Shapes
Assessment Practice

A. Fill in the circle next to the correct answer to each multiple-choice question.

1. What kind of triangle is this? 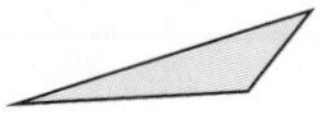

   Ⓐ acute scalene   Ⓑ obtuse isosceles   Ⓒ obtuse scalene   Ⓓ equilateral

2. Which of the following is a true statement?

   Ⓐ In an isosceles triangle, the angles opposite the equal sides are equal to each other.
   Ⓑ An obtuse triangle has three obtuse angles.
   Ⓒ The sum of the angles in an isosceles trapezoid is 540°.
   Ⓓ A convex polygon has at least one interior angle that is greater than 180°.

3. How many surfaces does an octagonal pyramid have in total?

   Ⓐ 6   Ⓑ 8   Ⓒ 9   Ⓓ 10

4. How many surfaces does an octagonal prism have in total?

   Ⓐ 6   Ⓑ 8   Ⓒ 9   Ⓓ 10

5. If a pyramid has 6 faces, what type of solid is it?

   Ⓐ triangular pyramid   Ⓒ pentagonal pyramid
   Ⓑ rectangular pyramid   Ⓓ hexagonal pyramid

6. What is the sum of the interior angles of a 14-gon?

   Ⓐ 1,080°   Ⓑ 1,260°   Ⓒ 1,400°   Ⓓ 2,160°

B. Complete the two parts below. Show all your work. Use additional paper if necessary.

The figure to the right is a regular heptagon, or 7-sided figure.

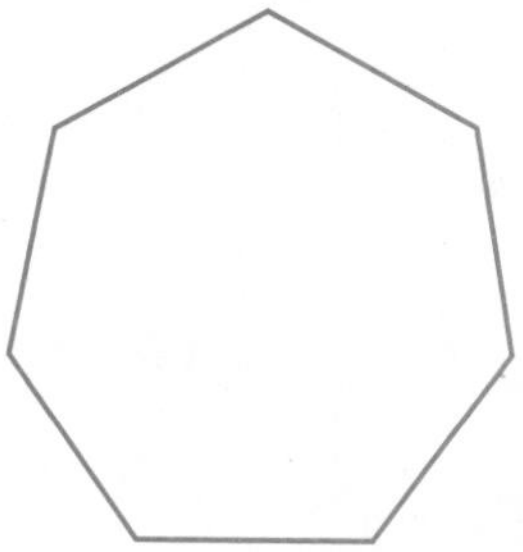

Part A Explain how to find the sum of the interior angles of this figure. Do the calculations and show all your work. You may write on the figure to show what you are doing.

Part B Explain how to find the measure of one interior angle of this figure. Perform the calculations and give your answer to the nearest degree.

SYMMETRY, SIMILARITY, AND TRANSFORMATIONS

This lesson addresses Benchmarks MA.B.1.3.4, MA.C.2.3.1, MA.C.2.3.2, and MA.C.3.3.1 of the Sunshine State Standards.

The Challenge

Examine these figures. Which figure is symmetrical? Which figure will tessellate? What would a reflection of Figure 2 across the dotted line look like? Make sketches, if necessary. Explain your answers.

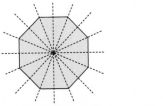
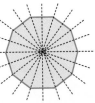

Learning the Ropes

Shapes have many properties that not only are fascinating to study but also have a huge variety of practical applications. In this lesson, you will learn about some of these properties.

Math in History
The telescope and the microscope were invented in the Netherlands in the early 1600s and were further developed by the great Italian astronomer Galileo Galilei (1564–1642). Telescopes and microscopes bend light rays to project images that are geometrically similar to the shapes of the real objects. The similar images, projected to our eyes or to a camera, preserve the shapes of the objects while changing their size. These inventions made modern astronomy and biology possible.

Symmetry. A **symmetrical** figure is one that can be divided into two matching halves. Each half is a mirror image of the other. The line that divides the figure into matching halves is called the **line of symmetry,** or **axis of symmetry.**

Some polygons are symmetrical and some are not. The regular pentagon to the right is symmetrical. The line of symmetry down the middle divides it into two mirror images. If you were to fold the figure along the line of symmetry, one half would fit exactly over the other half.

The irregular pentagon to the right is *not* symmetrical. It cannot be divided into two symmetrical halves.

A polygon can have more than one line of symmetry. A square has four lines of symmetry. How many lines of symmetry does a regular octagon have? a regular dodecagon? How many lines of symmetry do you think a circle has?

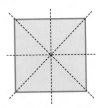

Since ancient times, mathematicians have marveled at how bees construct their honeycombs using tessellated regular hexagons. If they used equilateral triangles or squares, their honeycombs would use more wax to hold the same amount of honey. Of these three tessellating regular polygons, the hexagon offers the most area per unit of perimeter (and therefore, the most space in each cell), so it is the most efficient design.

Honeycomb shape	Perimeter	Side	Area (square units)
Equilateral triangle	1	$\frac{1}{3}$	0.048
Square	1	$\frac{1}{4}$	0.063
Regular hexagon	1	$\frac{1}{6}$	0.072

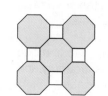

Tessellations. A tessellation is a set of polygons that fill a plane surface with no gaps and no overlapping. Floor tiles and checkerboards are examples of tessellated planes.

Some regular polygons tessellate, and some do not. Squares and equilateral triangles tessellate.

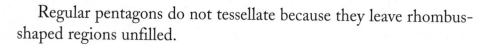

Regular pentagons do not tessellate because they leave rhombus-shaped regions unfilled.

Regular hexagons tessellate. This formation is found in nature in honeycombs and in insects' compound eyes, as well as in architecture.

Regular polygons with more than six sides do not tessellate. However, some tessellate with other regular polygons. For example, squares and regular octagons of certain sizes tessellate with each other.

Dodecagons tessellate with equilateral triangles and squares. What other regular polygons tessellate with each other?

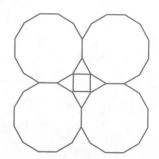

Many irregular polygons and other closed figures tessellate. As you can see in the first example below, parallelograms tessellate.

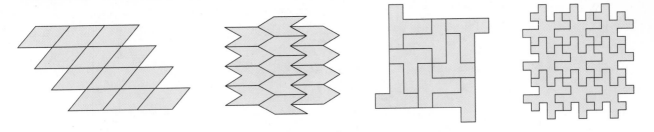

Congruence and Similarity. Congruent shapes are the same size and shape. Mirror images are also considered congruent. The **corresponding,** or matching, angles and sides of congruent shapes are congruent, as shown below.

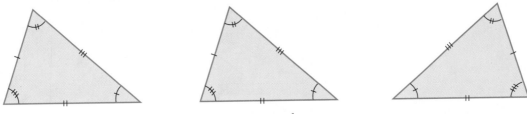

congruent shapes

Similar shapes are the same shape, but not the same size. The corresponding angles of congruent shapes are congruent. The corresponding sides are **proportional,** meaning that their lengths are in the same ratio. For example, if the base of the first triangle below is twice as long as the base of the third triangle, then each of the other sides of the first triangle will be twice as long as the matching sides of the third triangle. (See Lesson 1.4, "Fractions, Ratios, and Proportions.")

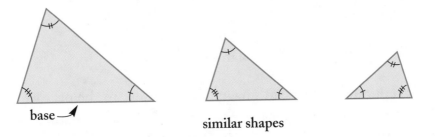

base

similar shapes

Transformations. A transformation, or **manipulation,** is what you do when you move, enlarge, or shrink a polygon. There are four kinds of transformation. Three of them—reflections (flips), translations (slides), and rotations (turns)—keep the polygons the same size and shape. In other words, the transformation is congruent to the original shape. The last kind of transformation involves enlargement or reduction, which changes the size of the polygon but keeps the shape the same. In other words, enlargements and reductions create shapes that are similar to the original.

A **reflection,** or **flip,** creates a mirror image that is congruent to the original image, with corresponding sides and angles that are equal. The new image and the original image are equidistant from the **line of reflection.**

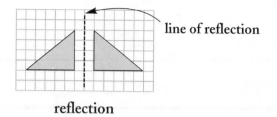

line of reflection

reflection

A **translation,** or **slide,** creates a congruent image whose sides are parallel to the corresponding sides of the original image. The arrow shows that in this translation, every point of the original image is moved two units down and six units to the right.

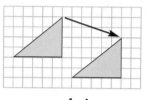

translation

A **rotation,** or **turn,** moves the image around a point. This point can be anywhere inside or outside the image, or on the image itself. The rotated image is still congruent to the original image. In this rotation, the arrow shows that the angle of rotation is 90° counterclockwise.

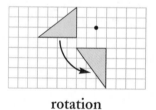

rotation

An **enlargement** or **reduction** creates an image that is similar to the original image; the corresponding angles are the same size, but the sides are on a different **scale.** In other words, the lengths of all the sides have been multiplied (or divided) by the same number. In an enlargement, the corresponding sides are proportionally larger; in a reduction, the corresponding sides are proportionally smaller.

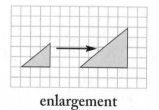

enlargement

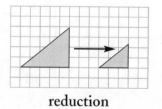

reduction

Some photocopiers can enlarge or reduce images. The size of the image is expressed as a percent; the original image is considered to be 100%. An image with sides that are half as long as in the original is a 50% reduction. An image whose sides are four times as long as in the original is a 400% enlargement.

Another way to describe the amount of enlargement or reduction is the scale factor. A $3 \times 4 \times 5$ triangle that is enlarged by a scale factor of 2 becomes a $6 \times 8 \times 10$ triangle. The ratio of the length of any side of the enlarged figure to the corresponding side of the original figure is the **scale factor.** The proportions between corresponding pairs of sides will also be equal. For example, in our enlarged triangle, the ratio of the smallest side to the largest is $6:10$. This ratio is the same as the ratio between the corresponding sides in the original triangle, which is $3:5$.

If you know that two shapes are similar, you can use the technique of **indirect measurement,** in which known proportions or ratios are used to determine the lengths of unknown sides.

EXAMPLE   The two polygons below are similar. What is the unknown length x?

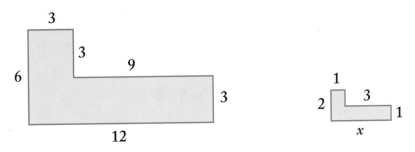

First, you determine the scale factor. In this case, it is $3:1$, or a reduction of one-third ($\frac{1}{3}$, or 33%). Since the length of the side of the original figure corresponding to x in the reduced figure is 12, the length of x is $\frac{12}{3} = 4$.

Creating Three-Dimensional Figures. You can rotate a two-dimensional figure around a line to produce a three-dimensional figure. For example, what would happen if you rotated a rectangle around one of its sides? Suppose you keep that side in a fixed position and let the rectangle spin around it. The blur created by the spinning rectangle would be in the shape of a cylinder. Similarly, a right triangle spinning around one of its legs would make a cone shape. What shape would be formed by a circle rotating around its diameter? around a line outside it?

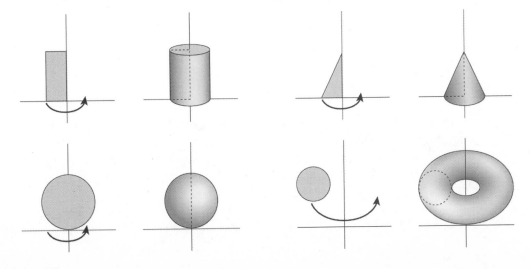

Meeting the Challenge

To answer the Challenge, you must choose which figure is symmetrical and which one will tessellate. You must also draw a reflection of the second figure.

STEP 1: To determine which shape is symmetrical, draw a line through the middle of each figure. Check to see which figure has one side that matches the other side. Only Figure 1 can be divided into two mirror-image halves. Therefore, it is symmetrical.

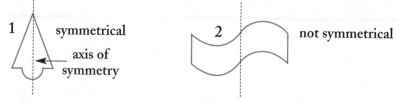

STEP 2: Now determine which shape tessellates. Draw similar, congruent shapes next to and below the shapes. Which shapes fit together without any spaces in between? The semicircular part on the bottom of each triangle in Figure 1 will not fit the edges of the figures next to it. Only Figure 2 tessellates; the shapes fit together with no gaps and no overlapping.

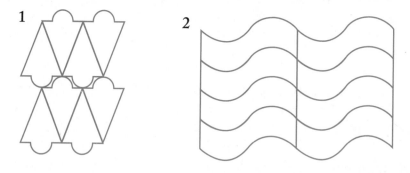

STEP 3: Draw a line next to Figure 2 and think of it as a mirror. Draw the mirror image of the figure on the other side of the line. The new figure is a reflection, or flip, of the original figure. If the image were folded in half, each line of the figure on the left would match (align with) a line in the figure on the right.

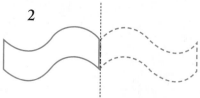

Another Way You can create more complex figures that tessellate by taking a regular polygon that tessellates, carving a piece out of it, and performing a transformation on the piece. For example, if you start with a square, draw a triangle inside it, and slide the triangle, you get a polygon that tessellates.

Name_____ Class _____ Date _____

Try It Yourself

A. Fill in the circle next to the correct answer to each multiple-choice question.

1. What manipulation(s) must you do to the figure on the left in order to create the figure on the right?

   Ⓐ slide

   Ⓑ flip and turn 45° counterclockwise

   Ⓒ flip and slide

   Ⓓ flip and turn 120° clockwise

2. The figure on the left has been reduced and rotated 90° clockwise to produce the figure on the right. What is the length of side a?

   Ⓐ 3

   Ⓑ 2

   Ⓒ 1

   Ⓓ $\frac{4}{3}$

3. Which transformations of the figure to the right will create an image that is not congruent?

   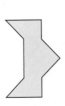

   Ⓐ flip and slide

   Ⓑ turn and reduce

   Ⓒ turn and slide

   Ⓓ rotate 360°

B. Complete the activity below.

On the grid, draw an irregular polygon that tessellates.

Try It Yourself

A. Fill in the circle next to the correct answer to each multiple-choice question.

1. Which of the following manipulations might you do to a photo to make a poster?
   - Ⓐ reflection
   - Ⓑ translation
   - Ⓒ rotation
   - Ⓓ enlargement

2. Which of the following transformations might you do to a poster on your wall, in order to make it closer to a window?
   - Ⓐ flip
   - Ⓑ slide
   - Ⓒ turn
   - Ⓓ reduce

3. Which of the following manipulations might you do to a painting that is hanging at an angle?
   - Ⓐ reflection
   - Ⓑ translation
   - Ⓒ rotation
   - Ⓓ enlargement

4. Which of the following transformations might you do to a page in a book?
   - Ⓐ flip
   - Ⓑ slide
   - Ⓒ rotate
   - Ⓓ reduce

B. Complete the three parts below. Show all your work.

Choose one of these figures for each part of the activity.

1    2    3

Part A Draw a tessellation using one of the figures.

Part B Rotate another one of the figures 90° clockwise.

Part C Enlarge the third figure by a scale factor of 2.

THE PYTHAGOREAN THEOREM

This lesson addresses Benchmarks MA.B.2.3.1 and MA.C.3.3.1 of the Sunshine State Standards.

The Challenge

To bike to your friend Casey's house, you can take one road 8 miles north, then another road 6 miles east. If you were to take a bike path straight from your house to Casey's house, how much shorter would the ride be?

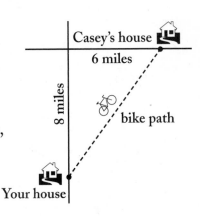

Math in History

Pythagoras of Samos (569–475 B.C.) has been called the first pure mathematician, but he thought of himself as much more than a mathematician. He believed that there was only one subject—philosophy—which at that time included the study of mathematics, astronomy, theology, logic, ethics, and music. Pythagoras held that the basic nature of the world is mathematical. He saw mathematics as an intellectual discipline of great power and beauty that held keys to the physical and spiritual world.

Learning the Ropes

The **Pythagorean theorem** is the most famous theorem in geometry. A **theorem** is a conclusion that follows logically from what is already known. The Pythagorean theorem is an equation that states a relationship among the sides of a right triangle.

The side that is opposite the right angle in a right triangle is called the **hypotenuse.** The other two sides are called **legs.** The Pythagorean theorem relates the length of the hypotenuse to the lengths of the legs. Study the diagram to the right.

What is the area of square A? of square B? of square C? What do you notice about the sum of the areas of square A and square B?

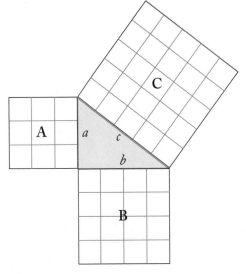

You see that the sum of the areas of squares A and B is equal to the area of square C. In the case of the shaded triangle shown in the diagram, side a is 3 units long, and side b is 4 units long. The area of square A is a^2, or 9, and the area of square B is b^2, or 16. The sum of these two areas is 25, which is equal to the area of square C, or c^2.

Math in Use: Construction Although Pythagoras gets the credit for proving the theorem that bears his name, the Babylonians had discovered it about a thousand years earlier. It is still enormously important today, not only to scientists and mathematicians but also to architects and builders, who use the principle to make sure that the rooms they build are perfect rectangles, and to lay out the foundation of buildings.

The triangle on the previous page works neatly with whole numbers, but the same principle works with *any* right triangle. If a and b are the lengths of the legs of the triangle and c is the length of the hypotenuse, the Pythagorean theorem says that $a^2 + b^2 = c^2$. If you know the hypotenuse and one of the legs, you can use this formula to find the other leg: $a = \sqrt{c^2 - b^2}$.

$$a^2 + b^2 = c^2$$

The Pythagorean theorem

$$a = \sqrt{c^2 - b^2}$$

Solving for the length of a leg

In addition to the set {3, 4, 5}, there are other sets of three whole numbers that can be used to make right triangles. For example, the set {5, 12, 13} gives the equation $5^2 + 12^2 = 13^2$. (Check to see if this equation is true!) Other sets are {7, 24, 25} and {8, 15, 17}. If you multiply all three numbers in one of these sets by any whole number, you will get another set of three numbers that works in the Pythagorean formula, $a^2 + b^2 = c^2$. For example, multiply each number in the set {3, 4, 5} by 7 to get {21, 28, 35}. A triangle with sides of these lengths would be a right triangle; plug the numbers into the Pythagorean theorem and see for yourself.

Meeting the Challenge

To answer the Challenge, you have to find the length of the bike path, which is the hypotenuse of a right triangle.

STEP 1: You know that the triangle formed by the roads and the bike path is a right triangle because the roads run due north and due east. You know the lengths of the two legs. Put the numbers into the Pythagorean theorem to find the length of the bike path, which is the hypotenuse of the right triangle.

$$a^2 + b^2 = c^2 \qquad 8^2 + 6^2 = c^2$$

STEP 2: Solve the equation to find c, the length of the bike path.

$$8^2 + 6^2 = c^2 \qquad 64 + 36 = c^2 \qquad 100 = c^2 \qquad c = 10$$

STEP 3: Calculate the distance you would travel by road (8 miles + 6 miles = 14 miles) and subtract the length of the bike path (10 miles) to find how much shorter the bike path would be.

$$14 \text{ miles} - 10 \text{ miles} = 4 \text{ miles}$$

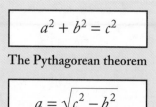

The answer to the Challenge is that you would save 4 miles by taking the bike path, which is 10 miles long, compared to the route on the roads, which is 14 miles long.

Name_____   Class _____   Date _____

Try It Yourself

A. Fill in the circle next to the correct answer to each multiple-choice question.

1. What is the length of side a?

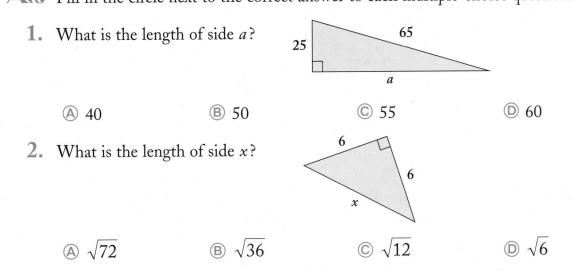

   Ⓐ 40   Ⓑ 50   Ⓒ 55   Ⓓ 60

2. What is the length of side x?

   Ⓐ $\sqrt{72}$ Ⓑ $\sqrt{36}$ Ⓒ $\sqrt{12}$ Ⓓ $\sqrt{6}$

3. Ellen has a square piece of fabric that is 2 feet on each side. She cuts it in half diagonally to make 2 triangular pieces for scarves. She wants to put a fringe around the edges of the scarves. Which expression shows how much fringe she needs for 1 scarf?

   Ⓐ 2 ft + 2 ft + 3 ft   Ⓑ 2 ft + 2 ft + 4 ft   Ⓒ 2 ft + 2 ft + 5 ft   Ⓓ 2 ft + 2 ft + $\sqrt{8}$ ft

B. Complete the two parts below. Show all your work.

Suppose you want to fly from your hometown to a city 500 miles southwest of you, but there are no direct flights. You have to fly through a major city 300 miles south, then take another plane west to your destination.

Part A Draw a diagram showing the direct route between the cities and the route through the major city. Write and solve an equation that shows the distance of the second leg (westward) of your trip.

Part B Calculate how many miles longer your trip is than a direct flight would be.

Try It Yourself

A. Fill in the circle next to the correct answer to each multiple-choice question.

1. What is the length of side x?

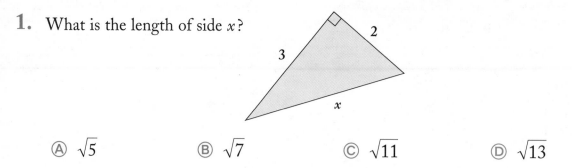

Ⓐ $\sqrt{5}$ Ⓑ $\sqrt{7}$ Ⓒ $\sqrt{11}$ Ⓓ $\sqrt{13}$

2. Kara is doing origami, the Japanese art of paper-folding. She starts with a square piece of paper that is 4 inches on each side, and she folds each corner into the middle:

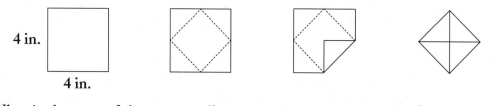

What is the area of the new smaller square in square inches (in.²)?

Ⓐ 2 in.²   Ⓑ 4 in.²   Ⓒ 8 in.²   Ⓓ 12 in.²

3. A rectangular computer monitor is 16 inches wide. It has a diagonal measure of 20 inches. How high is it?

Ⓐ 12 in.   Ⓑ 14 in.   Ⓒ 16 in.   Ⓓ 18 in.

B. Complete the two parts below. Show all your work.

Haywood Park is 1200 meters long and 500 meters wide. Stacy and Kelly were planning to run around the perimeter of the park. Stacy ran all the way around, but Kelly ran along two sides and then cut back to the starting point by running diagonally across the park.

Part A Draw a diagram of the park showing the girls' routes. Calculate how far Stacy ran.

Part B Calculate how far Kelly ran.

EXTENDED-RESPONSE QUESTION PRACTICE

The figure below (*ABCD*) is a rhombus. Each blue line inside the figure is parallel to two sides of the figure.

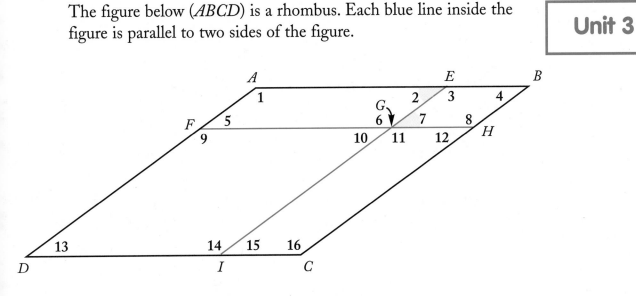

Part A List all the angles that are congruent to ∠7.

Part B Tell why each angle is congruent to ∠7. The first one has been done for you.

Angle:	Reason why that angle is congruent to ∠7:
∠2	∠2 and ∠7 are alternate interior angles formed by the intersection of transversal *EI* with lines *AB* and *FH*, which are parallel to each other.

Unit 3

Part C List all the angles that are supplementary to ∠7.

Part D Does figure *ABCD* have any lines of symmetry? If so, draw them on the figure and explain why they are lines of symmetry.

Part E Can figure *ABCD* tessellate? Why or why not? Explain and illustrate your answer.

✔ If you have trouble with this problem, review the following lessons:
   3.1, "Points, Lines, and Angles"
   3.2, "Two- and Three-Dimensional Shapes"
   3.3, "Symmetry, Similarity, and Transformations"

ESTIMATING MEASUREMENTS

This lesson addresses Benchmark B.3.3.1 of the Sunshine State Standards.

The Challenge

Diane goes to the store to buy a tablecloth, but she doesn't know the dimensions of her table. The tablecloths come in three lengths: 52 inches, 84 inches, and 108 inches. Her table seats 3 people on each side. How can she estimate the length of her table? Which tablecloth should she buy?

Learning the Ropes

Estimating measurements is helpful for finding ballpark sizes of large objects. The trick is to compare the object to something whose dimensions you know. For instance, you can estimate the height of a ceiling or a tree by comparing it to your own height.

EXAMPLE Shanice is organizing a dance-a-thon to raise money for the theater program. She needs to mark off a dance floor that is 25 feet by 25 feet, but she doesn't have a tape measure. How can she mark off the area?

To measure lengths without a tape measure, you can use the length of your foot or your stride. If Shanice knows that her stride is about 2.5 feet long, she can walk about 10 steps to determine where to mark off the dance floor.

To estimate the height of a building or a house, you can estimate the height of each story and multiply by the number of stories. Most stories in commercial buildings are about 12 feet in height, and stories in houses are about 10 feet in height.

Another method of estimating dimensions is by using your arm span, which is approximately equal to your height. You can also measure your hand span and use that as a way to estimate measurements. You can make a ruler out of your body by taking measurements, such as the distance between the floor and your knees, or the floor and your hips.

Math in History

In 1958, Oliver Smoot, a student at the Massachusetts Institute of Technology, measured the length of the Harvard Bridge, which connects Boston and Cambridge, Massachusetts. Instead of using a standard tool, like a tape measure, he used a nonstandard tool—himself. He and some friends used paint to mark over 360 body lengths, or Smoots. One Smoot is equal to about 5 feet, 7 inches. The Harvard Bridge is 364.4 Smoots and one ear, or about 2,000 feet long. The tradition has been continued, and every year the Smoot marks on the bridge are repainted.

Math in Use: Monetary Conversions   When you visit a foreign country, you are faced with the challenge of figuring out the monetary system, which is doubly tricky when a different measurement system is used as well. Good estimating skills can help you change prices and measurements into units you are more familiar with. For example, the Mexican peso was recently worth about 11 cents in U.S. dollars. Mexico uses the metric system, so you are likely to find items in the grocery store sold by the kilogram, which is equivalent to about 2.2 pounds. You would probably feel disoriented trying to work with prices given in pesos per kilogram, but if you do the conversion, you find that 1 peso per kilogram was recently about the same as 5¢ per pound. Knowing this fact, you can do quick estimates to see if you are getting a good deal.

To estimate distance, you must compare the unknown distance to a distance you do know. For example, you probably know how far your school is from your home. You can use that distance to estimate how far other locations are from your home. You can estimate distances by comparing how long it takes you to get to school with how long it takes you to get to other places.

You can also estimate the weight of an object by comparing it to an object whose weight you know. For example, if you get familiar with the feel of a one-pound piece of cheese or a five-pound bag of sugar, you can estimate the weight of a package you want to mail. An envelope with four sheets of paper weighs approximately one ounce.

You probably have a fairly good idea of how long one minute or one hour is. You can estimate unknown timespans by comparing them to times you do know, like the length of a one-hour class or a half-hour television show. Temperature can be more difficult to estimate, particularly with Celsius temperatures, which may not be as familiar. Try to become aware of how you feel—or how much clothing you need to wear—at different temperatures.

Having a good sense of approximate lengths, distances, weights, volumes, and so on will help you estimate measurements accurately and make good decisions based on your estimates.

Meeting the Challenge

To answer the Challenge, you must explain a method that Diane can use to estimate the dimensions of her table.

Step 1: Diane can estimate the length of her table by figuring out how much space each person at the table gets. She can guess that each person gets approximately 2 feet. Therefore, the table is about 6 feet long.

Step 2: Convert 6 feet into inches to find which tablecloth Diane should buy.

$$6 \text{ feet} \times \frac{12 \text{ inches}}{1 \text{ foot}} = 72 \text{ inches}$$

The answer to the Challenge is that Diane should buy the 84-inch tablecloth.

Name_____ Class _____ Date _____

Try It Yourself

A. Fill in the circle next to the correct answer to each multiple-choice question.

1. Which of the following is the best estimate of the diameter of a tire on a car?

   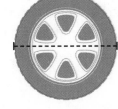

   Ⓐ 1 ft   © 4 ft

   Ⓑ 2 ft   Ⓓ 5 ft

2. Akira is ordering meat for an eighth-grade barbecue. He needs to order enough meat for 100 hamburgers. If he plans to make 4 hamburgers per pound, which of the following is the most reasonable figure for the amount of meat he should buy?

   Ⓐ 4 lb   Ⓑ 25 lb   © 200 lb   Ⓓ 400 lb

3. Shauna is working in her garden. She needs to buy bulbs to plant in the garden, which is 6 feet long and 6 feet wide. The bulbs must be planted at least 8 inches apart from each other. The bulbs are sold by the dozen. How many dozen bulbs should Shauna buy?

   Ⓐ 4 dozen   Ⓑ 7 dozen   © 14 dozen   Ⓓ 20 dozen

4. If "a pint's a pound the world around," which of the following is the best estimate of the weight of 4 gallons of milk?

   Ⓐ 12 oz   Ⓑ 2 lb   © 5 lb   Ⓓ 30 lb

5. Your house is 2 stories high. A tree growing next to your house is almost half as tall as the house. Which of the following is the best estimate for the height of the tree?

   Ⓐ 10 ft   Ⓑ 20 ft   © 30 ft   Ⓓ 60 ft

B. Complete the activity below.

A group of volunteers is cultivating the neighborhood garden. They wish to purchase some fertilizer for the garden, but they do not know the square footage. Describe a method that they could use to estimate the square footage.

Try It Yourself

A. Fill in the circle next to the correct answer to each multiple-choice question.

1. Evan works as a chef for a catering company. He is preparing soup for a dinner party that 35 people will be attending. If each person will be served about 2 cups of soup, approximately how much soup should he make?

   Ⓐ about 5 gal   Ⓑ about 9 gal   Ⓒ about 12 gal   Ⓓ about 18 gal

2. Which of the following is the best estimate of the volume of a refrigerator?

   Ⓐ 200 ft³   Ⓑ 100 ft³   Ⓒ 20 ft³   Ⓓ 200 in.³

3. While hiking on a trail, Mrs. Doyle wonders how far she has gone. She knows that it takes her 15 minutes to walk to the store, which is about $\frac{3}{4}$ of a mile away. If she has hiked for $1\frac{1}{2}$ hours, which of the following is the best estimate of how far she has hiked?

   Ⓐ $1\frac{1}{2}$ mi   Ⓑ 3 mi   Ⓒ $4\frac{1}{2}$ mi   Ⓓ 9 mi

4. Your scout troop is sponsoring a pancake breakfast in the Community House. The hall you will be using measures 50 feet by 50 feet. You should allow an area about 10 feet by 7 feet for each table with its chairs. Which of the following is the most reasonable estimate for the maximum number of tables (with chairs) you could put in the hall?

   Ⓐ 10 tables   Ⓑ 35 tables   Ⓒ 150 tables   Ⓓ 200 tables

B. Complete the two parts below. Show all your work.

Trini and her brother go to a theater to watch a movie. Her brother asks her how large the movie screen is and how many seats the theater holds.

Part A Explain how she can estimate the dimensions of the screen.

Part B Explain how she can estimate the number of seats in the theater.

PRECISION, ACCURACY, AND SIGNIFICANT DIGITS

This lesson addresses Benchmark B.2.3.2 of the Sunshine State Standards.

The Challenge

Amalia is fascinated by the elephant at the zoo. The trainer tells her that the elephant has recently weighed in at 9,450 pounds on the large-animal scale, which measures to the nearest 10 pounds. Today, the elephant is wearing a headdress that weighs 18.5 pounds. Perched on her head is a little bird that weighs 4 ounces. What is the total weight of the elephant, the headdress, and the bird? Give your answer to the most reasonable degree of precision.

Learning the Ropes

When you are counting, it is possible to give an *exact* number. For example, you could say that there are exactly three people in a room, or there are exactly 17 coins in your pocket. When you measure, however, it is impossible to give an exact figure. No matter how good your measuring instrument is, you can never say *exactly* how long or how deep or how heavy something is. You can get closer and closer to the real measurement, but you can never give a measurement with complete certainty.

Suppose that you are weighing bananas on a scale at a grocery store. The scale goes from 0 to 10 pounds. Each half-pound is marked on the scale. The best you can do is tell the weight of the bananas to the nearest half-pound. It would be unreasonable to estimate the measurement at 3.527 pounds. It would be reasonable to say that the bananas weigh about 3.5 pounds.

Precision. How **precise** a measurement is, or its **precision,** depends upon the quality of the measuring tool. A scientific scale, which can measure to the thousandths place, is more precise than a spring scale at a grocery store because a scientific scale gives measurements in smaller units.

Uncertainty. Suppose you have a tape measure marked off in inches. You measure a window and find the width to be closest to 38 inches. You know it is more than 37 inches and less than 39 inches. In fact, if you have measured carefully, you know that it is more than $37\frac{1}{2}$ inches because if it were less, you would have read it as 37 inches. In the same way, it is less than $38\frac{1}{2}$ inches because if it were more, you would have read it as 39 inches.

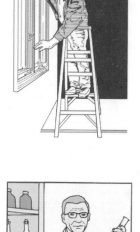

With this measuring tool, you can say that the window is between $37\frac{1}{2}$ and $38\frac{1}{2}$ inches wide. Anyone else who measures the window correctly will find a value in that same interval. The **uncertainty** is the interval, or space, around your measurement within which the true measurement lies, in this case, plus or minus $\frac{1}{2}$ inch (+/− 0.5 in.). The smaller the uncertainty in a measurement, the greater the precision. For example, some instruments can measure millionths of a second; their uncertainty is very tiny!

Accuracy. When you perform experiments in science class, you are often trying to find a value that is already known. That is, the value is known by your teacher and by scientists, but you have to figure it out! The closer your measurement is to the true value, the more **accurate** it is. For example, suppose you do an experiment to determine the boiling point of a certain liquid. You do your experiment and calculations and find that the boiling point is 201°F. Your partner finds that the temperature (boiling point) is 194°F. Then your teacher tells you that the true value is actually 199°F. Whose value is more accurate?

Error. The amount by which a number differs from the true value is called the **error.** Suppose you and a friend set your watches by the school clock, which is a very good one. One month later, when it is noon by the school clock, your watch reads 11:59 and your friend's reads 12:04. What is the error of your watch? of your friend's watch?

Math in Use: Space Science On June 4, 1996, a French *Ariane 5* rocket blew up shortly after launch. The disaster was due to incompatibility between two computer programs. One of the programs generated a very large number with 64 significant digits. It sent this information to another program that was not set up to handle such large numbers. The program generated a diagnostic error, which the rocket's computer then falsely interpreted as flight data. The computer made a flight correction that caused the rocket to veer off course and explode! So, as you can see, the number of significant digits in a calculation can sometimes be extremely important!

Significant Digits. If someone told you there were exactly 3,412,691,777,023 grains of sand on a beach, would you believe it? Of course not; it would be impossible to count the exact number of grains of sand. It might be reasonable to say that there are about 3.4 trillion grains of sand. If you can give the number only to the nearest 100 billion, then all the digits after the 10-billions place are meaningless; no matter what they are, they will not change the digit in the 100-billions place.

When you work with measurements, you have to decide which digits are **significant digits,** ones that represent actual measurements and should be taken into account when you do your calculations. For example, in a huge number with many zeros at the end, the zeros are usually not significant, since the places they represent are so small compared to places farther to the left.

Determining Whether Digits Are Significant. To find out the number of significant digits a measurement has, follow the rules in the box below.

1. The digits 1–9 are always significant.
   EXAMPLES 5,622 cm and 1.259 cm each have 4 significant digits.

2. Zeros between significant digits are always significant.
   EXAMPLES 20,109 in. and 3,025.5 m each have 5 significant digits.

3. Zeros ending a whole number are not usually considered significant. They often suggest that the number has been rounded.
   EXAMPLES 1000 mm and 2,000,000 mm each have 1 significant digit.

4. Leading zeros before a number are not usually considered significant. These zeros just set the place value of the decimal.
   EXAMPLES 0.003 mm and 0.00007 mm each have 1 significant digit.

5. Zeros at the end of a decimal are always significant. People leave such zeros in place to indicate how precise a measurement was.
   EXAMPLES 23.600 ft and 0.25000 in. each have 5 significant digits.

6. In scientific notation, every digit in the base number is significant.
   EXAMPLES 9×10^3 ft and 1×10^{17} in. each have 1 significant digit.
   9.19×10^3 ft and 1.00×10^{17} in. each have 3 significant digits.

Performing Operations with Measurements. When you work with measurements, you have to remember that they are not exact. To do calculations, you have to take into account how precise each measurement is. Suppose you want to add two measurements, 3.76 miles and 5 miles. Your second measurement is good only to the closest mile; it might really be only 4.5 miles, or maybe as much as 5.5 miles. Therefore, the sum can be good only to the nearest mile (ones place). You would add the two numbers, then round: 3.76 miles + 5 miles = 8.76 miles ≈ 9 miles. The greatest precision you can achieve is that of the least precise measurement.

When scientists perform experiments, they want to find results that are as accurate and precise as possible with the least error and the least uncertainty. They have developed rules for using significant digits when working with measurements so that the conclusions they reach are as true and as meaningful as they can be. You need to remember that measurement is never exact, but you can make meaningful statements about the things you observe.

Meeting the Challenge

To answer the Challenge, you must add the weights and decide which digits in your answer are significant.

STEP 1: Add the weights of the elephant, the headdress, and the bird. The bird weighs 4 ounces, which is the same as one-quarter pound, or 0.25 pound.

$$
\begin{array}{r}
9,450.00 \\
18.50 \\
+\ 0.25 \\
\hline
9,468.75
\end{array}
$$

STEP 2: You know that the bird is weighed to the nearest ounce, which is only a fraction of a pound. The headdress is weighed at least to the nearest half-pound. The elephant herself, however, is weighed only to the nearest 10 pounds, which means that the value could be off by as much as 5 pounds. Therefore, the fractions of a pound in the weights of the bird and the headdress are meaningless. Your answer can be, at best, to the nearest 10 pounds. If you round to the nearest 10 pounds, you will find that the combined weight is about 9,470 pounds.

The answer to the Challenge is that the combined weight of the elephant, the headdress, and the bird is about 9,470 pounds. This answer has the same degree of uncertainty (to the nearest 10 pounds, or +/− 5 pounds) and the same number of significant digits as the elephant's weight, which is the least precise of the three weights.

Another Way When thinking about significant digits, remember the saying, "A chain is only as strong as its weakest link." Likewise, a calculation is only as precise as the weakest, or least precise, measurement used in the calculation. Always make sure that your result has the same number of significant digits as this "weakest link." To do this, round the result if necessary. When rounding, follow these steps:

Step 1: Find the digit that you wish to round.
Step 2: If the digit to the right is ≥ 5, round up.
Step 3: If the digit to the right is ≤ 4, round down.

As noted above, uninterrupted zeros before a decimal point, as in the numbers 2,000 and 1,000,000, are usually not considered significant because they usually result from rounding. However, use your common sense. If the number is exact (as in the statement "The Senate has exactly 100 members"), then the zeros are significant. Twenty-five percent of the members (100 × 0.25) would be expressed to two significant digits, not to one. Twenty-five percent of the senators = 100 × 0.25 = 25.

Name_____ Class _____ Date _____

Try It Yourself

A. Tell how many significant digits are in each number.

1. 1.236 _____

2. 2,000,000,000 _____

3. 5.0 _____

4. 0.0005 _____

B. Fill in the circle next to the correct answer to each multiple-choice question.

1. Which of the following is the most *precise* measurement?
Ⓐ 0.1 m   Ⓑ 3.50 m   Ⓒ 6.523 m   Ⓓ 17,000 m

2. A steel rod is certified by a machine company to be 8 inches long. Four students measure the rod and find the following lengths. Which measurement is the most *accurate*?
Ⓐ 7.93 in.   Ⓑ 8.12 in.   Ⓒ 8.2 in.   Ⓓ 8.235 in.

3. What is the uncertainty in a measurement that is correct to the nearest 100 miles?
Ⓐ +/− 15 mi   Ⓑ +/− 10 mi   Ⓒ +/− 50 mi   Ⓓ +/− 100 mi

C. Complete the two parts below. Show all your work. Use additional paper if necessary.

For his chemistry experiment, Jumaine uses a scientific scale to measure substances before and after they are heated, as shown in the chart.

Part A Find the difference between the masses before and after heating for each substance.

Substance A _____

Substance B _____

Substance C _____

Substance D _____

Substance	Mass before heating	Mass after heating
JUMAINE'S MEASUREMENTS (IN GRAMS)		
A	2.003	1.210
B	11.05	10.91
C	0.35	0.05
D	6.01	2.57

Part B What would happen to his measurements if Jumaine used a scale that measures to the nearest gram? Explain your answer.

Try It Yourself

4.2 Precision, Accuracy, and Significant Digits
Assessment Practice

A. Fill in the circle next to the correct answer to each multiple-choice question.

1. Which of the following numbers has the greatest number of significant digits?

Ⓐ 9,000,000,000 Ⓑ 120.26 Ⓒ 100,000.0 Ⓓ 0.0072589

2. How many significant digits are in the number 3.90×10^{22}?

Ⓐ 2 Ⓑ 3 Ⓒ 5 Ⓓ 7

3. You measure a piece of wood to the nearest inch and find it to be 26 inches long. What is the interval of uncertainty in your measurement?

Ⓐ 20 in. to 30 in.

Ⓑ 25 in. to 27 in.

Ⓒ 25.5 in. to 26.5 in.

Ⓓ 25.75 in. to 26.25 in.

4. You are trying to find the distance you have traveled using the following formula: rate × time = distance. Your rate is 12 miles per hour, and your time is 10.5 seconds. How many significant digits will be in your answer?

Ⓐ 1 Ⓑ 2 Ⓒ 3 Ⓓ 4

B. Complete the two parts below. Show all your work.

Students in Mrs. Friedman's class measure a piece of wire. Their measurements are shown to the right.

WIRE MEASUREMENTS (IN INCHES)

Student	Length
Julio	3
Tisha	3.5
Becca	4
Jae-sung	3.4

Part A Mrs. Friedman tells the students that the manufacturer of the wire claims it is 3.82 inches long. By that measure, which student's measurement is most accurate? Explain your answer.

Part B Which student's measurement has the most error? Explain your answer.

CONVERTING CUSTOMARY AND METRIC UNITS

This lesson addresses Benchmark B.2.3.2 of the Sunshine State Standards.

The Challenge

Eva is a professional mountain climber. She is training to climb Mount McKinley in Alaska and Mount Rainier in Washington. Mount McKinley is 20,320 feet high, and Mount Rainier is 14,411 feet high. What is the difference in height, in miles, between the two mountains? Round your answer to the nearest tenth of a mile.

Math in History

In September of 1999, the Mars *Climate Orbiter,* a U.S. space-craft meant to be the first Martian weather satellite, crashed into the surface of the red planet. What caused the orbiter to crash? Unfortunately, the company that built the satellite sent navigation information to NASA's Jet Propulsion Laboratory (JPL) in customary units. The JPL engineers thought that they were receiving metric units. The failure to convert the units sent the satellite 100 kilometers lower into the Martian atmosphere than planned. Heat from friction and other stresses destroyed the $125 million craft.

Learning the Ropes

Sometimes when you work with measurements, you must convert between units. To do this, you must set up an expression that uses a **conversion fraction.** A conversion fraction is a ratio that expresses the relationship between two units. A conversion fraction is equal to 1 because its numerator is equal to its denominator.

EXAMPLES
$$\frac{1 \text{ foot}}{12 \text{ inches}} = 1 \qquad \frac{36 \text{ inches}}{1 \text{ yard}} = 1 \qquad \frac{1 \text{ kilometer}}{1000 \text{ meters}} = 1$$

To convert a measurement from one unit to another, multiply the measurement by the conversion fraction that has the units you need in the numerator and the units you have in the denominator. Then the units you have cancel each other out and the answer is in the units you need.

EXAMPLE The Tour de Spain is a 2925-kilometer bicycle race. How many meters long is the race?

$$2925 \text{ kilometers} \times \frac{1000 \text{ meters}}{1 \text{ kilometer}} \begin{array}{l} \leftarrow \text{ units you need} \\ \leftarrow \text{ units you have} \end{array}$$

$$2925 \text{ \sout{kilometers}} \times \frac{1000 \text{ meters}}{1 \text{ \sout{kilometer}}} = 2,925,000 \text{ meters}$$

Converting in the metric system is easy because you must multiply or divide by a power of 10. To multiply by a power of 10, move the decimal point to the *right* as many places as there are zeros in the power of 10. To divide by a power of 10, move the decimal point over to the *left* as many places as there are zeros in the power of 10.

Math in Use: Sports In the United States, we use the customary measurement system (inches, feet, yards, miles, etc.) for most purposes. However, many sports, such as swimming and track, commonly make use of the metric system (centimeters, meters, kilometers, etc.). When a young American is told that he is going to be running a 400-meter race, he might need to convert this measurement into yards to understand how far that is. To do the calculation, simply set up an equation using a conversion fraction:

400 meters $\times \frac{1 \text{ yard}}{0.9144 \text{ meters}} = 400 \div 0.9144 \approx 437$ yards.

Be careful when you convert between square units or between cubic units. The conversion fraction for square feet to square yards is not the same as the conversion fraction for feet to yards. Though 1 yard is equal to 3 feet, 1 square yard is actually equal to 9 square feet.

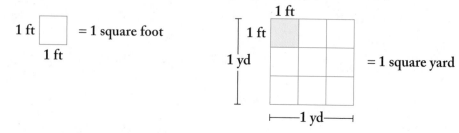

Meeting the Challenge

To answer the Challenge, you must convert the difference in height into miles.

STEP 1: Find the difference in height between the two mountains.

20,320 feet − 14,411 feet = 5,909 feet

STEP 2: Use the appropriate conversion fraction to convert the difference into miles.

$$5,909 \text{ feet} \times \frac{1 \text{ mile}}{5,280 \text{ feet}} = \frac{5,909 \text{ miles}}{5,280} \approx 1.119 \text{ miles}$$

The answer to the Challenge is that the difference between the heights of Mount McKinley and Mount Rainier, to the nearest tenth of a mile, is about 1.1 miles.

The tables on the following pages give common conversion fractions for customary and metric units.

Another Way There are two ways of doing conversions when you are performing calculations. You can either perform the calculations first and then convert your answer, or you can convert the units you are working with first and then perform the calculations.

Calculate first:

8 gallons + 6 gallons = 14 gallons

14 gallons $\times \frac{4 \text{ quarts}}{1 \text{ gallon}} = 56$ quarts

Convert first:

144 inches − 36 inches =

12 feet − 3 feet = 9 feet

Conversion Fraction Tables

All fractions in these tables are equal to 1.

Length in Metric Units

millimeters ↔ meters	$\dfrac{1\text{ millimeter (mm)}}{0.001\text{ meter (m)}}$	$\dfrac{1\text{ meter (m)}}{1000\text{ millimeters (mm)}}$
centimeters ↔ meters	$\dfrac{1\text{ centimeter (cm)}}{0.01\text{ meter (m)}}$	$\dfrac{1\text{ meter (m)}}{100\text{ centimeters (cm)}}$
meters ↔ kilometers	$\dfrac{1\text{ meter (m)}}{0.001\text{ kilometer (km)}}$	$\dfrac{1\text{ kilometer (km)}}{1000\text{ meters (m)}}$

Length in Customary (English) Units

inches ↔ feet	$\dfrac{1\text{ inch (in.)}}{0.083\text{ foot (ft)}}$	$\dfrac{1\text{ foot (ft)}}{12\text{ inches (in.)}}$
inches ↔ yards	$\dfrac{1\text{ inch (in.)}}{0.028\text{ yard (yd)}}$	$\dfrac{1\text{ yard (yd)}}{36\text{ inches (in.)}}$
feet ↔ yards	$\dfrac{1\text{ foot (ft)}}{0.33\text{ yard (yd)}}$	$\dfrac{1\text{ yard (yd)}}{3\text{ feet (ft)}}$
feet ↔ miles	$\dfrac{1\text{ foot (ft)}}{0.000189\text{ mile (mi)}}$	$\dfrac{1\text{ mile (mi)}}{5{,}280\text{ feet (ft)}}$
yards ↔ miles	$\dfrac{1\text{ yard (yd)}}{0.000568\text{ mile (mi)}}$	$\dfrac{1\text{ mile (mi)}}{1{,}760\text{ yards (yd)}}$

Length: Metric ↔ Customary (English)
(conversions given are approximate)

centimeters ↔ inches	$\dfrac{1\text{ centimeter (cm)}}{0.3937\text{ inch (in.)}}$	$\dfrac{1\text{ inch (in.)}}{2.54\text{ centimeters (cm)}}$
centimeters ↔ feet	$\dfrac{1\text{ centimeter (cm)}}{0.0328\text{ foot (ft)}}$	$\dfrac{1\text{ foot (ft)}}{30.48\text{ centimeters (cm)}}$
meters ↔ feet	$\dfrac{1\text{ meter (m)}}{3.28\text{ feet (ft)}}$	$\dfrac{1\text{ foot (ft)}}{0.3048\text{ meter (m)}}$
kilometers ↔ miles	$\dfrac{1\text{ kilometer (km)}}{0.6214\text{ mile (mi)}}$	$\dfrac{1\text{ mile (mi)}}{1.6093\text{ kilometers (km)}}$

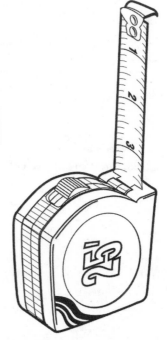

Capacity in Metric Units

milliliters ↔ liters	$\dfrac{1 \text{ milliliter (mL)}}{0.001 \text{ liter (L)}}$	$\dfrac{1 \text{ liter (L)}}{1000 \text{ milliliters (mL)}}$
liters ↔ kiloliters	$\dfrac{1 \text{ liter (L)}}{0.001 \text{ kiloliter (kL)}}$	$\dfrac{1 \text{ kiloliter (kL)}}{1000 \text{ liters (L)}}$

Capacity in Customary (English) Units

teaspoons ↔ tablespoons	$\dfrac{1 \text{ teaspoon (tsp)}}{0.33 \text{ tablespoon (tbsp)}}$	$\dfrac{1 \text{ tablespoon (tbsp)}}{3 \text{ teaspoons (tsp)}}$
tablespoons ↔ fluid ounces	$\dfrac{1 \text{ tablespoon (tbsp)}}{0.5 \text{ fluid ounce (fl oz)}}$	$\dfrac{1 \text{ fluid ounce (fl oz)}}{2 \text{ tablespoons (tbsp)}}$
fluid ounces ↔ cups	$\dfrac{1 \text{ fluid ounce (fl oz)}}{0.125 \text{ cup (c)}}$	$\dfrac{1 \text{ cup (c)}}{8 \text{ fluid ounces (fl oz)}}$
cups ↔ pints	$\dfrac{1 \text{ cup (c)}}{0.5 \text{ pint (pt)}}$	$\dfrac{1 \text{ pint (pt)}}{2 \text{ cups (c)}}$
cups ↔ quarts	$\dfrac{1 \text{ cup (c)}}{0.25 \text{ quart (qt)}}$	$\dfrac{1 \text{ quart (qt)}}{4 \text{ cups (c)}}$
pints ↔ quarts	$\dfrac{1 \text{ pint (pt)}}{0.5 \text{ quart (qt)}}$	$\dfrac{1 \text{ quart (qt)}}{2 \text{ pints (pt)}}$
quarts ↔ gallons	$\dfrac{1 \text{ quart (qt)}}{0.25 \text{ gallon (gal)}}$	$\dfrac{1 \text{ gallon (gal)}}{4 \text{ quarts (qt)}}$

Capacity: Metric ↔ Customary (English)
(conversions given are approximate)

liters ↔ quarts	$\dfrac{1 \text{ liter (L)}}{1.06 \text{ quarts (qt)}}$	$\dfrac{1 \text{ quart (qt)}}{0.94 \text{ liter (L)}}$
liters ↔ gallons	$\dfrac{1 \text{ liter (L)}}{0.26 \text{ gallon (gal)}}$	$\dfrac{1 \text{ gallon (gal)}}{3.79 \text{ liters (L)}}$

Mass and Weight in Metric Units

milligrams ↔ grams	$\dfrac{1 \text{ milligram (mg)}}{0.001 \text{ gram (g)}}$	$\dfrac{1 \text{ gram (g)}}{1000 \text{ milligrams (mg)}}$
grams ↔ kilograms	$\dfrac{1 \text{ gram (g)}}{0.001 \text{ kilogram (kg)}}$	$\dfrac{1 \text{ kilogram (kg)}}{1000 \text{ grams (g)}}$

Mass and Weight in Customary (English) Units

ounces ↔ pounds	$\dfrac{1 \text{ ounce (oz)}}{0.0625 \text{ pound (lb)}}$	$\dfrac{1 \text{ pound (lb)}}{16 \text{ ounces (oz)}}$
pounds ↔ tons	$\dfrac{1 \text{ pound (lb)}}{0.0005 \text{ ton (T)}}$	$\dfrac{1 \text{ ton (T)}}{2{,}000 \text{ pounds (lb)}}$

Mass and Weight: Metric ↔ Customary (English)
(conversions given are approximate)

grams ↔ ounces	$\dfrac{1 \text{ gram (g)}}{0.035 \text{ ounce (oz)}}$	$\dfrac{1 \text{ ounce (oz)}}{28.35 \text{ grams (g)}}$
kilograms ↔ pounds	$\dfrac{1 \text{ kilogram (kg)}}{2.2 \text{ pounds (lb)}}$	$\dfrac{1 \text{ pound (lb)}}{0.454 \text{ kilogram (kg)}}$

Name_____ Class _____ Date _____

Try It Yourself

A. Fill in the circle next to the correct answer to each multiple-choice question.

1. How many kilometers are in 556 centimeters?
   - Ⓐ 0.00556 km
   - Ⓑ 0.556 km
   - Ⓒ 5.56 km
   - Ⓓ 55,600 km

2. How many full days are in $8\frac{1}{2}$ years? Use 365 days = 1 year.
   - Ⓐ 310 days
   - Ⓑ 2,920 days
   - Ⓒ 3,102 days
   - Ⓓ 3,102.5 days

3. How many minutes are in 15 years? Use 365 days = 1 year.
   - Ⓐ 7,884,000 min
   - Ⓑ 131,400 min
   - Ⓒ 21,600 min
   - Ⓓ 8,700 min

B. Complete each grid. Write your answer at the top and fill in the numbered circles.

1. How many millimeters are in 346 centimeters?

3. How many quarts are in 24 gallons?

2. How many yards are in 327 feet?

4. How many seconds are in 8 hours?

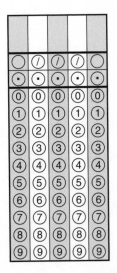

Try It Yourself

A. Fill in the circle next to the correct answer to each multiple-choice question.

1. How many inches are in 3.45 feet?
   - Ⓐ 41.4 in.
   - Ⓑ 20.7 in.
   - Ⓒ 15.45 in.
   - Ⓓ 0.29 in.

2. How many milliliters are in 2.6 liters?
   - Ⓐ 26,000 mL
   - Ⓑ 2600 mL
   - Ⓒ 260 mL
   - Ⓓ 0.0026 mL

3. How many miles are in 4,400 yards?
   - Ⓐ 0.25 mi
   - Ⓑ $0.8\overline{3}$ mi
   - Ⓒ 2.5 mi
   - Ⓓ 1,760 mi

4. How many inches are in 1 mile?
   - Ⓐ 5,280 in.
   - Ⓑ 10,560 in.
   - Ⓒ 63,360 in.
   - Ⓓ 760,320 in.

B. Complete the two parts below. Show all your work.

For a project on suspension bridges, Ray created a chart presenting the lengths of the longest suspension structures. Each length in the chart reflects the length of the bridge's main span.

Part A How many yards long is the main span of the Tsing Ma Bridge?

LONGEST SUSPENSION BRIDGES	
Bridge	**Length (feet)**
Akashi Kaikyo Bridge Kobe and Awaji-shima, Japan	6,532
Storebaelt Halsskov-Sprogoe, Denmark	5,328
Humber Yorkshire and Lincolnshire, England	4,626
Jiangyin Yangtze Jiangsu Province, China	4,544
Tsing Ma Hong Kong, China	4,518

Part B The historic Hal Adams Bridge over the Suwannee River in Florida is 420 feet long between its towers. How many miles *longer* is the Akashi Kaikyo Bridge's main span? Round your answer to the nearest tenth of a mile.

MEASURING LENGTH, PERIMETER, AND CIRCUMFERENCE

This lesson addresses Benchmarks B.1.3.1 and B.3.3.1 of the Sunshine State Standards.

The Challenge

Antoine is helping the landscape crew set up for an outdoor concert at his school. He first marks the perimeter of a grassy area with string to let workers know where to put up fences. Then he marks with string a circle where the stage will be. If one spool of string is 150 feet long, how many spools does Antoine need to mark the concert area and the stage?

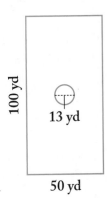

100 yd

13 yd

50 yd

Math in History

Using geometry, the ancient Greek mathematician Eratosthenes (275–194 B.C.) was able to figure out that the circumference of Earth is about 25,000 miles. Unfortunately, many later thinkers did not know of Eratosthenes' result. Some even thought that the world was flat! Once he knew the circumference, it was an easy matter for Eratosthenes to calculate Earth's diameter: $d = c \div \pi \approx 25{,}000$ miles $\div 3.14 \approx 8{,}000$ miles. Since the radius is half the diameter, the radius of Earth is about 4,000 miles.

Learning the Ropes

When measuring length, here are some important points to remember:

1. Choose the right instrument for the scale of the measurement.
   EXAMPLE Use a car odometer, not a ruler, to measure the distance between two cities.

2. You can measure up to the limit of the instrument.
   EXAMPLE If a tape measure is divided into tenths of inches, you can measure to the nearest foot, inch, or tenth of an inch. You cannot measure to the nearest hundredth of an inch.

3. Make multiple measurements to make sure your figures are all in the same ballpark and are reliable.

4. Keep in mind significant digits when calculating measurements.

The **perimeter** of a shape is the distance around the outside of the shape. The perimeter of any shape is calculated by adding the lengths of all the sides. **Circumference** is the perimeter of a circle. To calculate circumference, you must first find the diameter. The **diameter (d)** is the distance across the center of a circle. The **radius (r)** is half of the diameter.

circumference

radius (*r*)

diameter (*d*)

diameter = 2*r*

Carpenters have a saying that they learn as apprentices—"Measure twice, cut once." When they measure the length of a piece of wood twice, carpenters make sure that their measurement is correct, and they avoid wasting materials. This is a good tip to keep in mind for your own projects!

To find the circumference, multiply the diameter by the constant pi (π). A **constant** is a symbol that always stands for the same number. The constant pi represents the ratio between the circumference and the diameter of any circle.

$$\pi = \frac{\text{circumference}}{\text{diameter}} \qquad \text{circumference} = \pi \times \text{diameter} = \pi \times 2 \times \text{radius} = 2\pi r$$

Pi is an infinite, nonrepeating decimal. Usually we use an approximation of pi, 3.14 or $\frac{22}{7}$. Professor Yasumasa Kanada, of the University of Tokyo, has calculated pi to more than 1.24 trillion decimal places!

Meeting the Challenge

To answer the Challenge, you must find out how many feet of string Antoine will use to mark the perimeter of the concert area and the circumference of the stage.

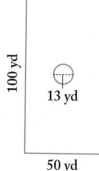

100 yd

13 yd

50 yd

STEP 1: Calculate the perimeter of the concert area.

perimeter = 2(length) + 2(width)

perimeter = 2(100 yards) + 2(50 yards)

perimeter = 300 yards

STEP 2: Calculate the circumference of the stage area. Use 3.14 as an approximation of π.

circumference = $\pi \times$ diameter

circumference $\approx 3.14 \times 13$ yards

circumference ≈ 40.82 yards ≈ 41 yards

STEP 3: Add the perimeter of the grassy area and the circumference of the circle.

combined perimeters = 300 yards + 41 yards

combined perimeters = 341 yards

STEP 4: Convert the combined perimeters from yards to feet.

$$341 \text{ yards} \times \frac{3 \text{ feet}}{1 \text{ yard}} = 1{,}023 \text{ feet}$$

STEP 5: Divide the combined perimeters, in feet, by the number of feet in one spool of string to find out how many full spools Antoine will use.

1,023 feet $\div$ 150 feet ≈ 6.8

The answer to the Challenge is that Antoine needs 7 spools of string to mark the perimeter of the concert area and the circumference of the stage.

Name_____ Class _____ Date _____

Try It Yourself

A. Complete each grid. Write your answer at the top and fill in the numbered circles.

1. An air vent is a rectangle with a perimeter of 36 inches. If the width of the vent is 8 inches, what is the length, in inches?

2. The perimeter of a square stable is 69.2 meters. What is the length of each side of the stable, in meters?

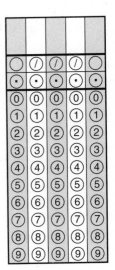

B. Complete the two parts below. Show all your work. Use additional paper if necessary.

Simon draws a diagram for a fence around a garden using the scale shown below.

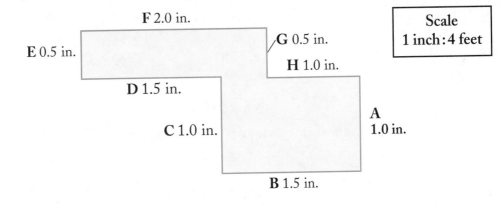

F 2.0 in.

E 0.5 in.

G 0.5 in.

H 1.0 in.

D 1.5 in.

C 1.0 in.

A 1.0 in.

B 1.5 in.

Scale
1 inch : 4 feet

Part A Calculate the actual length of each side in feet.

A _____ B _____ C _____ D _____

E _____ F _____ G _____ H _____

Part B Calculate the perimeter of the garden in feet.

Try It Yourself

A. Fill in the circle next to the correct answer to each multiple-choice question.

1. What is the perimeter of a metal plate in the shape of an equilateral triangle with each side measuring 23.54 centimeters?

    Ⓐ 69.162 cm   Ⓑ 69.62 cm   Ⓒ 70.162 cm   Ⓓ 70.62 cm

2. A hubcap has a regular pentagon design with each side measuring 12 inches. What is the perimeter?

    Ⓐ 36 in.   Ⓑ 48 in.   Ⓒ 60 in.   Ⓓ 72 in.

3. What is the circumference of a circular bottle with a radius of 6.25 centimeters? Use 3.14 as an approximation of π. Round to the nearest hundredth of a centimeter.

    Ⓐ 19.63 cm   Ⓑ 39.25 cm   Ⓒ 122.66 cm   Ⓓ 490.63 cm

B. Complete the three parts below. Show all your work.

Dominique has 40 feet of fencing. He is trying to decide how to set it up.

Part A What is the diameter of a circular fenced area with a circumference of 40 feet? Use 3.14 as an approximation of π. Round your answer to the nearest tenth of a foot.

Part B What is the length of one side of a square fenced area whose perimeter is 40 feet?

Part C On your own paper, draw three other rectangles that have a perimeter of 40 feet. Label the lengths of the sides.

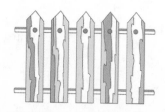

MEASURING AREA

This lesson addresses Benchmarks B.1.3.1 and B.3.3.1 of the Sunshine State Standards.

The Challenge

The members of the Theater Club are designing a castle set for their next play. They want to know the total area that needs to

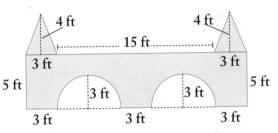

be painted so they can buy enough paint. The plan of the castle is above; the area to be painted is shaded. What is the area of the castle that needs to be painted? Round your answer to the nearest square foot. Use 3.14 as an approximation of π.

Learning the Ropes

Area is the measurement of the space within the perimeter of a shape. Area is always expressed in square units, as in $A = 3$ ft^2.

Here are formulas for calculating area for various polygons.

Name	Figure	Area	Key
triangle	h / b	$\frac{1}{2}bh$	$b = $ base $h = $ height (or **altitude**)
square	s, s, s, s	s^2	$s = $ length of side
rectangle	w, l, w, l	$l \times w$	$l = $ length $w = $ width
parallelogram	h / b	bh	$b = $ base $h = $ height
trapezoid	b / h / a	$\frac{1}{2}(a + b) \times h$	$b = $ base $h = $ height
circle	r	πr^2	$r = $ radius

Math in History

Archimedes was a Greek mathematician who lived in Syracuse (on the island of Sicily) from around 287 to 212 B.C. Archimedes wrote a treatise called *On the Measurement of the Circle.* In this work, he estimated the value of pi (π) by figuring the area of a polygon with 95 sides! Based on these calculations, Archimedes concluded that $3\frac{10}{71} < \pi < 3\frac{10}{70}$ This was an excellent estimate, much closer than the estimates of 3 and $3\frac{1}{4}$ used by the Hebrews and the Babylonians.

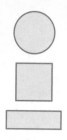

Meeting the Challenge

To answer the Challenge, you must calculate the area of each part of the castle.

STEP 1: Calculate the areas of the two corner triangles.

Area of 1 triangle = $\frac{1}{2}$ × base × height = $\frac{1}{2}$ × 3 ft × 4 ft = 6 ft^2

Area of 2 triangles = 6 ft^2 × 2 = 12 ft^2

STEP 2: Calculate the total area of the rectangular wall, including the spaces within the arches.

Length of rectangular wall = 3 ft + 15 ft + 3 ft = 21 ft

Area of rectangular wall = length × width = 21 ft × 5 ft = 105 ft^2

STEP 3: Calculate the area of the spaces within the arches. Since each arch is a half-circle, you can use the formula for finding the area of a circle. Express your answer to the nearest square foot.

Area of a circle = $\pi r^2 \approx 3.14 \times (3 \text{ ft})^2 \approx 3.14 \times 9 \text{ ft}^2 \approx 28.26 \text{ ft}^2 \approx 28 \text{ ft}^2$

STEP 4: Subtract the area of the space within the arches from the area of the rectangular wall, and add the area of the two corner triangles.

Area of castle = (Area of rectangular wall − Area of space in arches) + Area of 2 corner triangles

$\approx (105 \text{ ft}^2 - 28 \text{ ft}^2) + 12 \text{ ft}^2$

$\approx 77 \text{ ft}^2 + 12 \text{ ft}^2$

$\approx 89 \text{ ft}^2$

The answer to the Challenge is that the area of the castle the students must paint is about 89 ft^2.

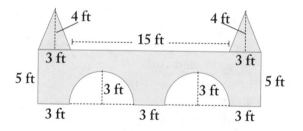

Name_____ Class _____ Date _____

Try It Yourself

A. Complete each grid. Write your answer at the top and fill in the numbered circles.

1. Calculate the area of the triangle below. Give your answer in square feet.

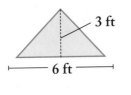

3 ft

6 ft

3. Calculate the side of a square whose area is 144 square inches. Give your answer in inches.

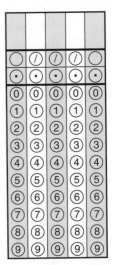

2. Shane ordered a triangular sail for his sailboat. The sail has 44 square feet of canvas. The height of the sail is 11 feet. What is the length of the bottom of the sail, in feet?

11 ft

4. Carrie has a rectangular piece of construction paper that is 9 inches by 12 inches. If she divides it in half diagonally, what is the area in square inches of each triangular piece?

B. Complete the activities below. Show all your work. Use your own paper.

1. Calculate the area of the trapezoid to the right.

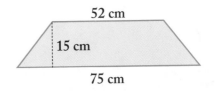

52 cm

15 cm

75 cm

2. Calculate the area of a circle with a diameter of 3 meters. Use 3.14 as an approximation of π.

Try It Yourself

A. Fill in the circle next to the correct answer to each multiple-choice question.

1. What is the diameter, in feet, of a circle that covers 50 square feet? Use 3.14 as an approximation of π, and round your answer to the nearest foot.

   Ⓐ 2 ft   Ⓑ 4 ft   Ⓒ 8 ft   Ⓓ 16 ft

2. What is the area of this parallelogram?

   Ⓐ 416 square units

   Ⓑ 208 square units

   Ⓒ 84 square units

   Ⓓ 42 square units

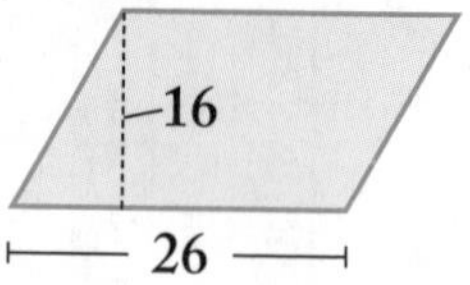

3. What is the difference in area between a triangle that has a height of 15 feet and a base of 20 feet and a rectangle that has a length of 15 feet and a width of 20 feet?

   Ⓐ 0 ft^2 Ⓑ 75 ft^2 Ⓒ 150 ft^2 Ⓓ 225 ft^2

4. What is the area of this shape?

   Ⓐ 30 square units

   Ⓑ 36 square units

   Ⓒ 42 square units

   Ⓓ 48 square units

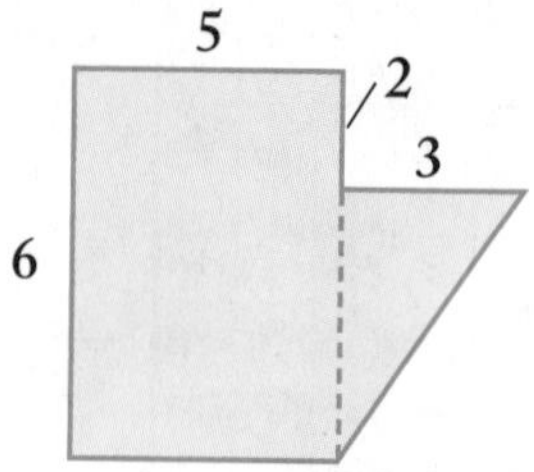

B. Complete the two parts below. Show all your work.

Yoon-jung needs to buy ceiling tiles for her office. Each tile is 1.5 feet by 1.5 feet. The office is 18 feet long and 9 feet wide.

Part A Calculate the area of her office.

Part B How many tiles does Yoon-jung need? Explain how you got your answer.

MEASURING VOLUME AND CAPACITY

This lesson addresses Benchmarks B.1.3.1 and B.3.3.1 of the Sunshine State Standards.

The Challenge

The shallow end of a pool is 4 feet deep. The deep end is 11 feet deep. The pool is 15 feet long and 10 feet wide. The depth of the pool begins to increase 7 feet from the shallow end of the pool. What is the volume of the pool in cubic feet?

Learning the Ropes

A **polyhedron** is a solid figure with flat sides called **faces.** A **prism** is a polyhedron with two congruent and parallel faces. A **pyramid** is a polyhedron whose base is a flat surface and whose other faces are triangles that meet at one point.

Other solid figures have curved surfaces. A **cylinder** is a figure with two circular congruent bases that are parallel. A **cone** is a figure that has a circular base and a curved surface that comes to a point. A **sphere** is a round, solid figure, like a ball.

To calculate the **volume** of these solid figures—that is, the amount of space they take up—use the formulas in the chart below. Notice that calculating volume always involves multiplying three dimensions. Therefore, volume is measured in cubic units, like cubic feet (ft^3).

Math in History
Archimedes, the Greek mathematician whom we have met before in this book, was the discoverer of an important principle about volume. According to legend, one day while taking a bath, he realized that a body placed in water displaces, or moves, an amount of water equal in volume to that of the body itself. Legend has it that Archimedes was so excited by his discovery that he jumped up and ran through the streets shouting "Eureka," Greek for "I've found it." Today, we use this principle for measuring volume by noting how much the water in a cylinder rises when an object is placed into the cylinder.

Name	Figure	Volume	Name	Figure	Volume
rectangular prism		$l \times w \times h$	rectangular pyramid		$\frac{1}{3}(lw)h$
triangular prism		Bh B = area of base of prism h = height of prism	cone		$\frac{1}{3}(\pi r^2)h$
cylinder		$\pi r^2 \times h$	sphere		$\frac{4}{3}\pi r^3$

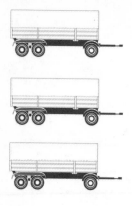

A measure that is related to volume is capacity. The **capacity** of a container is the amount that it can hold. Some customary units of capacity are teaspoon, fluid ounce, cup, quart, and gallon. One cup is equal to 8 fluid ounces, about the amount in a medium-sized glass of milk. There are 4 cups in a quart and 4 quarts in a gallon. In the metric system, we use milliliters, liters, and kiloliters to measure capacity. Milliliters are tiny units used for measuring liquid medicine, for example. A milliliter contains a few drops of liquid. A liter is slightly bigger than a quart. To find the equivalents for all these measures of capacity, see the conversion tables in Lesson 4.3, "Converting Customary and Metric Units."

Meeting the Challenge

To answer the Challenge, you must mentally separate the drawing into two different shapes and then calculate the volume of each shape.

STEP 1: Look at the pool as two parts— a rectangular prism and a triangular prism.

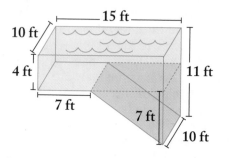

STEP 2: Calculate the volume of the rectangular prism.

Volume of a rectangular prism = length × width × height

$$= 15 \text{ ft} \times 10 \text{ ft} \times 4 \text{ ft}$$
$$= 600 \text{ ft}^3$$

STEP 3: Calculate the volume of the triangular prism (deeper part).

Volume of a triangular prism = area of base of prism × distance between the bases

$$= (\tfrac{1}{2} \times 8 \text{ ft} \times 7 \text{ ft}) \times 10 \text{ ft} = 280 \text{ ft}^3$$

STEP 4: Add the volumes of the two parts of the pool together to determine the total volume of the pool.

Total volume of pool = volume of rectangular prism + volume of triangular prism

$$= 600 \text{ ft}^3 + 280 \text{ ft}^3$$
$$= 880 \text{ ft}^3$$

The answer to the Challenge is that the volume of the pool is 880 cubic feet.

Name_____ Class _____ Date _____

Try It Yourself

A. Complete each grid. Write your answer at the top and fill in the numbered circles.

1. Calculate the volume of the rectangular pyramid below. Give your answer in cubic centimeters.

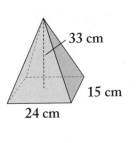

33 cm

15 cm

24 cm

2. Calculate the width of a box that has a volume of 1,120 cubic inches, a height of 7 inches, and a length of 16 inches. Give your answer in inches.

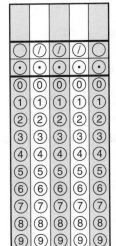

B. Complete each activity below. Show all your work.

1. What is the volume of an inflated exercise ball with a radius of 2 feet? Use 3.14 as an approximation of π. Round your answer to the nearest cubic foot.

2 ft

2. Calculate the volume, in cubic inches, of a can that is 4.5 inches high and has a diameter of 4 inches. Use 3.14 as an approximation of π.

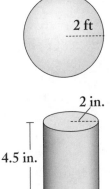

2 in.

4.5 in.

C. Complete the two parts below. Show all your work.

A dentist's office has both paper cups and paper cones for water. The cylindrical paper cups are 2.5 inches tall and have a 2-inch-wide opening. The paper cones are 4 inches tall and have a 3-inch-wide opening. Which shape holds more water?

Part A Calculate the volume of each cup.

Part B Calculate the volume of each cone.

Try It Yourself

A. Fill in the circle next to the correct answer to each multiple-choice question.

1. If the volume of a cube is 125 cubic inches, what is the length of each side?
   Ⓐ 4 in.   Ⓑ 5 in.   Ⓒ 25 in.   Ⓓ 31.25 in.

2. The outside dimensions of a metal box are 30 centimeters by 15 centimeters by
   20 centimeters. The inside dimensions of the box are 28 centimeters by 13 centimeters
   by 18 centimeters. What is the volume of the metal used to make the box?
   Ⓐ 1224 cm³   Ⓑ 2448 cm³   Ⓒ 6552 cm³   Ⓓ 9000 cm³

3. If you double the radius and the height of a cone, by what factor do you increase the
   volume?
   Ⓐ by 2   Ⓑ by 4   Ⓒ by 6   Ⓓ by 8

4. What is the volume of a storage unit that is 10 feet long, 8 feet wide, and 8 feet high?
   Ⓐ 64 ft³   Ⓑ 80 ft³   Ⓒ 160 ft³   Ⓓ 640 ft³

5. Raul is putting boxes in a storage unit shaped and sized like the one in question 4.
   The boxes are approximately 2 feet by 1 foot by 1 foot. Which of the following is the
   best estimate of the maximum number of boxes that will fit in the storage unit?
   Ⓐ 150   Ⓑ 300   Ⓒ 450   Ⓓ 600

B. Complete the three parts below. Show all your work.

You are trying to figure out how big a cylinder must be in order to hold a sphere.

Part A Calculate the dimensions of the smallest cylinder that can
hold a sphere whose diameter is 4 inches.

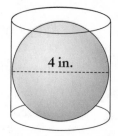

Part B What is the volume of such a cylinder? Use π in your answer.

Part C What is the volume of the smallest cylinder that can hold a sphere whose diameter
is x? Express the relationship as an algebraic equation. On your own paper, explain how
you found your answer.

MEASURING SURFACE AREA

This lesson addresses Benchmarks B.1.3.1 and B.3.3.1 of the Sunshine State Standards.

Math in History

Ancient scholars believed that everything in the world was made of four elements, put together in different quantities. These four elements were earth, water, fire, and air. The Pythagoreans of ancient Greece associated these elements with four regular polyhedra:

tetrahedron
= fire

cube = earth

octahedron
= air

icosahedron
= water

The Challenge

Suppose you were making a cylindrical canister and a box for tennis balls. How many square inches of plastic would you need to make a canister just big enough to hold three tennis balls, each 2.5 inches in diameter? How much plastic would you need to make a box just wide and tall enough to hold three tennis balls? Which shape container is a more efficient use of plastic? What is the surface area of one tennis ball? Round your answers to the nearest tenth of a square inch.

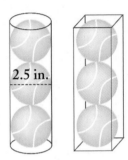

2.5 in.

Learning the Ropes

Surface area is the area of the outside of a three-dimensional figure. To calculate the surface area of a polyhedron, add the areas of all its faces.

Surface Area of Rectangular Solids. To find the surface area of a rectangular prism, which is one type of solid, add the areas of the top, bottom, left side, right side, front, and back.

Calculate the area of the top or bottom face by multiplying the length by the width.

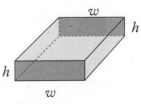

Calculate the area of the left or right face by multiplying the length by the height.

Then calculate the area of the front or back face by multiplying the width by the height.

To simplify the calculation, you can multiply the area of one face from each pair of congruent, parallel faces by 2:

Surface area of rectangular solid = $2(lw) + 2(lh) + 2(wh)$

Surface Area of Cylinders. To find the surface area of a cylinder, you must add the areas of the two circular bases to the area of the curved surface. The area of the two circular bases is equal to $2(\pi r^2)$. Think of the area of the curved surface as if it were the label on a can; it is equal to $2\pi rh$, the circumference of the circular base multiplied by height of the cylinder.

r = radius of circular base
h = height of cylinder

$$\text{Surface area of cylinder} = 2\pi r^2 + 2\pi rh$$

Surface Area of Spheres. There is a special formula for the surface area of a sphere, since it has no flat surfaces.

$$\text{Surface area of sphere} = 4\pi r^2$$

r = radius of sphere

Meeting the Challenge

To answer the Challenge, you must calculate the surface areas of the cylinder, the rectangular prism, and the sphere.

STEP 1: The smallest cylinder that could hold three tennis balls would have to be 2.5 inches in diameter and tall enough for three balls to be stacked on top of each other: 3×2.5 inches = 7.5 inches. The radius of the circular base would be half of the diameter of the ball: 2.5 inches ÷ 2 = 1.25 inches. Substitute the dimensions into the formula for the surface area of a cylinder.

$$\text{Surface area of cylinder} = 2\pi r^2 + 2\pi rh$$
$$= 2 \times \pi \times (1.25 \times 1.25) + 2 \times \pi \times 1.25 \times 7.5$$
$$\approx 9.8 + 58.9 \approx 68.7 \text{ square inches}$$

STEP 2: Find the dimensions of the smallest box that could hold three tennis balls. The box would have to be 2.5 inches long, 2.5 inches wide, and 7.5 inches high. Substitute the dimensions into the formula to find the surface area of a rectangular solid, or prism.

$$\text{Surface area of rectangular solid} = 2lw + 2lh + 2wh$$
$$= (2 \times 2.5 \times 2.5) + (2 \times 2.5 \times 7.5) + (2 \times 2.5 \times 7.5)$$
$$= 12.5 + 37.5 + 37.5 = 87.5 \text{ square inches}$$

STEP 3: To find the surface area of one tennis ball, substitute the radius of the ball ($r = 1.25$ in.) into the formula to calculate the surface area of a sphere.

$$\text{Surface area of a sphere} = 4\pi r^2$$
$$= 4(3.14)(1.25 \times 1.25)$$
$$= 19.625 \approx 19.6 \text{ square inches}$$

Try It Yourself

A. Complete each grid. Write your answer at the top and fill in the numbered circles.

1. What is the surface area of a number cube whose sides are each 2 centimeters long? Give your answer in cubic centimeters.

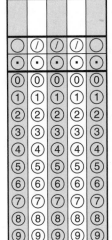

2. Marta is painting the outside of a wooden toy box 4 feet long, 2 feet wide, and 2 feet tall. What is the area of the surface she must paint, in square feet, including the bottom of the box?

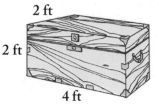

2 ft

2 ft

4 ft

B. Complete each activity below. Show all your work. Use your own paper.

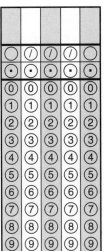

24 in.

36 in.

1. A trash can is 36 inches tall and has a diameter of 24 inches. How much metal, in square inches, is needed to make the trash can without the lid? Use 3.14 as an approximation of π.

2. What is the surface area of a sphere with a diameter of 24 inches? Use 3.14 as an approximation of π.

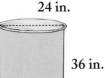

24 in.

C. Complete the three parts below. Show all your work. Use your own paper.

A square can with a width of 2.2 inches and a height of 5 inches has nearly the same volume as a round can with a diameter of 2.5 inches and a height of 5 inches or a spherical container with a diameter of 3.6 inches.

Part A To the nearest square inch, how much metal is needed to make the square can?

Part B To the nearest square inch, how much metal is needed to make the round can?

Part C To the nearest square inch, how much metal is needed to make the sphere?

Try It Yourself

A. Fill in the circle next to the correct answer to each multiple-choice question.

1. What is the length of a cube whose surface area is 216 square inches?

   Ⓐ 3 in.   © 8 in.

   Ⓑ 6 in.   Ⓓ 36 in.

2. Ms. Min paints a wooden dowel (cylindrical stick) that has a height of 10 inches and a diameter of 3 inches. Approximately how many square inches does she paint?

   Ⓐ 61 in.²   © 108 in.²

   Ⓑ 101 in.²   Ⓓ 245 in.²

3. A rectangular fish tank has 4 glass sides, a glass top, and a glass bottom. It is 2 feet long, 1 foot wide, and 1.5 feet high. How many square inches of glass are in the whole fish tank?

   Ⓐ 13 in.²   ©   936 in.²

   Ⓑ 156 in.²   Ⓓ 1,872 in.²

4. What is the surface area of a jewelry box that is 17 centimeters long, 10 centimeters wide, and 12 centimeters high?

   Ⓐ 74 cm²   © 548 cm²

   Ⓑ 307 cm²   Ⓓ 988 cm²

B. Complete the two parts below. Show all your work. Use additional paper.

Julio buys a basketball for Ming's birthday. He places the basketball inside a square box. The radius of the basketball is 12 centimeters.

Part A What is the surface area of the smallest box that can hold the basketball?

Part B What is the surface area of the basketball? Use 3.14 as an approximation for π.

© GREAT SOURCE. COPYING IS PROHIBITED.

EFFECTS OF CHANGING DIMENSIONS

This lesson addresses Benchmarks B.1.3.1, B.1.3.3, and B.3.3.1 of the Sunshine State Standards.

The Challenge

A candle maker creates a rectangular mold to use to make candles. The mold is 2 inches wide, 2 inches long, and 4 inches tall. To make larger candles, he creates a mold whose dimensions are 3 times the dimensions of the original. How many times greater is the area of the top of the larger mold? How many times greater is the volume of the larger mold?

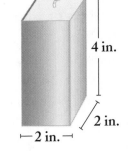

Math in History
The ancient Greeks often did mathematical calculations by drawing in the sand. When we say that a number is squared, as in 4^2, we are recognizing the fact that 4×4 can be represented as a square of 16 dots in the sand. Note that by drawing lines in the sand, we can illustrate the fact that every squared integer is a sum of consecutive odd numbers: Try this yourself for square numbers larger than 4^2, such as 5^2, 6^2, and 7^2.

Learning the Ropes

In the 1950s and 1960s, Hollywood studios created a string of horror movies about giant creatures. The usual story line went something like this: An atomic bomb test takes place in the desert. Radiation from the blast causes a scorpion (or some other creature) to grow to enormous size. The creature then heads off and attacks Los Angeles (or some other city). Of course, nuclear radiation doesn't have these effects, but the old Hollywood creature features do raise an interesting question: What happens to the area and volume of something when its overall size, or **scale**, increases or decreases?

Effects of Changes in One Dimension. First, let's look at what happens when you change one dimension of a figure. You know that the area of a rectangle (A) is equal to the length (l) times the width (w). If you double the length, the area also doubles:

Area of original rectangle = $l \times w$

Area of new rectangle = $2l \times w$

What happens to the circumference of a circle if you double the diameter? Think of the formula for circumference:

Circumference of original circle = πd

Circumference of new circle = $2\pi d$

Effects of Changes in Scale on Area. When you **scale** a figure, you enlarge it or shrink it by multiplying or dividing *each* of its dimensions by the same amount. All the dimensions of the new figure are proportional to those of the old figure. What happens to the area of a figure when you scale it? Let's consider an example.

Suppose that you have a rectangle that is 2 inches by 3 inches:

3 in.

2 in.

The area of this rectangle is the length times the width. That's 2 in. × 3 in., or 6 in.².

Now let's see what happens when both dimensions of the rectangle are doubled:

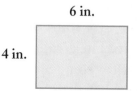

6 in.

4 in.

Notice that each side is twice as long as it was before. The area of the new rectangle is 4 in. × 6 in., or 24 in.². Notice that the area of the larger rectangle is 4 times the area of the smaller rectangle. In other words, when an object doubles in each dimension, its area becomes 4 times as large.

Area of original rectangle = $l \times w$

Area of rectangle that is doubled in each dimension = $2l \times 2w$, or $2^2 \times lw$, or $4lw$

In general, whenever the dimensions of an object increase or decrease by some factor, its area increases or decreases as the square of the factor. Suppose that you have a rectangle with area A. If you triple the dimensions of the rectangle, the new area is $3^2 \times A$, or $9A$. If you halve the size of the rectangle, the new area is $(\frac{1}{2})^2 \times A$, or $\frac{1}{4}A$.

Effects of Changes in Scale on Volume. To find out how the volume of an object changes as its dimensions increase or decrease, you can follow a similar procedure.

Suppose that you have a cube that is 3 inches on each side:

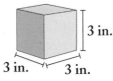

3 in.

3 in.   3 in.

The formula for the volume of a cube (V) is length (l) times width (w) times height (h). In this case, it is 3 in. × 3 in. × 3 in., or 27 in.^{3}.

Now let's see what happens when each side of the cube is doubled:

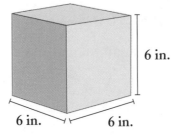

6 in.

6 in.   6 in.

Notice that each side is twice as long as it was before. The volume of the new cube is 6 in. × 6 in. × 6 in., or 216 in.^{3}. The volume of the larger cube is 8 times the volume of the smaller cube. In other words, when the dimensions of an object double, its volume is increased by a factor of 8.

Volume of original cube = $l \times w \times h$

Volume of cube whose dimensions are doubled = $2l \times 2w \times 2h$, or $2^3 \times lwh$, or $8lwh$

In general, whenever the dimensions of an object increase or decrease by a factor, its volume increases or decreases as the cube of the factor. Suppose that you have a cube with volume V. If you triple the dimensions of the cube, the new volume is $3^3 \times V$, or $27V$. If you halve the dimensions, the new volume is $(\frac{1}{2})^3 \times V$, or $\frac{1}{8}V$.

Another Way As you have seen in this lesson, to calculate the increase or decrease in area or volume, simply start with the original area or volume and multiply it by the amount of the increase or decrease squared (in the case of area) or cubed (in the case of volume). Another way is simply to begin with the original formula for area and to multiply each part of the formula by the amount of the increase or decrease. For example, suppose that you want to halve the dimensions of a rectangle. What is the resulting area? The area of the original rectangle is $l \times w$. The area of the new rectangle is $\frac{1}{2}l \times \frac{1}{2}w = \frac{1}{4}lw$.

Meeting the Challenge

To answer the Challenge, you must compare the top areas and the volumes of the two candle molds.

Step 1: Calculate the areas of the tops of the smaller and larger molds.

Area = length × width

Smaller mold:

length = 2 inches

width = 2 inches

Area = 2 inches × 2 inches = 4 square inches

Larger mold:

length = 2 inches × 3 = 6 inches

width = 2 inches × 3 = 6 inches

Area = 6 inches × 6 inches = 36 square inches

Step 2: Calculate the volumes of the smaller and larger molds.

Volume = length × width × height

Smaller mold:

length = 2 inches

width = 2 inches

height = 4 inches

Volume = 2 inches × 2 inches × 4 inches = 16 cubic inches

Larger mold:

length = 2 inches × 3 = 6 inches

width = 2 inches × 3 = 6 inches

height = 4 inches × 3 = 12 inches

Volume = 6 inches × 6 inches × 12 inches = 432 cubic inches

Step 3: Compare the areas. The area of the top of the small mold is 4 square inches, and the area of the top of the large mold is 36 square inches. The ratio is equal to 4 : 36, or 1 : 9. The area of the large mold is 9 times as large as that of the small mold. Since the large mold's dimensions are 3 times greater than those of the small mold, the formula to find the area is (3 × length) × (3 × width), or 9 × length × width.

Step 4: Compare the volumes. The volume of the small mold is 16 cubic inches, and the volume of the large mold is 432 cubic inches. The ratio is equal to 16 : 432, or 1 : 27. The volume of the large mold is 27 times as large as that of the small mold. The formula to find the volume of the larger mold is (3 × length) × (3 × width) × (3 × height), or 27 × length × width × height.

The answer to the Challenge is that the top of the large mold is 9 times larger than the top of the small mold, and the large mold's volume is 27 times larger than the small mold's volume.

Try It Yourself

A. Fill in the circle next to the correct answer to each multiple-choice question.

1. If the length and width of a rectangular screen are reduced by half, what happens to the area?

   Ⓐ The area is reduced to $\frac{1}{8}$ the original size.

   Ⓑ The area is reduced to $\frac{1}{4}$ the original size.

   Ⓒ The area is cut in half.

   Ⓓ The area is increased to 4 times the original size.

2. Joel's insects are preserved in rectangular glass prisms. If the dimensions of one are each increased to 5 times their original size, what happens to the volume?

   Ⓐ It increases by a factor of 5.   Ⓒ It increases by a factor of 25.

   Ⓑ It increases by a factor of 15.   Ⓓ It increases by a factor of 125.

3. Which of the following changes will produce the largest area for a tile floor?

   Ⓐ doubling both dimensions of a 3-ft × 6-ft rectangle

   Ⓑ halving both dimensions of a 12-ft × 24-ft rectangle

   Ⓒ tripling both dimensions of a 2-ft × 4-ft rectangle

   Ⓓ doubling either dimension of a 6-ft × 7-ft rectangle

B. Complete the three parts below. Show all your work. Use additional paper.

Civil engineers are designing a wishing pool for the town square. They design a circular pool that has a diameter of 8 feet. The mayor tells the civil engineers to double the diameter of the pool.

Part A How many times greater will the circumference of the new pool be?

Part B How many times greater will the area of the new pool be?

Part C If the depth is also doubled, how many times greater will the volume of the new pool be?

A. Fill in the circle next to the correct answer to each multiple-choice question.

1. A cubic yard of bark mulch measures 3 feet long, 3 feet wide, and 3 feet high. If it is spread at a depth of $\frac{1}{2}$ foot, how many square feet would a cubic yard of mulch cover at a depth of $\frac{1}{2}$ foot?

   Ⓐ 54 ft²   Ⓑ 36 ft²   Ⓒ 27 ft²   Ⓓ 18 ft²

2. Construction workers expand a room by adding on to the house. The original room is 12 feet long and 10 feet wide. They extend the length of the room by 6 feet. Which of the following statements is *true*?

   Ⓐ The area of the expanded room is 120 ft².

   Ⓑ The area of the expanded room is 6 ft² greater than the area of the original room.

   Ⓒ The area of the original room is half the area of the expanded room.

   Ⓓ The area of the original room is $\frac{2}{3}$ the area of the expanded room.

3. Ginny packs her old clothes into boxes. She has a box that is 17 inches × 11 inches × 8 inches. She finds a second box whose volume is 8 times larger than the first box. What could the dimensions of the second box be?

   Ⓐ 17 in. × 11 in. × 16 in.   Ⓒ 136 in. × 88 in. × 64 in.

   Ⓑ 8.5 in. × 22 in. × 16 in.   Ⓓ 34 in. × 22 in. × 16 in.

B. Complete the two parts below. Show all your work.

One cylindrical container measures 3 inches high with a radius of 2 inches. Another cylindrical container has a height of 6 inches and a radius of 4 inches.

Part A Using the measures given, write an expression for the circumference of the small container. Write another expression for the circumference of the large container. (You may use π in your expressions.) Then write a ratio comparing the circumferences of the small and large containers:

$$\frac{\text{circumference of small container}}{\text{circumference of large container}} = \underline{\hspace{3cm}} = \underline{\hspace{2cm}}$$

Part B Do the same with the volume. How many times greater is the volume of the second container?

$$\frac{\text{volume of small container}}{\text{volume of large container}} = \underline{\hspace{3cm}} = \underline{\hspace{2cm}}$$

MEASURING WEIGHT, MASS, AND DENSITY

This lesson addresses Benchmarks B.1.3.1 and B.3.3.1 of the Sunshine State Standards.

The Challenge

Erica learned in science class that a person who weighs 100 pounds on Earth would weigh only about 5 pounds on Pluto. Later that evening, she watched a science fiction movie about a mission to that small, icy, distant planet. The astronauts in the movie were studying the rocks on Pluto. One of the rocks, whose volume was 0.5 cubic meter, weighed 100 pounds on Pluto. How much would it weigh on Earth? What is its mass in kilograms? What is its density in kilograms per cubic meter?

Learning the Ropes

When you step on a bathroom scale, you find out how much you weigh. **Weight** measures the force with which gravity is pulling you down. Your weight is different on other planets because the gravity is different. In the United States, weight is usually measured in customary units such as ounces and pounds.

Mass is the amount of matter in an object. Mass is not related to gravity, so your mass is the same—no matter what planet you are on. Mass is almost always measured in metric units such as grams and kilograms.

Math in History
Objects have weight because of gravity. Most people have heard the legend that Isaac Newton "discovered" the theory of gravity when he saw an apple fall from a tree. The truth is that Newton reasoned something like this: Picture a ball thrown from a high tower. It has two forces working on it, the force with which it was thrown outward and the force of gravity. The combination of these forces causes the ball to fall in a curve. If the ball is thrown hard enough, however, gravity and the force of the throw will balance one another and the ball will "fall" in a continuous curve called an *orbit*.

CUSTOMARY WEIGHT		
Weight Unit	**Abbreviation**	**Conversion**
ounce	oz	1 ounce = 0.0625 pound
pound	lb	1 pound = 16 ounces
ton	T	1 ton = 2,000 pounds

METRIC MASS		
Metric Mass Unit	**Abbreviation**	**Conversion**
milligram	mg	1 milligram = 0.001 gram
gram	g	1 gram = 1000 milligrams
kilogram	kg	1 kilogram = 1000 grams
metric ton	T	1 metric ton = 1000 kilograms

Weight and mass are measured with spring scales or balance scales. In some countries that use the metric system, recipes use measurements of mass ("10 grams of sugar"), while in the United States, recipes use measurements of volume ("3 cups of flour") or weight ("5 pounds of ground beef").

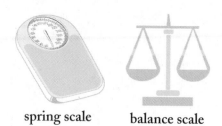

spring scale   balance scale

Density is mass per unit volume. An object's density is the amount of matter it has in a given space. To find density, you need to measure mass and volume.

Density is found using the formula $D = \frac{m}{V}$, where m is mass and V is volume. For example, if the mass of an object is 35 g and its volume is 10 cm³, its density is $\frac{m}{V} = \frac{35 \text{ g}}{10 \text{ cm}^3} = 3.5$ g/cm³.

Meeting the Challenge

To answer the Challenge questions, you must calculate the rock's weight on Earth, its mass in kilograms, and its density in kilograms per cubic meter.

STEP 1: Since an object that weighs 100 pounds on Earth weighs 5 pounds on Pluto, you can use this relationship to make a conversion fraction equal to 1, with the units you need in the numerator and the ones you have in the denominator.

$$100 \text{ lb on Pluto} \times \frac{100 \text{ lb on Earth}}{5 \text{ lb on Pluto}} = 2{,}000 \text{ lb on Earth}$$

STEP 2: Since you now know the rock's weight in pounds on Earth, you can calculate its mass by converting pounds to kilograms.

$$2{,}000 \text{ lb} \times \frac{1 \text{ kg}}{2.2 \text{ lb}} \approx 900 \text{ kg}$$

STEP 3: The mass of the rock is the same on Pluto as on Earth. Since density is a measure of mass per unit of volume, and you know the mass and the volume of the rock, you can now calculate its density.

$$\text{Density} = \frac{900 \text{ kg}}{0.5 \text{ m}^3} \approx 1800 \text{ kg/m}^3$$

The answer to the Challenge is that the rock would weigh about 2,000 pounds on Earth, it has a mass of about 900 kilograms, and its density is 1800 kilograms per cubic meter.

Name_____ Class _____ Date _____

Try It Yourself

A. Complete each grid. Write your answer at the top and fill in the numbered circles.

1. A pound of mushrooms costs $2.08. How much would 24 ounces of mushrooms cost?

2. Dana measured the mass of a stone to be 80 grams. Its volume was 29 cubic centimeters. What was the density of the stone? Give your answer in grams per cubic centimeter (g/cm³).

B. Complete each activity below. Show all your work. Use your own paper.

1. Ella goes to Poland to visit relatives. To make dessert for her family, she goes to the market to buy 3 pounds of strawberries. In Poland, fruit is sold by the kilogram. The market sells strawberries in $\frac{1}{4}$-kilogram baskets. Ella knows that 1 kilogram is equal to about 2.2 pounds. How many baskets of strawberries must she buy to make her dessert?

2. One package of cookies weighs 500 grams. Each cookie weighs about 20 grams and contains 80 calories. About how many calories are in the whole package?

C. Complete the three parts below. Show all your work. Use your own paper.

Sean's doctor gives him a bottle that contains 150 cubic centimeters (cc) of a liquid medicine. Sean is supposed to take 1 tablespoon each day.

Part A The liquid in the bottle weighs 210 grams. What is the density of the liquid, in grams per cubic centimeter?

Part B If there are about 60 tablespoons in 1 liter, how many tablespoons are in the whole bottle of liquid medicine? (Remember that there are 1000 cc in 1 L.)

Part C What is the approximate mass (in grams) of 1 tablespoon of the medicine?

Try It Yourself

A. Fill in the circle next to the correct answer to each multiple-choice question.

1. How many milligrams are in 3.1 kilograms?

   Ⓐ 3100 mg   Ⓑ 31,000 mg   © 310,000 mg   Ⓓ 3,100,000 mg

2. How many ounces are in 0.8 pound?

   Ⓐ 0.05 oz   Ⓑ 12.8 oz   © 128 oz   Ⓓ 800 oz

3. How many metric tons are in 6725 kilograms?

   Ⓐ 3.3625 T   Ⓑ 6.725 T   © 3362.5 T   Ⓓ 6,725,000 T

4. How many pounds are in 3.35 tons?

   Ⓐ 0.001675 lb   Ⓑ 0.00335 lb   © 3,350 lb   Ⓓ 6,700 lb

5. How many pounds are in 128 ounces?

   Ⓐ 8 lb   Ⓑ 16 lb   © 2,048 lb   Ⓓ 128,000 lb

B. Complete the two parts below. Show all your work.

As part of a math and science competition, students are shown three solids made of the same material: a cylinder 2 feet high with a base diameter of 1 foot, a sphere with a diameter of 1.5 feet, and a rectangular prism measuring 2 feet × 1 foot × 1 foot.

Part A Explain how you can calculate which object has the greatest mass.

Part B Perform the calculations and rank the objects in order of their mass, from least to greatest. You may use π in your calculations.

MEASURING RATE AND VELOCITY

This lesson addresses Benchmarks B.1.3.2 and B.3.3.1 of the Sunshine State Standards.

The Challenge

Celia's office is 10 miles south of her home. On her way to work, she goes 60 miles per hour. Coming home, there is a lot of traffic, so she can go only 30 miles per hour. What is her average speed for the whole round trip? What is her velocity going home?

Learning the Ropes

The speedometer of a car measures how many miles a car would travel in one hour if it continued at the speed indicated. The speedometer shows the rate at which the car moves. **Rate** is the measurement of the distance traveled per unit of time. The word *per* means "for every." A rate of 55 miles per hour means that a car would travel 55 miles for every hour that it maintained that speed. This rate is abbreviated as 55 mph.

When you include the direction you are going, you are telling your **velocity.** If a car is traveling north at a rate of 55 miles per hour, the car has a velocity of 55 miles per hour north.

To calculate rate, divide the distance traveled by the time it takes to go that distance.

$$rate = \frac{distance}{time}$$

You can change the rate formula around to calculate distance or time. To calculate distance, multiply the rate by the time. To calculate time, divide the distance by the rate.

$$distance = rate \times time \qquad time = \frac{distance}{rate}$$

EXAMPLE How long would it take a bicyclist to travel 15 miles if she goes 12 miles per hour?

$$time = distance \div rate$$

$$time = 15 \text{ miles} \div 12 \text{ miles per hour} = 1.25 \text{ hours}$$

Rate is not limited to units of distance and time. It can also describe one quantity per unit of another, or the relationship between two units. For example, local governments set tax rates that show the amount of tax a home owner must pay per $1,000 for the value of his or her home.

Math in History

Galileo Galilei was an Italian physicist and astronomer who lived from 1564 to 1642. By studying the movement of balls rolling down inclined planes, Galileo figured out that objects do not fall at a constant rate. Instead, the rate increases with time. In fact, in the absence of air resistance, every object falls to Earth at a rate that increases by 32 feet per second every second. After 1 second, an object is falling at a rate of 32 feet per second. After 2 seconds, the object is falling at a speed of 64 feet per second. How fast would it be falling after 3 seconds?

The money placed into a bank account is called the **principal.** The extra money the principal earns is called the **interest. Simple interest** is a flat rate paid for a period of time. For example, $100 at an annual rate of simple interest of 10% would, at the end of a year, increase to $110. **Compound interest** increases the value of money much more rapidly, by adding the interest earned to the principal and then calculating the interest on this new (larger) amount. At a 10% annual compound interest rate, $100 would be equal to $100 × 1.1, or $110, after the first year; $110 × 1.1, or $121, after the second year; and so on.

EXAMPLE In a famous hot dog-eating contest, Kazutoyo Arai set a record. He ate 25 hot dogs in 12 minutes, or more than 2 hot dogs per minute. If a contestant can eat 1.5 hot dogs per minute, how many could he eat in 12 minutes?

$$\text{number of hot dogs} = \text{rate} \times \text{time} \qquad \frac{1.5 \text{ hot dogs}}{1 \text{ minute}} \times 12 \text{ minutes} = 18 \text{ hot dogs}$$

Now try another example: A bank gives an annual interest rate of 5% on savings accounts. The rate is therefore $\frac{0.05}{1 \text{ year}}$. At this rate, if you deposit $122 for one year, how much interest will you receive?

$$\text{interest} = \text{rate} \times \text{amount in bank} \qquad \frac{0.05}{1 \text{ year}} \times \$122 = \$6.10/\text{year}$$

Meeting the Challenge

To answer the Challenge, you must use the formulas that relate rate, time, and distance to calculate Celia's average speed to and from work. To tell Celia's velocity going home, you need to know her direction as well as her speed.

STEP 1: Calculate how much time it takes Celia to get to work in the morning.

time = distance ÷ rate   10 miles ÷ 60 miles per hour = $\frac{1}{6}$ hour

$\frac{1}{6} \times 60$ minutes = 10 minutes

STEP 2: Calculate how much time it takes Celia to drive home from work.

time = distance ÷ rate   10 miles ÷ 30 miles per hour = $\frac{1}{3}$ hour

$\frac{1}{3} \times 60$ minutes = 20 minutes

STEP 3: Calculate Celia's average rate for her trip to and from the office.

average rate = total distance ÷ total time

total distance = 10 miles + 10 miles = 20 miles

total time = 10 minutes to work + 20 minutes from work = 30 minutes, or $\frac{1}{2}$ hour

20 miles ÷ $\frac{1}{2}$ hour = 40 miles per hour

STEP 4: Velocity includes both speed and direction. The problem states that Celia's speed on the homeward trip is 30 miles per hour. We know that she is heading north because her office is south of her home, so her home must be north of her office. Therefore, her velocity is 30 miles per hour north.

Try It Yourself

A. Fill in the circle next to the correct answer to each multiple-choice question.

1. A machine can manufacture 12 pens in 1 minute. How many minutes will it take to manufacture 216 pens?

    Ⓐ 12 min   Ⓑ 18 min   Ⓒ 24 min   Ⓓ 36 min

2. A band states that 5% of every ticket purchase goes to charity. If a ticket costs $40, how many tickets would the band have to sell to donate $1,000 to charity?

    Ⓐ 50 tickets   Ⓑ 125 tickets   Ⓒ 250 tickets   Ⓓ 500 tickets

3. The distance between the moon and Earth is about 239,000 miles. Light travels at about 186,000 miles per second. How long does it take light to travel from the moon to Earth? Round your answer to the nearest tenth of a second.

    Ⓐ 0.08 sec   Ⓑ 0.3 sec   Ⓒ 0.8 sec   Ⓓ 1.3 sec

4. A 12-month bank CD pays interest at an annual rate of 4.3%. At this rate, how much interest will you receive on $5,000 when the CD matures at the end of 12 months?

    Ⓐ $21.50   Ⓑ $215.00   Ⓒ $415.00   Ⓓ $430.00

B. Complete the two parts below. Show all your work.

A small car can go about 36 miles on 1 gallon of gas. The car's gas tank can hold 12 gallons. A new car that uses both electric and gas power can go 68 miles on 1 gallon of gas. This car can go about 700 miles on 1 tank of gas.

Part A How many gallons of gas would the first car use on a 700-mile trip? Round to the nearest gallon.

Part B How many gallons of gas can the second car's tank hold? Round to the nearest gallon.

Try It Yourself

A. Fill in the circle next to the correct answer to each multiple-choice question.

1. If a car travels 55 kilometers per hour, how far would it travel in 3 hours?
   Ⓐ 0.05 km   Ⓑ 16.5 km   Ⓒ 18.3 km   Ⓓ 165 km

2. At the Bermuda Aquarium, Museum, and Zoo, there is a 145,000-gallon aquarium that displays fish, turtles, and seals around a coral reef. If water can be pumped into the aquarium at a rate of 65 gallons per minute, about how long would it take to fill the tank?
   Ⓐ about 30 min   Ⓒ about 37 hr
   Ⓑ about 2 hr   Ⓓ about 2,230 hr

3. A new roller coaster at an amusement park has a track that is 7,920 feet long. If it averages 60 miles per hour, about how many minutes would it take to complete two trips around the whole track?
   Ⓐ 2.25 min   Ⓑ 3 min   Ⓒ 3.25 min   Ⓓ 22.5 min

B. Complete the two parts below. Show all your work.

Trust Bank pays a yearly interest rate of 4.0% on the first $2,000 in a bank account. On any amount over $2,000, the bank gives an interest rate of 3.0%.

Part A If Roland deposits $3,260 in the bank, how much interest will he earn in a year?

Part B National Bank offers 3.8% per year on the first $2,000 and 3.4% per year on everything over $2,000. Which bank will give Roland more interest per year on his money? Explain your answer.

EXTENDED-RESPONSE QUESTION PRACTICE

1. The Langmuir family is having a problem with fire ants. They have discovered a fire ant mound on their property.

   Unit 4

   Part A Calculate the total volume of the mound. In the box below, you will find all the information you need in order to make your estimate. Explain the steps you take to find your answer.

   > To calculate the volume of a mound, first measure the following three lengths in meters:
   >
   > a = length of long axis
   > b = length of short axis
   > c = height of mound
   >
   > The formula for the mound's volume is $V = 0.524 \times a \times b \times c$.
   >
   > Mr. Langmuir measures the mound with an old boot. The mound is about 2 boot-lengths on its long axis, one and a half boot-lengths on its short axis and about one boot-length in height.
   >
   > Mr. Langmuir's boot is about 0.3 meter long.

   Part B There are about 1.67 million ants per cubic meter of mound. Using this fact, about how many ants are in the mound? Round your answer to the nearest ten thousand.

✔ If you have trouble with this problem, review the following lessons:
   4.1, "Estimating Measurements"
   4.3, "Converting Customary and Metric Units"
   4.6, "Measuring Volume and Capacity"
   4.10, "Measuring Rate and Velocity"

Unit 4

2. A farmer is preparing to buy hay and store it in his barn. Use the information in the box below to answer the questions that follow.

> A bale of hay measures approximately 1.5 feet by 2 feet by 3 feet.
>
> One bale weighs about 50 pounds.
>
> The hay costs $5 per bale, but if the farmer buys the hay by the ton, he saves 20% of the cost of buying individual bales.

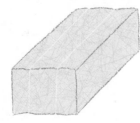

Part A What is the volume (in ft³) of 1 bale of hay? Show your work.

Part B What is the surface area (in ft²) of 1 bale? Show your work.

Part C How many bales make 1 ton of hay? Show your work.

Part D How much money will the farmer save on each ton of hay if he buys it by the ton rather than by the individual bale? Explain how you found your answer.

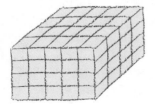

Part E To store the bales, the farmer plans to make stacks weighing about 2 tons each. Each stack will be 5 bales wide, 4 bales high, and 4 bales deep, as shown in the diagram to the right. What are the dimensions of each stack? Show your work.

Part F Suppose that the estimated weight of a bale is accurate only to the nearest 10 pounds. In other words, some bales might weigh as little as 45 pounds; others might weigh as much as 55 pounds. What is the least that 1 stack of hay would weigh? What is the most? Explain your answers.

✔ If you have trouble with this problem, review the following lessons:
   4.1, "Estimating Measurements"
   4.2, "Precision, Accuracy, and Significant Digits"
   4.3, "Converting Customary and Metric Units"
   4.4, "Measuring Length, Perimeter, and Circumference"
   4.5, "Measuring Area"
   4.6, "Measuring Volume and Capacity"
   4.7, "Measuring Surface Area"
   4.9, "Measuring Weight, Mass, and Density"
See also Lesson 1.5, "Decimals and Percents."

DATA COLLECTION: SAMPLING

This lesson addresses Benchmarks MA.E.1.3.1 and MA.E.23.3.1 of the Sunshine State Standards.

The Challenge

Ms. Oiseaux's eighth-grade science class is studying birds. One group of students was assigned to come up with a list of birds that are common in the county where they live. The students spent a Saturday afternoon at a nearby lake taking notes on all the birds that they saw there. They saw two egrets, one roseate spoonbill, a blue heron, and three cormorants. They reported to the class that the most common birds in the county were egrets and cormorants. What sampling technique did the students use, and what is the problem with this technique?

Learning the Ropes

You have probably heard it said that we live in an information age. When people gather information in a systematic manner, as when they conduct a poll or do a scientific experiment, the information that they gather is called **data.**

Populations and Samples. Usually, people are interested in gathering data about a particular group of things. For example, a restaurant owner might want to gather information about the likes and dislikes of his or her customers. The mayor of a city might want to gather information about the wishes of the voters in the city. A forest ranger might want to gather information about the trees in a state park. The entire group of items, people, or subjects about which one wishes to gather information is called the **population.**

Math in History

Among the earliest applications of mathematics to social science was the work of an English clothing salesman named John Graunt, who lived from 1620 to 1674. Graunt became interested in rates of birth and death. He was the first to recognize that slightly more men than women are born each year. He also discovered that mortality rates were higher in cities than in the country. Since Graunt's time, the science of **statistics**—the gathering and analysis of data, has grown to become indispensable to the work of governments, businesses, and social scientists of all kinds.

Deadlock

Often, the population is so big that gathering information from or about every member of the population would be too time-consuming and expensive. For example, suppose that a movie studio is trying to decide which of three stars should play the lead role in a new film. The studio cannot simply ask every potential movie-goer which star would be best, because the population of movie-goers contains many millions of people.

Data-gatherers deal with this problem by choosing a subset of the entire population from which to gather information. Such a subset is called a **sample.** The process of gathering data from or about a sample is called **sampling.**

Principles of Sampling. Obviously, for a sample of a population to reflect the population as a whole, it has to be **representative.** In other words, the sample should be a smaller version of the population. To ensure that a sample is representative, one should follow these rules:

RULES FOR SAMPLING
1. Randomness. The elements in the sample group should be chosen **randomly.** That is, every member of the population should have an equal chance of being chosen.
2. Independence. Each act of choosing should be **independent** from every other act of choosing. That is, choosing one or more members for the sample group should not make choosing other members more or less likely.
3. Size of Sample. The sample size should be large enough to reflect the diversity of the whole population. (There are sophisticated mathematical techniques for helping to ensure that a sample is large enough, but those techniques are beyond the scope of this book.)
4. Similarity of Sample and Population. The sample should have the same weighting of elements and relevant characteristics as is found in the total population. For example, if the total population contains 49 percent women and 51 percent men, then the sample should, too, if it is to reflect the population as a whole.

A sample that does not follow these rules is said to be **biased.** Suppose that you wanted to find out what people in the United States think about changing the driving age to eighteen in every state. If, to find out, you interviewed only people in Arkansas or only teenagers, you would have an unrepresentative, and therefore biased, sample.

Methods of Sampling. People use many different techniques for choosing samples. Here are some common ones:

SAMPLING METHODS
1. Simple Random Sampling. The researcher picks elements from the population at random. One way of doing this is to assign each member of the population a number, put the numbers in a hat, mix them up, and then draw numbers. Another way is to use a computer program to assign numbers to each member and then use a computer program that generates random numbers equal to or less than n, where n represents the number assigned to the last member in the population (such as 100, if there are 100 members of the population).
2. Systematic Sampling. The researcher chooses every nth member of the population, where n is some arbitrary small number. For example, a theater owner might interview every twentieth customer.
3. Stratified Sampling. The researcher divides the population into groups. Then the researcher determines the percentage that each group represents within the population. Next, the researcher chooses elements at random from each group, making sure that the percentages in the sample are the same. Thus, for example, if you know that females make up 51 percent of the U.S. population and males make up 49 percent, you might take a sample of 100 people, 51 of whom are female and 49 of whom are male.
4. Opportunity Sampling. This is the least accurate but easiest method of sampling. The researcher simply takes the first elements of the population that he or she encounters. Opportunity samples are often biased.

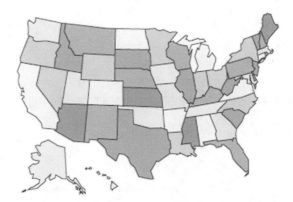

Meeting the Challenge

To answer the Challenge, you must identify what type of sampling the students used and explain the problems with their technique.

Step 1: Determine what the population is. The population in the Challenge is the birds living in the students' county.

Step 2: Think about whether the sample—birds at one lake—is representative of the total bird population for the county. Depending on their feeding and nesting habits, different birds tend to live in different areas, or habitats. Some birds live in cities, while others live in suburban or rural areas. Even among water birds, some kinds live near the sea, while others live around bodies of fresh water, like lakes or ponds. The students have chosen to look only at birds living around a particular lake at a certain time of year. Therefore, the sample is not representative of the bird population as a whole.

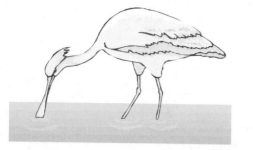

Step 3: The students' choice of this one location ensured that the sampling was not random. Think about how they sampled the population. They went to a lake that was convenient because it was nearby, and they observed whatever birds came along at that time. The sample is not representative of the total population, and it was not drawn randomly and independently.

The students have used an opportunity sample. Therefore, it is a biased sample that contains a greater percentage of water birds than the whole population would. By going during the daytime, the students also missed the birds that are nocturnal. In addition, they may have counted some birds that were migrating through the area but are not year-round residents.

The answer to the Challenge is that the students used an opportunity sampling method. As a result, their sample does not reflect the whole population.

Another Way In all school subjects, you either learn about something by studying its parts, or you learn about something's parts by examining the whole. Statistical sampling is a way to understand something (a population) by studying just a part of it (the sample). Another way to think about sampling is to think of a building: You are trying to learn all about a whole building by studying a few of its bricks. That is why it is important to study enough bricks and to choose them carefully. If you choose only one brick and you happen to get the only cracked one in the whole building, you might assume that the whole building is crumbling, when in fact it is in very good shape!

Name_____ Class _____ Date _____

Try It Yourself

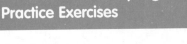

A. Fill in the circle next to the correct answer to each multiple-choice question.

1. The Student Council is organizing a dance and must decide on a theme. They ask every fifth student who walks through the school entrance what kind of dance he or she would like to have. What kind of sampling technique does the Student Council use?

   (A) simple random sampling

   (B) systematic sampling

   (C) stratified sampling

   (D) opportunity sampling

2. Dr. Dewey is conducting a survey about how the patients like his services. In order to find out whom to ask, he puts the names of his patients in a box and draws out names. What kind of sampling technique is Dr. Dewey using?

   (A) simple random sampling

   (B) systematic sampling

   (C) stratified sampling

   (D) opportunity sampling

3. Professor Huang wants to know whether a class on American women poets would be popular among students attending the college where she teaches. She asks the students in her Introduction to Women's Studies class about it. What kind of sampling technique is Professor Huang using?

   (A) random sampling

   (B) systematic sampling

   (C) stratified sampling

   (D) opportunity sampling

B. Complete the activity below.

A new movie theater has opened, and the manager wants to know if people like the theater. Explain how she could use systematic sampling to select her sample.

Try It Yourself

A. Fill in the circle next to the correct answer to each multiple-choice question.

1. All the students at Springside Middle School are voting to select a new mascot to represent the school. Patricio wants to predict which mascot will be chosen, so he interviews a random sample of students from each grade (sixth, seventh, and eighth). What kind of sampling does Patricio use?

   Ⓐ simple random sampling
   Ⓑ systematic sampling
   Ⓒ stratified sampling
   Ⓓ opportunity sampling

2. The manager of a concert hall has a new system of giving away backstage passes. Every person waiting in line puts his or her name into a bucket. Any person whose name is drawn receives two backstage passes. What kind of sampling technique does the concert hall manager use?

   Ⓐ simple random sampling
   Ⓑ systematic sampling
   Ⓒ stratified sampling
   Ⓓ opportunity sampling

3. On a farm, it is important to know the amount of nutrients in the soil. A farm worker is testing the quality of her soil. She divides the farm into 20 equal plots and takes one sample of soil from each plot. What kind of sampling technique does the farm worker use?

   Ⓐ simple random sampling
   Ⓑ systematic sampling
   Ⓒ stratified sampling
   Ⓓ opportunity sampling

B. Complete the two parts below.

A radio station holds a contest to answer the question *Who is the most popular rock star of all time?* The announcer at the station asks the first 10 callers on a Saturday afternoon.

Part A What kind of sample is this? Explain your answer.

Part B Explain why this sample is biased.

DISPLAYING DATA: SIMPLE GRAPHS

This lesson addresses Benchmarks MA.E.1.3.1 and MA.E.3.3.1 of the Sunshine State Standards.

Math in History

Percentages are often used in pie charts because both pie charts and percentages are used to show how the parts of something relate to the whole. The whole of something, of course, is 100 percent. Half of it would be 50 percent, and so on. The term *percent* comes from the Latin words *per centum,* meaning "out of a hundred," so fifty percent means, literally, 50 out of a hundred.

The Challenge

Dana wants to give a presentation to her sales staff about business expenses. She has collected data over the last six months. The results are shown in the chart to the right. Use the data to create a bar graph and a percent circle graph.

EXPENSES FOR LAST SIX MONTHS	
Type of Expense	**Total Spent**
Advertising	$1.5 million
Inventory	$4.5 million
Building	$4.5 million
Salaries	$6.0 million
Taxes	$1.5 million

Learning the Ropes

Once you have collected your data, you will want to find the best way to display it. There are many ways to display data, depending upon what you want to show. In this lesson, you will learn some simple ways to present data graphically, including circle graphs (pie charts), bar and column graphs, pictographs, and Venn diagrams.

Circle Graphs. One common way to present data is using a **circle graph,** or **pie chart.** In this type of graph, the whole circle or pie represents the whole of something. The circle is divided into sections, each representing a part of the whole. You can compare the sizes of parts readily, so circle graphs are often used for simple comparisons. The circle graphs on the next page show the time Sue-Wei spent building a bookcase for her classroom.

On circle graphs, data can be displayed as raw numbers, percentages, or fractions. To express the data as fractions, use the raw number for the numerator and the total number for the whole as the denominator. To express the data as a percent of the whole, divide the raw number by the total. Then multiply the quotient by 100.

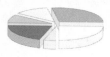
The first graph to the right shows how many hours Sue-Wei spent doing each step in the process of making her bookcase. The graph directly below shows the time for each individual task as a fraction of the whole time. The third graph shows the same information as percents.

STEPS IN BOOKCASE CONSTRUCTION (HOURS)

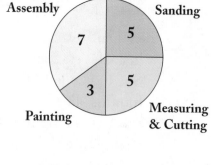

STEPS IN BOOKCASE CONSTRUCTION (FRACTIONS)

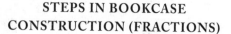
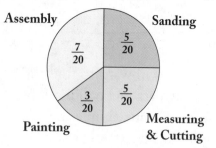

STEPS IN BOOKCASE CONSTRUCTION (PERCENTS)

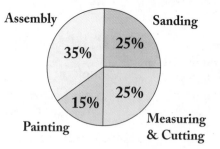

Pictographs and Bar Graphs. Another way to present data is in the form of a pictograph or a bar graph. A **pictograph** uses pictures to represent data. In the first graph at the top of the next page, each picture of a bicycle represents the sale of 5,000 bicycles. Pictographs help you to get a general idea of differences between categories.

Data that can be presented in a pictograph can also be shown in a bar graph. A **bar graph** uses vertical or horizontal bars, instead of pictures, to represent data. Bar graphs generally show more detail than pictographs, which show only rounded numbers rather than exact ones. A bar graph shows categories of data on one axis and numbers on the other. By looking at a bar graph, you can quickly see which categories are biggest and which are smallest. A graph with vertical bars, such as the graph at the top of the next page, is also called a **column graph.** If you were to switch the axes of a column graph, the bars would be horizontal, but the data would be the same.

In the graphs below, the same data is presented in two different ways. Which graph is easier to read? Which one gives more details?

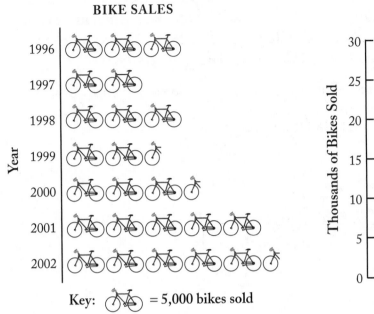

BIKE SALES

1996
1997
1998
1999
2000
2001
2002

Year

Key: = 5,000 bikes sold

BIKE SALES

Thousands of Bikes Sold

30
25
20
15
10
5
0

96 97 98 99 00 01 02
Year

Venn Diagrams. A **Venn diagram** is a data display that shows relationships among groups of items. In particular, it shows when items belong to more than one group. This table shows club membership at three schools. To make Venn diagrams for the data, use two circles or ovals to show the two kinds of clubs. Label the circles *S* for ski and *C* for chess, as shown below.

CLUB MEMBERSHIP			
	Madison	**Adams**	**Lincoln**
Ski Club	28	34	34
Chess Club	20	21	14
Both Clubs	6	0	14

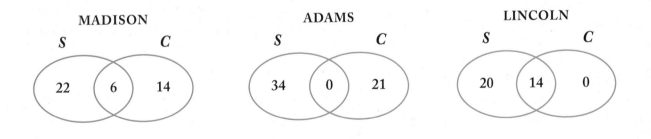

MADISON

S   *C*

22   6   14

ADAMS

S   *C*

34   0   21

LINCOLN

S   *C*

20   14   0

Another Way You can often get a better understanding of a data set by displaying it in several different ways. Try a table *and* a bar graph. Try switching the columns and rows in a table, or switching the horizontal and vertical axes on graphs. A graphing calculator or a computer graphing program can help you try out different displays.

Meeting the Challenge

To answer the Challenge, you must create a bar graph and a percent circle graph.

Step 1: To create the bar graph, let one axis show the type of expense and the other axis show the total spent, in millions of dollars. Label each axis. You will need to mark your numerical axis in units of millions of dollars, from 0 to 6.

Step 2: Draw a rectangular bar for each data value from the table. Title your graph.

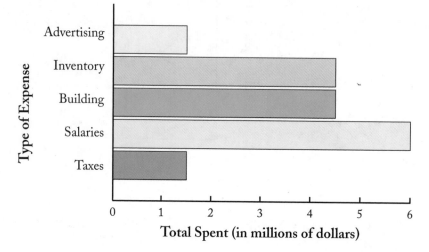

EXPENSES FOR LAST SIX MONTHS

Step 3: To calculate the percentages for each type of expense, you need to find the total of all expenses. Then divide each expense by the total and multiply by 100 to find the percentage.

$$1.5 \div 18 = 0.083 = 8.3\%$$
$$4.5 \div 18 = 0.25 = 25\%$$
$$6.0 \div 18 = 0.333 = 33.3\%$$

Step 4: Draw the percent circle graph. Each section should show the portion of the total that was spent on each category. Label each section with the type of expense and the percent. Title your graph.

EXPENSES FOR LAST SIX MONTHS

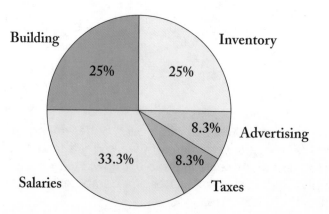

Name_____ Class _____ Date _____

Try It Yourself

A. Fill in the circle next to the correct answer to each multiple-choice question.

WHICH SERVICES SHOULD GET MORE MONEY?	
public education	48%
police department	52%
fire department	36%
street cleaning	17%
parks department	23%
other	14%

1. The table shows the results of a survey. Which type of graph is most appropriate for displaying this information?
   Ⓐ bar graph
   Ⓑ circle graph
   Ⓒ pictograph
   Ⓓ Venn diagram

2. The Venn diagram below shows the number of people who saw a popular movie in the theater, at home, or both. How many people saw the movie at home?
   Ⓐ 22
   Ⓑ 109
   Ⓒ 163
   Ⓓ 141

THEATER   HOME

87 141 22

3. The circle graph shows a survey of 2,500 people. How many chose cats?
   Ⓐ 25
   Ⓑ 125
   Ⓒ 625
   Ⓓ 1,000

FAVORITE PET

Other 10%
Fish 5%
Bird 15%
Dog 45%
Cat 25%

4. According to the circle graph, how many people like birds best?
   Ⓐ 5   Ⓑ 37   Ⓒ 150   Ⓓ 375

B. Complete the two parts below.

Part A On your own paper, draw a bar graph of the data in the table to the right.

Part B On your bar graph, draw a bar for the predicted number of subscribers for 2003. Use a different type of shading for this bar in order to distinguish between actual values and a predicted value. Assume that the general trend in number of subscribers continues.

NEWSPAPER SUBSCRIBERS IN SMALLVILLE					
Year	1998	1999	2000	2001	2002
Number	93	108	145	217	342

Try It Yourself

A. Fill in the circle next to the correct answer to each multiple-choice question.

1. A needlework shop took four surveys of their customers. Which of the surveys would be most appropriate for display on a Venn diagram?

   Ⓐ number of people who bought quilting supplies each year for the last five years

   Ⓑ number of people who knit, number who embroider, and number who do both

   Ⓒ percents of people who chose knitting, embroidery, quilting, weaving, or other as their favorite craft

   Ⓓ percent of those surveyed who do any or all of the following: knit, crochet, embroider, quilt, weave

2. The double bar graph shows the answers to a survey about homework. Which group of people feels most strongly that students have too much homework?

   Ⓐ students

   Ⓑ parents

   Ⓒ teachers

   Ⓓ grandparents

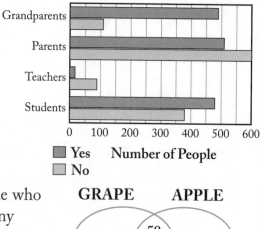

DO STUDENTS HAVE TOO MUCH HOMEWORK?

■ Yes   Number of People
■ No

3. The Venn diagram at right shows the number of people who like grape juice, apple juice, and orange juice. How many people like grape juice and apple juice but not orange juice?

   Ⓐ 59   Ⓒ 180

   Ⓑ 155   Ⓓ 301

GRAPE   APPLE

40   59   56
75   121   48
21

ORANGE

4. How many people like all three kinds of juice?

   Ⓐ 59   Ⓑ 121   Ⓒ 182   Ⓓ 303

B. Complete the two parts below.

Part A On your own paper, make a rough sketch of a circle graph that would display this data. Label each sector.

Part B Give the size of each sector of the graph in degrees of arc (of a circle). Explain how you found the number of degrees for each sector.

NUMBER OF VOTES IN SCHOOL ELECTION	
Bynes	85
Smith	142
Zola	186
Porter	43
Didn't Vote	17

DISPLAYING DATA: LINE GRAPHS AND SCATTER PLOTS

This lesson addresses Benchmarks MA.E.1.3.1 and MA.E.3.3.1 of the Sunshine State Standards.

Math in History
Policy makers in business and government often use line graphs to analyze changes over time. Such graphs can show trends and help people to make predictions about the future. For example, stock market prices in the United States often fluctuate considerably over short periods of time. However, if one plots those prices over a long period—for the past 75 years, for example—one sees a clear, strong upward direction, indicating that stocks are good investments over the long term.

The Challenge

Since 1970, the U.S. Census Bureau has kept a record of the number of people enrolled in college. The chart to the right shows the data. Create a line graph displaying the number of people enrolled in college. Then write two statements analyzing the data and draw a conclusion from them. Is your conclusion valid?

COLLEGE ENROLLMENT	
Year	**No. of People**
1970	6,000,000
1975	8,000,000
1980	8,500,000
1985	9,000,000
1990	9,500,000
1995	10,000,000

Learning the Ropes

There are still other ways of displaying data, depending upon what you want to show. Line graphs help you to see trends in data. Scatter plots show whether or not there is a correlation between sets of data.

Line Graphs. While pie charts compare parts of a whole, **line graphs** show how the data changes over time. The **scales** (evenly spaced marks) on the x-axis often show units of time. The scales on the y-axis are units of the quantity you are studying. Line graphs help to show **trends,** or changes in a particular direction. For example, researchers say that because of advances in medicine, people are living longer. The trend is that the average life span of people in the United States is increasing. A line graph can show the overall pattern of changes.

EXAMPLE   The line graph to the right shows the number of athletes who have attended basketball camp each year. The line graph shows a trend: Basketball camp attendance has gone up over the years. Though there was a drop in attendance from Year 1 to Year 2, the number of athletes going to basketball camp has increased overall.

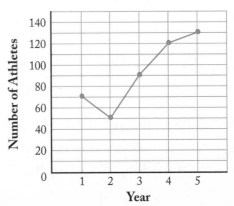

BASKETBALL CAMP ATTENDANCE

Math in Use: Interpreting Research   Scatter plots are useful for researchers in the social sciences who are trying to determine if there is a correlation between two sets of data. For example, a psychologist studying a certain disorder might make a scatter plot of different factors, such as family history or birth order, to see if the factors have any relationship to the disorder. Even if a correlation is found, however, further study is necessary to determine if one condition *causes* another, or if both are connected to some other factor.

You can also use a line graph to **extrapolate** what will happen beyond the known range of your data—that is, to estimate future values based on values you already know. As you observe the trends in the data on a line graph, you can make **projections,** or predictions, based on the direction in which the data is changing. A reasonable projection of our data would be that about 140 to 150 athletes will attend basketball camp in Year 6. Similarly, graphs of weather patterns and trends in the temperature allow weather forecasters to predict what the weather will be like. Weather patterns, however, have many more variables and are far more complicated!

Scatter Plots. Graphs can also be useful for showing whether or not there is a relationship, or **correlation,** between two sets of data. For example, you may want to know if there is a relationship between the ages of students in your class and their heights. A **scatter plot,** or **scattergram,** is a graph that displays points for ordered pairs of numbers on a coordinate grid. A scatter plot can show a positive correlation, a negative correlation, or no correlation.

You graph data on a scatter plot in the same way that you graph values for *x* and *y* on a coordinate graph. The graph below shows the ages and heights of 12 girls. It shows age data along the *x*-axis and height data along the *y*-axis.

GIRLS' AGES AND HEIGHTS

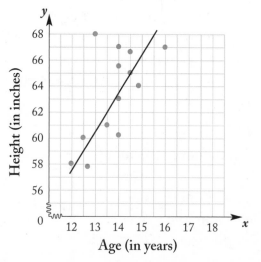

The jagged line ($\lessgtr$) on the *y*-axis indicates that the height scale skips from 0 to 56 inches. The jagged line ($\sim\!\!\wedge\!\!\sim$) on the *x*-axis indicates that the age scale skips from 0 to 12 years.

The points are scattered on the graph, but they show a general trend that as age increases, height also increases. Notice that the points seem to go upward to the right. This means that the graph shows a **positive correlation;** that is, both age and height increase together during the teenage years.

To examine the trend more accurately, you can draw a line through the scatter plot, touching or almost touching as many points as you can. This is called a **line of best fit.** You can use the line of best fit to make predictions about other data that are not shown on the graph.

Some data may show a **negative correlation;** as one quantity increases, the other decreases. Marla asked her classmates how much time they spent watching television and playing computer games the week before a big math test. Then she graphed her classmates' scores on the test, along with their television and computer time.

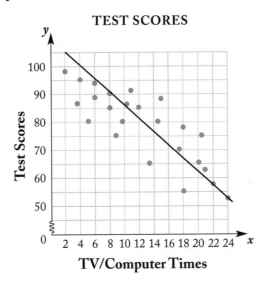

TEST SCORES

Notice that the points seem to go downward to the right. In general, the more time a student spent watching television and playing computer games, the lower his or her score on the test.

Some scatter plots show **no correlation;** one quantity does not affect the other. For example, Adrian graphed his classmates' heights and their scores on a history test.

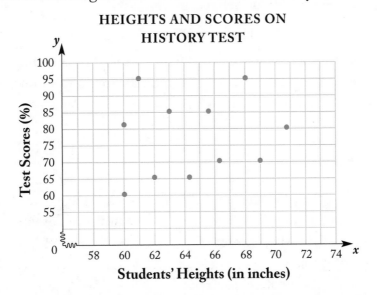

HEIGHTS AND SCORES ON HISTORY TEST

The points are randomly distributed, showing that there is no correlation between a student's height and his or her ability to do well on a test. Since there is no trend, you cannot draw a line of best fit.

Meeting the Challenge

To answer the Challenge, you must create a line graph and interpret the data.

STEP 1: Write the years along the *x*-axis, and label that axis "Year."

STEP 2: Write numbers up the *y*-axis. Label that axis of your graph "Number of People (in millions)," so that 1 stands for 1 million.

STEP 3: Plot the points and connect them with line segments.

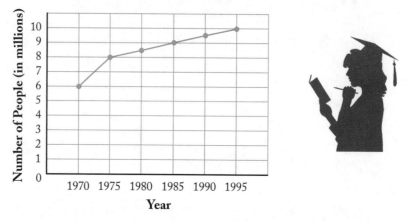

COLLEGE ENROLLMENT

STEP 4: Interpret the data, and write two statements summarizing your analysis.

1) In 1970, about 6 million people were enrolled in college, and in 1995, about 10 million people were enrolled.

2) The number of people who were enrolled in college increased by about half a million during each five-year period from 1975 to 1995.

STEP 5: Write a conclusion about the data shown in the graph.

Conclusion: The number of people enrolled in college in the United States is increasing over time. Based on the data provided, this conclusion is valid because the graph shows an upward trend in college enrollment.

Another Way As you have seen in this lesson, one way to determine how much data has changed over time is to make a line graph, plotting the data points and drawing lines connecting them. Yet another way is to determine the slope of the line between data points by using the formula $\frac{y_1-y_2}{x_1-x_2}$. In the example on the first page of the lesson, the change in basketball camp attendance from the first year to the second year is $\frac{50-70}{2-1} = \frac{-20}{1} = -20$. A negative slope indicates a change that is in a downward direction. From the second year to the third year, the slope is $\frac{90-50}{3-2} = \frac{40}{1} = 40$, indicating a change in a positive direction.

Name_____ Class _____ Date _____

Try It Yourself

A. Use the line graph below to answer the multiple-choice questions. Fill in the circle next to the correct answer to each question.

The line graph to the right shows how the average price of a video cassette recorder (VCR) changed between 1985 and 1997.

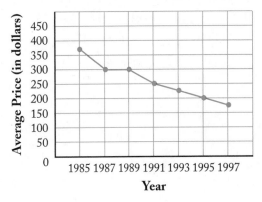

AVERAGE PRICE OF A VCR

1. What trend does the line graph show?
   Ⓐ The average price of a VCR increased sharply between 1985 and 1997.
   Ⓑ The average price of a VCR increased slowly between 1985 and 1997.
   Ⓒ The average price of a VCR remained unchanged between 1985 and 1997.
   Ⓓ The average price of a VCR slowly decreased between 1985 and 1997.

2. Which of the following choices is the best estimate of the difference between the average price of a VCR in 1985 and in 1997?
   Ⓐ $400   Ⓑ $300   Ⓒ $200   Ⓓ $150

B. Complete the two parts below. Use your own paper.

During election time, one candidate, Ms. Phillips, said that property taxes had been lowered several times over the past few years. Another candidate, Mr. Simm, said that taxes had been raised. The scatter plot to the right illustrates trends in property taxes over the last few years.

Part A Write a sentence explaining what the scatter plot tells about the town's taxes.

Part B Draw a line of best fit. Does the graph show a positive correlation, a negative correlation, or no correlation? Explain your answer.

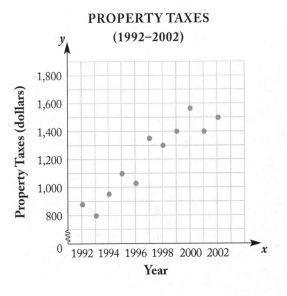

PROPERTY TAXES
(1992–2002)

Try It Yourself

A. Use the line graph to the right to answer the multiple-choice questions. Fill in the circle next to the correct answer to each question.

The line graph shows the data collected by the U.S. Census Bureau about the populations of California and Florida since 1900.

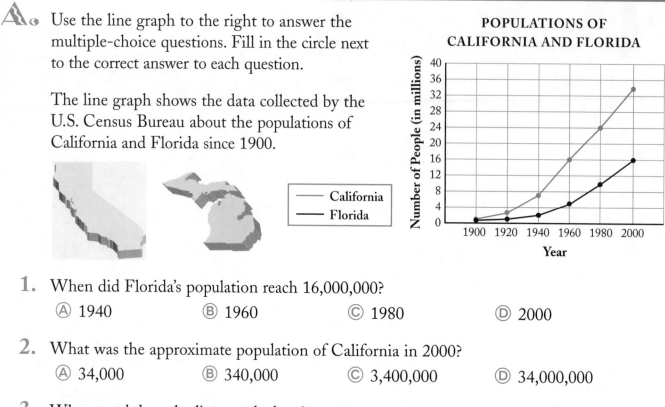

1. When did Florida's population reach 16,000,000?

ⓐ 1940   ⓑ 1960   ⓒ 1980   ⓓ 2000

2. What was the approximate population of California in 2000?

ⓐ 34,000   ⓑ 340,000   ⓒ 3,400,000   ⓓ 34,000,000

3. What trend does the line graph show?

ⓐ The populations of California and Florida increased slightly between 1900 and 2000.

ⓑ The populations of California and Florida grew significantly in the twentieth century.

ⓒ The populations of California and Florida decreased between 1960 and 1980.

ⓓ The populations of California and Florida doubled in size between 1980 and 2000.

B. Complete the two parts below. Use your own paper.

Kiara has collected data from her classmates about the type of video games they enjoy playing the most. Marlon wants to show how the number of people who have bought video game systems has increased each year.

Part A What is the best type of graph to show Kiara's data? Explain your answer.

Part B What type of graph should Marlon use to show his data? Explain your answer.

DISPLAYING DATA: HISTOGRAMS AND RELATED GRAPHS

This lesson addresses Benchmarks MA.E.1.3.1 and MA.E.3.3.1 of the Sunshine State Standards.

The Challenge

Ms. Vasquez, a science teacher, has 100 students altogether. Her students' grades on a recent exam improved dramatically from the previous exam, so she wants to create a graph that displays the grades earned by her students. The display must show this information without using individual names, and it must fit on a single piece of paper that can be sent home with progress reports. How could she do this?

EXAM GRADES	
Grade	**Number of Students**
A	24
B	33
C	22
D	15
F	6

Learning the Ropes

Data can be organized and displayed in many forms, including tables, Venn diagrams, pictographs, bar and column graphs, circle graphs, and line graphs. Some methods are especially useful for illustrating how data is grouped or clustered. This quality is sometimes called the **spread** or **distribution** of the data.

Histograms. A **histogram** is like a bar graph, except that the scale along one of the axes shows numerical **intervals,** or ranges, instead of **discrete** (individual) numbers. In a histogram, there are no spaces in between the shaded areas representing each interval.

The histogram to the right shows the average amount of time that a group of honor-roll students spent reading for pleasure each day. What can you tell about the reading times? How many students are in the group altogether?

AVERAGE TIME SPENT READING FOR ENJOYMENT

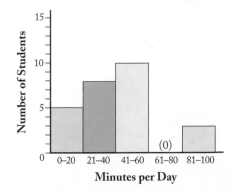

Math in History
When data is displayed clearly, it can be understood easily and used wisely. Histograms have been crucial in displaying health care data clearly since the late 1850s. Florence Nightingale, a pioneer in nursing, continued her campaign for better medical care after she returned from the Crimean War in Turkey. She compiled death statistics from British hospitals and put the data in histogram form. Her data showed administrators the need for changes in hospital procedures. Those changes reduced death rates from infection and continue to save lives today.

Math in Use: Scientific Studies   Data sets collected by scientists doing research can be very large, complex, and varied. It is often more practical (and necessary) to display data frequency in terms of intervals or ranges as opposed to exact values. Think about a research study on the relationship between time spent exercising and heart disease. If you studied 1,000 people, it would be very difficult to plot individual data for all 1,000 subjects. Histograms, frequency polygons, and stem-and-leaf charts can display these kinds of data in a meaningful way through the use of intervals.

As you can see, histograms are a good way to show how data can be broken down or sorted into groups. Can you think of some other contexts where sorting data into groups or ranges might be important? (Hint: Think of special "letters" your teacher gives you.)

Frequency Polygons. A **frequency polygon** is a special kind of line graph that serves many of the same purposes as a standard histogram. **Frequency** refers to how often the points of a data set fall within a certain interval. Frequency polygons use straight lines to connect the midpoints of the intervals, as shown on the first graph below. The graph is in the shape of a polygon because the straight lines between the midpoints form a closed figure when joined with the x-axis. The middle graph below, which is based on the same data as the first graph, is a **cumulative frequency polygon.** This graph is **cumulative** because each point shows the sum of all the frequencies up to and including the given interval. Notice that the cumulative frequency for all the intervals up to and including the last one is 80, which is the total of the frequencies of all the intervals. The **cumulative relative frequency polygon** is the same as the middle graph except that it shows the cumulative frequencies on the y-axis as percents, up to a total of 100%, rather than as actual numbers of data points.

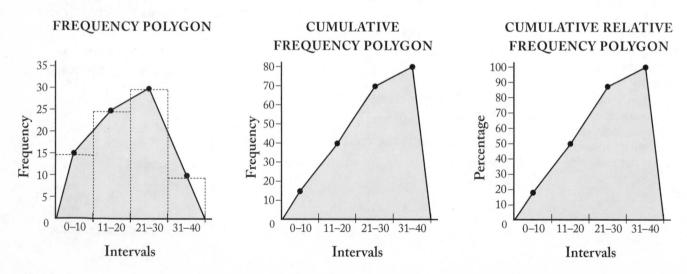

Stem-and-Leaf Plots. Another way to graph data according to its grouping is with stem-and-leaf plots, which, like histograms, show how data falls within various ranges. Unlike histograms, however, **stem-and-leaf plots** display the value of every single member of the data set. These useful plots clearly highlight the frequency of each value within the displayed intervals. Stem-and-leaf plots make it easy to spot the particular range in which the data falls most frequently or most infrequently. They do this with their placement of **stems,** which stand for reasonable intervals (often multiples of ten), and the more precise **leaves,** which complete each value. Together, the stem values on the left and the leaves on the right describe the exact value of each piece of data. For example, look at the stem-and-leaf plot below.

**AGES OF U.S. PRESIDENTS
AT INAUGURATION**

Stem	Leaves
4	2, 3, 6, 6, 7, 8, 9, 9
5	0, 0, 1, 1, 1, 1, 2, 2, 4, 4, 4, 4, 4, 5, 5, 5, 5, 6, 6, 6, 7, 7, 7, 7, 8
6	0, 1, 1, 1, 2, 4, 4, 5, 8, 9

4|2 = 42 years old

Note that you can easily see important facts about the data. For example, the youngest president at inauguration was 42; the oldest was 69; and most of the 43 U.S. presidents were inaugurated when they were in their 50s.

Another Way   If you are having trouble understanding the way data is displayed in stem-and-leaf plots, first focus on one piece of information at a time. Choose a "stem" value from the left side of the plot, then mentally match it with a single "leaf" value on the right side of the same line of the plot, no matter how far to the right it may be. Then say, write, or picture the stem number, followed immediately by the leaf number. For example, "4…7" becomes 47, the value of one data point. After some practice, you'll be doing this quickly, reading and understanding the values without even thinking about how to do it. Remember that a stem-and-leaf plot is really just a special, logically ordered list!

Meeting the Challenge

To answer the Challenge, you must figure out a way to represent a large amount of data in a relatively small space, and do so without naming the individuals behind the data. The best way to display the information and accomplish Ms. Vasquez's goals is with a histogram.

STEP 1: Choose a title for the graph. Then draw the axes and label them appropriately.

STEP 2: Choose a vertical scale and horizontal intervals that make sense for the situation. It is safe to assume from the information given that many of the students performed well on the exam.

STEP 3: Plot the information as solid bars, with no space between data intervals. Remember that the sum of the number of students in all the grade ranges must add up to the total number of students who took the test!

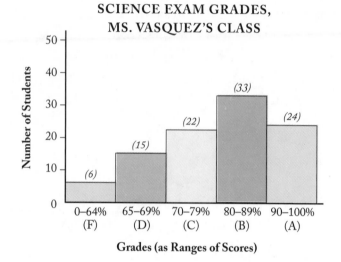

SCIENCE EXAM GRADES, MS. VASQUEZ'S CLASS

Try It Yourself

A. Fill in the circle next to the correct answer to each multiple-choice question.

1. Given the data set 45, 25, 54, 38, and 57, how many stem values (numbers on the left) would you be likely to use when creating a stem-and-leaf chart of the data?
   Ⓐ 2   Ⓑ 3   Ⓒ 4   Ⓓ 5

2. What does one axis of a histogram always represent?
   Ⓐ degrees Fahrenheit   Ⓒ individual units
   Ⓑ an interval or group   Ⓓ weight

3. Which of the following would be the best method of displaying 10 data points so that the exact values of the highest and lowest data points are visible?
   Ⓐ histogram   Ⓒ frequency polygon
   Ⓑ cumulative polygon   Ⓓ stem-and-leaf plot

B. Complete the activity below.

The table to the right contains the individual weights of a football team's starting offense. Create a histogram using the data. Choose appropriate intervals for your x-axis. Also, remember that the sum of the frequencies of all the intervals must be the same as the total number of data points—in this case, players.

FOOTBALL PLAYERS' WEIGHTS	
Position	**Weight**
center	298
guard	310
guard	321
tackle	289
tackle	283
tight end	265
quarterback	207
running back	215
fullback	251
wide receiver	169
wide receiver	187

Try It Yourself

A. Fill in the circle next to the correct answer to each multiple-choice question.

1. A group of 20 high school students all scored 90% or higher on their driver's education midterm. If there were 25 students in the whole class, what would the shape of a histogram representing the breakdown of their scores look like?
   - Ⓐ It would show a value for each score.
   - Ⓒ It would be higher on the right.
   - Ⓑ It would be higher on the left.
   - Ⓓ It would have spaces in between columns.

2. In a stem-and-leaf plot of the data set 25, 15, 43, 18, and 47, which values would be the two "leaves" on the right side of the last line?
   - Ⓐ 4 and 7
   - Ⓑ 1 and 5
   - Ⓒ 5 and 7
   - Ⓓ 3 and 7

3. A histogram would be the best method to show which of the following?
   - Ⓐ how data changes over time
   - Ⓑ what portion of the total data is represented by each data point
   - Ⓒ the breakdown of a large quantity of data within ranges
   - Ⓓ the exact value of each data point

B. Complete the three parts below.

For a math and social studies project, Bhavna asked people in her neighborhood to identify their favorite pro basketball team. She displayed the ages of all the people who chose the Miami Heat in the stem-and-leaf plot shown.

Part A How many people chose the Heat altogether?

Part B How many people in their twenties chose the Heat? How many 13-year-olds?

Part C What are the upper and lower extremes?

AGES OF MIAMI HEAT FANS	
Stem	Leaves
0	8, 9
1	0, 3, 3, 4, 6, 7, 7
2	3, 4, 7
3	3, 9
4	1, 7, 8
5	2, 2
6	1, 4, 4
7	0, 7, 7

$1 \mid 0 = 10$ years old

CENTRAL TENDENCIES AND BOX-AND-WHISKER PLOTS

This lesson addresses Benchmarks MA.E.1.3.1, MA.E.1.3.2, and MA.E.1.3.3 of the Sunshine State Standards.

The Challenge

The final test scores in Mr. Mercedes' physical science class ranged from 56 to 100, as follows: 75, 84, 87, 86, 68, 74, 70, 56, 74, 92, 69, 76, 100, 78, 72, 85, 88, and 95. What is the mean score? What is

the mode? What is the median score? What is the interquartile range? How many students scored below the first quartile? How many scored above the third quartile? Create a box-and-whisker plot for this data.

Learning the Ropes

One way to interpret data you have gathered is to calculate its central tendencies. **Central tendencies** give you information about what is typical in your data. Three measures of central tendency are the mean, median, and mode.

ARIEL'S PHONE TIME	
Day	**No. of Minutes**
Monday	120
Tuesday	60
Wednesday	10
Thursday	30
Friday	120
Saturday	180
Sunday	90

The chart to the left shows the number of minutes Ariel spent on the phone one week.

The **mean** is the average of the data set, in this case, the average amount of time Ariel spent on the phone per night. To calculate the mean, add all the values in the data and divide by the number of addends.

Mean time on phone per day
= total time on phone ÷ number of days
= $(120 + 60 + 10 + 30 + 120 + 180 + 90) ÷ 7$
= $610 ÷ 7 ≈ 87$

Ariel spent an average of about 87 minutes on the phone each night.

Math in History
The calculation of a mean, or average, relies on simple mathematical operations—addition and division—that are thousands of years old, so old that no one knows who first conceived of them. The concept of a mean, however, is very much a modern notion, one that permeates life in our industrial, scientific age.

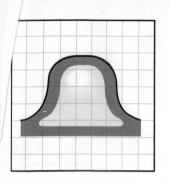

The **median** is the middle number in the data set. To find the median, you must first rearrange the data by size—from largest to smallest, or vice versa. Then, find the value that lies in the middle, where an equal number of values appear above and below it. If the number of values is even, and therefore there are two middle values, take the average of the middle values to find the median.

Day	Sat.	Mon.	Fri.	Sun.	Tues.	Thurs.	Wed.
Minutes	180	120	120	90	60	30	10

median, or middle point

The **mode** is the most frequently occurring number in the data set. To find the mode, find the value in the data that appears more often than any other value. Ariel spent 120 minutes on the phone on two different nights, Monday and Friday, so the mode is 120.

The **range,** which helps to describe how data is spread out, is the difference between the largest number and the smallest number in the data. The range of the data from the chart on Ariel's calls is 170 minutes $(180 - 10 = 170)$.

Box-and-Whisker Plots. A good way to display data and show its central tendencies is the **box-and-whisker plot.** This kind of plot shows the median, as well as two other important statistical measures—the first quartile and the third quartile.

The chart below shows the data for the number of DVDs rented daily during a two-week period at Videoland.

DAILY DVD RENTALS FOR TWO WEEKS														
Day	1	2	3	4	5	6	7	8	9	10	11	12	13	14
No. of Rentals	80	75	73	77	72	104	83	75	74	49	79	75	85	84

To create a box-and-whisker plot for the data set shown on the previous page, begin by arranging the data points in order from left to right. Identify the median—the middle value that divides the data into two equal groups. Then mark the extreme (lowest and highest) values—in this case, 49 and 104.

49 72 73 74 75 75 75 77 79 80 83 84 85 104

|

76
Median

$$\frac{75 + 77}{2}$$

The median of this set of data is 76. The **first quartile,** or **lower quartile,** is the median of the lower half of the data (from 49 to 76). That number is 74. The **third quartile,** or **upper quartile,** is the median of the upper half of the data (from 76 to 104). That number is 83.

To make the box-and-whisker plot, draw a number line that can include all your data points. Above the number line, draw a box from the first quartile to the third quartile, as shown.

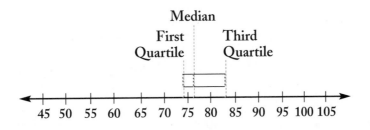

Then draw **whiskers**—line segments from the first and third quartiles to the extremes. The **extremes** are the lowest and highest values in the data set, in this case, 49 and 104.

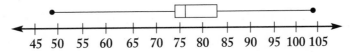

Once you have identified the first and third quartiles, you can find the **interquartile range** of the data, which is the difference between the first and third quartiles of the data set. The interquartile range of the set is 83 − 74, or 9. This number tells you that 50 percent of the time, the number of DVDs rented was between 74 and 83.

Another Way Remember that with box-and-whisker plots, the box represents the middle 50% of the data in terms of frequency. In other words, half of the data points fall within the range shown by the box. This is true regardless of the position within the box of the individual data points. Also, remember that the "middle half" of the data extends from the uppermost boundary of the first quarter of the data points to the beginning of the fourth quarter of the data points.

Meeting the Challenge

To answer the Challenge, find the central tendencies of this data and create a box-and-whisker plot using the scores given.

STEP 1: To find the mean of the scores, add them together and divide by the number of scores.

$75 + 84 + 87 + 86 + 68 + 74 + 70 + 56 + 74 + 92 + 69 + 76 + 100 + 78 + 72$
$+ 85 + 88 + 95 = 1,429$

$$1,429 \div 18 = 79.3\overline{888}$$
$$\approx 79$$

STEP 2: To determine the mode, find the score that appears most frequently. The only score that was received by more than one student is 74, so 74 is the mode.

STEP 3: To find the median, list the scores in numerical order. The median is the number in the middle of the list; an equal number of scores appear above and below the median. Since there are an even number of scores in this data set, take the average of the two scores in the middle: $(76 + 78) \div 2 = 77$.

56 68 69 70 72 74 74 75 76 78 84 85 86 87 88 92 95 100

First Quartile (72)   Median (77)   Third Quartile (87)

STEP 4: Now that you have arranged the scores in order and found the median, you can find the first and third quartiles and determine the interquartile range. The median of the lower half of the data—the first quartile—is 72, and the median of the upper half, or the third quartile, is 87. The interquartile range is 15: $87 - 72 = 15$. Four students scored below the first quartile, and four scored above the third quartile. Eight students in total scored outside the box.

STEP 5: Create a number line. Draw a box above the number line between the quartile values. Draw a vertical line through the median value, plot the extremes, and draw the whiskers. Your box-and-whisker plot should look like the one shown below.

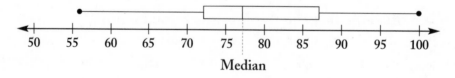

Median

Try It Yourself

A. Use the chart below to answer the multiple-choice questions. Fill in the circle next to the correct answer to each question.

Ms. Eltantawi prepares for a parent-teacher conference with Kareem's parents. She makes a chart of Kareem's previous math test scores.

KAREEM'S MATH SCORES	
Test	**Score (out of 100)**
1	96
2	91.5
3	64.5
4	89.5
5	96

1. What is Kareem's mean score on the math tests?
   - Ⓐ 96
   - Ⓒ 87.5
   - Ⓑ 91.5
   - Ⓓ 72.9

2. What is Kareem's median score on the math tests?
   - Ⓐ 96
   - Ⓑ 91.5
   - Ⓒ 87.5
   - Ⓓ 72.9

3. Which score is the mode of Kareem's scores on the math tests?
   - Ⓐ 96
   - Ⓑ 91.5
   - Ⓒ 87.5
   - Ⓓ 72.9

B. Complete the two parts below. Show all your work.

George asked 12 teenagers how much money they earned per hour at their summer jobs. The results are shown in the chart below.

HOURLY WAGES ($)
8 12 5 6 7 20 2 11 8 10 12 10

Part A On your own paper, make a box-and-whisker plot for the data in the chart.

Part B Describe how you determined the length of the box.

Try It Yourself

5.5 Central Tendencies and Box-and-Whisker Plots
Assessment Practice

A. Use the chart below to answer the multiple-choice questions. Fill in the circle next to the correct answer to each question.

The chart shows how much rain fell in a city in central California during the summer and early fall.

RAINFALL IN CITY	
Month	**Rainfall (inches)**
June	0.09
July	0.02
August	0.02
September	0.22

1. What is the mean rainfall during these months? Round to the nearest hundredth of an inch.

   Ⓐ 0.35 in. Ⓑ 0.09 in. Ⓒ 0.02 in. Ⓓ 0.009 in.

2. What is the median rainfall for these four months? Round to the nearest hundredth of an inch.

   Ⓐ 0.16 in. Ⓑ 0.12 in. Ⓒ 0.09 in. Ⓓ 0.06 in.

3. What amount of rainfall is the mode during this period?

   Ⓐ 0.35 in. Ⓑ 0.16 in. Ⓒ 0.09 in. Ⓓ 0.02 in.

B. Complete the three parts below. Use additional paper if necessary.

The annual salaries of six graduates of an engineering school are shown in the chart at the right.

ANNUAL SALARIES	
Graduate	**Salary**
1	$45,000
2	$50,000
3	$47,000
4	$45,000
5	$1,350,000
6	$36,000

Part A What are the measures of central tendency for this set of data? Show your work.

Mean: __________ Median: __________ Mode: __________

Part B Why is the mean so high, and why, in this case, are the median and mode better indicators of a typical salary for one of this school's graduates?

Part C On your own paper, create a box-and-whisker plot of the data.

INTRODUCTION TO PROBABILITY AND ODDS

This lesson addresses Benchmarks MA.E.2.3.1, MA.E.2.3.2, and MA.E.3.3.2 of the Sunshine State Standards.

Math in History
The foundations of probability were laid by French mathematician Blaise Pascal (1623–1662). Pascal worked out the theory of classical probabilities, based upon possible outcomes. For example, if there are four shirts of different colors in a drawer and you pull out one shirt, there are four possible outcomes. Later mathematicians applied the same techniques to describe probabilities based on historical frequencies, that is, on how often something has happened in the past.

The Challenge

Yolanda and Charise are sisters. Their father has asked them to take turns mowing the lawn once a week. They have to decide who will take the first week. Yolanda says to Charise, "OK. I'll shuffle these cards. Then, you pull one card from the deck. If the card that you pull is a ten or higher, I'll go first. If it is a nine or lower, you'll go first." The deck consists of 52 cards, with 13 cards (ace, 2, 3, 4, 5, 6, 7, 8, 9, 10, jack, queen, and king) in each of four suits (clubs♣, diamonds♦, hearts♥, and spades♠). The ace counts as the high card. What is the probability that Charise will pick a ten or higher? What are the odds in favor? The odds against? Is Yolanda offering her sister a fair deal? Why, or why not?

Learning the Ropes

There are many things in life that depend, at least in part, upon random events governed by chance. What is the likelihood that a person will experience some catastrophe such as a disease, an auto accident, a flood, a hurricane, or a tornado? What is the likelihood of winning a drawing? of having twins or triplets or quintuplets? of living to be 90 years old? 100? 120? The mathematics of **probability,** or likelihood, can be used to provide reasonable answers to such questions.

The Range of Probabilities. The probability (P) of an event, A, is always greater than or equal to zero and less than or equal to 1.

$$0 \leq P(A) \leq 1$$

If an event is **impossible**—if it could never occur—then it has a probability of 0.

If an event is absolutely **certain**—if it has to occur—then it has a probability of 1.

Cereal

Math in Use: Marketing   Market researchers often make use of probabilities based upon frequency to predict how consumers will react to products. For example, researchers might interview focus groups to find out which breakfast cereal people prefer. Suppose that 1,000 people are surveyed, with the following results:

Brand A	Brand B	Brand C	Other Brands
386	254	192	168

Assuming the sample is representative, the probability that a given consumer will buy brand A is thus $\frac{386}{1,000}$, or 38.6%.

An event that has a probability close to 1 is more likely to occur than one whose probability is close to 0. If there are two possible results and both have a probability of 0.5, then they are equally likely to occur—what we call a "50-50" chance.

The probability that an event will *not* occur—P(not A)—is equal to 1 minus the probability that it will occur: P(not A) = 1 – P(A).

The probability that an event *will* occur—P(A)—is equal to 1 minus the probability that it will not occur: P(A) = 1 – P(not A).

The probability that an event will occur plus the probability that it will not occur is 1: P(A) + P(not A) = 1. In other words, it is certain that either the event will occur or it will not!

Calculating Probabilities of Simple, Random Events. Simple, random events are those that are independent of one another and occur by chance. The classic example of a simple, random event is the flipping of a coin. What is the probability of getting heads when flipping a coin?

$$\text{probability of event A} = \frac{\text{number of favorable outcomes}}{\text{number of possible outcomes}}$$

To calculate the probability, we can use this formula:

$$P(A) = \frac{a}{a+b}$$

The letter A represents the event; *a* represents the number of possible **outcomes** that are favorable (getting heads), and *b* represents the number of possible outcomes that are unfavorable (not getting heads). For the coin toss, if A represents tossing heads, there are 2 possible outcomes, heads and tails. There is 1 possible favorable outcome and 1 possible unfavorable outcome. Therefore, the probability of A (getting heads) is $\frac{1}{1+1}$, which is $\frac{1}{2}$. This probability can be expressed as a fraction ($\frac{1}{2}$), as a ratio (1 : 2), as a decimal number (0.5), or as a percentage (50%). Probabilities are commonly expressed as percentages, as in the statement, "When you flip a coin, there is a 50% chance of getting heads."

A good way to find all the possible outcomes is to create a chart. For example, when you roll two number cubes, there are six possible outcomes for each cube. As shown in the chart below, there are 36 possible outcomes for the two cubes. What is the probability of rolling a total of 4? The favorable outcomes are shaded in the chart; the unfavorable outcomes are not.

	1	**2**	**3**	**4**	**5**	**6**
1	1,1	1,2	1,3	1,4	1,5	1,6
2	2,1	2,2	2,3	2,4	2,5	2,6
3	3,1	3,2	3,3	3,4	3,5	3,6
4	4,1	4,2	4,3	4,4	4,5	4,6
5	5,1	5,2	5,3	5,4	5,5	5,6
6	6,1	6,2	6,3	6,4	6,5	6,6

There are 3 favorable outcomes and 33 unfavorable outcomes, so the probability is $\frac{3}{3+33}$, or $\frac{3}{36}$, which is the same as $\frac{1}{12}$ or 0.083—a little over 8%.

Calculating Odds. Another way to express probabilities is as odds in favor or odds against. **Odds** are ratios of favorable outcomes to unfavorable outcomes, or vice versa.

$$\text{Odds in favor} = \frac{\text{number of favorable outcomes}}{\text{number of unfavorable outcomes}}$$

$$\text{Odds against} = \frac{\text{number of unfavorable outcomes}}{\text{number of favorable outcomes}}$$

For the number-cube example, the odds in favor are 3 to 33, which can be written in any of these ways:

- as words: three to thirty-three, which reduces to one to eleven
- as a ratio: $3:33$, which reduces to $1:11$
- as a fraction: $\frac{3}{33}$, which reduces to $\frac{1}{11}$

The odds against are 33 to 3, which can be written in any of these ways:

- as words: thirty-three to three, which reduces to eleven to one
- as a ratio: $33:3$, which reduces to $11:1$
- as a fraction: $\frac{33}{3}$, which reduces to $\frac{11}{1}$

Probabilities are most commonly expressed as percentages. Odds are most commonly expressed as ratios.

Meeting the Challenge

To answer the Challenge, you must find the number of possible outcomes, the number of favorable outcomes, and the number of unfavorable outcomes. Then, you must use the formulas to determine the probability and the odds in favor and against.

STEP 1: Determine the number of possible outcomes. There are 52 cards in a deck, so the number of possible outcomes is equal to 52.

STEP 2: Determine the number of favorable and unfavorable outcomes. For each suit in a deck of cards, there are 5 cards that are 10 or higher (10, jack, queen, king, and ace). There are four suits, so there are 5×4, or 20, possible favorable outcomes. The remaining outcomes are unfavorable $(52 - 20 = 32)$.

STEP 3: Calculate the probability of getting a 10 or higher.

$$\text{Probability} = \frac{\text{favorable outcomes}}{\text{total outcomes}} \qquad \frac{20}{52} = \frac{5}{13} \approx 0.38, \text{ or about } 38\%$$

STEP 4: Calculate the odds in favor.

$$\text{Odds in favor} = \frac{\text{favorable outcomes}}{\text{unfavorable outcomes}} \qquad 20:32, \text{ or } 5:8$$

STEP 5: Calculate the odds against.

$$\text{Odds against} = \frac{\text{unfavorable outcomes}}{\text{favorable outcomes}} \qquad 32:20, \text{ or } 8:5$$

The answer to the Challenge question is that Yolanda has offered her sister a bad deal. The probability that Charise will choose a card that is 10 or higher is only $\frac{5}{13}$, or about 0.38. The odds in favor are 5 to 8. The odds against are 8 to 5.

Another Way You know from the lesson that you can calculate the probability of an event A using the formula $P(A) = \frac{a}{a+b}$, where a is the number of favorable outcomes, and b is the number of unfavorable outcomes. You can also calculate this probability simply by dividing the number of favorable outcomes by the number of possible outcomes. This is because the number of possible outcomes equals the number of favorable outcomes plus the number of unfavorable outcomes.

Name________________________ Class __________ Date __________

Try It Yourself

5.6 Introduction to Probability and Odds Practice Exercises

A. Fill in the circle next to the correct answer to each multiple-choice question.

1. Which of the following expresses the probability that a single roll of a number cube with six faces will be an even number?

Ⓐ $\frac{1}{6}$ Ⓑ $\frac{1}{3}$ Ⓒ $\frac{1}{2}$ Ⓓ $\frac{2}{6}$

2. Which of the following expresses the odds in favor of rolling an even number with one number cube?

Ⓐ 1:2 Ⓑ 1:3 Ⓒ 1:1 Ⓓ 2:1

3. Which of the following expresses the odds against rolling an even number with one number cube?

Ⓐ 1:2 Ⓑ 1:3 Ⓒ 1:1 Ⓓ 2:1

B. Complete the two parts below.

A deck of cards has four suits: clubs (♣), diamonds (♦), hearts (♥), and spades (♠). Suppose you were to draw one card from each of two decks.

Part A Complete the following chart to show the set of all possible outcomes. The chart has been started for you.

	C♣	D♦	H♥	S♠
C♣	C, C	C, D		
D♦	D, C			
H♥				
S♠				

Part B Calculate the probabilities and odds below. Explain how you found each one.

Probability of drawing at least one diamond: ____________

Odds in favor of drawing at least one diamond: ____________

Odds against drawing at least one diamond: ____________

Try It Yourself

A. Fill in the circle next to the correct answer to each multiple-choice question.

1. Which of the following expresses the probability that one will draw a spade from a standard deck of 52 cards?

   Ⓐ $\frac{4}{52}$ Ⓑ $\frac{1}{13}$ Ⓒ $\frac{1}{4}$ Ⓓ $\frac{3}{26}$

2. What are the odds against drawing a spade from a standard 52-card deck?

   Ⓐ 4 : 1   Ⓑ 1 : 1   Ⓒ 3 : 1   Ⓓ 1 : 3

3. What are the odds in favor of drawing a queen or a 4 from a standard 52-card deck?

   Ⓐ 2 : 11   Ⓑ 11 : 2   Ⓒ 2 : 13   Ⓓ 13 : 2

B. Complete the two parts below.

A regular octahedron has eight sides. Suppose that you were to roll two regular octahedrons, each with the numbers 1–8 printed on its sides.

Part A Complete the following chart to show the set of all possible outcomes.

	1	2	3	4	5	6	7	8
1								
2								
3								
4								
5								
6								
7								
8								

Part B Calculate the probabilities and odds shown below. Explain how you found each one.

Probability of rolling a total of 6 or less: _____

Odds in favor of rolling a total of 6 or less: _____

Odds against rolling a total of 6 or less: _____

COUNTING STRATEGIES

This lesson addresses Benchmark MA.E.2.3.2 of the Sunshine State Standards.

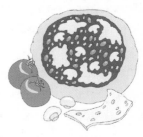

The Challenge

Kendra is making round and square pizzas for a party. She has three toppings—meat, peppers, and onions—and plans to put one topping on each pizza. How many different ways can she make a round or square pizza with one topping? What are they?

Learning the Ropes

In the previous lesson, you learned to find the probability of an event by making a chart showing all of the possible outcomes. You can also find possible outcomes by drawing diagrams, by using the counting principle, or by applying the formulas for permutations and combinations.

Diagrams. Look at the two spinners below. The first spinner has one white section and one blue section. The other spinner has four sections numbered 1, 2, 3, and 4. You can draw a **tree diagram** to find how many different ways you can get one color and one number on the spinners. The tree diagram shows the 8 possible outcomes of the spins.

Tree Diagram

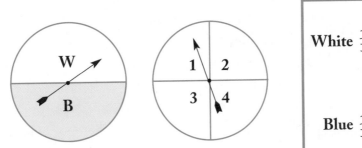

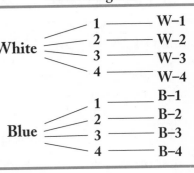

Another kind of diagram can be helpful in other situations. Suppose each player on your school golf team shakes hands with all of the other players on the team. If there are 4 players on the team—A, B, C, and D—how many handshakes are there? You might draw a diagram like the one to the right. The diagram shows that there are 6 handshakes altogether.

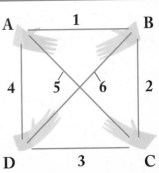

Math in Use: Designing and Scheduling   Permutations are used in many varied fields. Among the areas in which permutations are important are designing codes in cryptography, designing combination locks, producing workable schedules for large numbers of students and classes in schools, and creating automobile license plate numbers. They can even be used in designing stage and concert lighting.

Counting Principle. Sometimes you may need to find the number of possible outcomes when there are many choices involved. For example, suppose that you have 3 shirts, 4 pairs of pants, and 2 pairs of shoes. How many different outfits (each consisting of 1 shirt, 1 pair of pants, and 1 pair of shoes) can you make? It would take time to draw a diagram or to make a list or a chart. To find the number of different outfits quickly, you can use the **counting principle.** Just multiply the number of possibilities for each event.

(x choices of shirts) $\times$ (y choices of pants) $\times$ (z choices of shoes) = number of possible outcomes

    3 shirts $\times$ 4 pants $\times$ 2 pairs of shoes = $3 \times 4 \times 2 = 24$ outfits

Sometimes when one event happens, it reduces the number of choices for the next event. Suppose that a photographer is photographing a mother, a father, and a child for a family portrait. There are 3 places for the family members to sit. How many ways can the photographer arrange the three family members? He can choose any of the 3 people to sit in the first seat, but once he chooses 1 person, there are only 2 possibilities left for the second seat. By the time he comes to the last seat, there is only 1 person left. The equation that gives the total number of possible arrangements looks like this:

1st seat   2nd seat   3rd seat

3 choices $\times$ 2 choices $\times$ 1 choice = 6 possible arrangements

A short way to express the product $3 \times 2 \times 1$ is to use the use the **factorial** symbol (!). The product $3 \times 2 \times 1$ can be written as 3!, or "three factorial." The expression $n!$ means to multiply all integers from n down to 1.

Permutations. Sometimes the order or arrangement of items or events is important when making choices. A **permutation** is an arrangement in which order is important. In the example above, each different arrangement of the three family members is a permutation.

You can use the counting principle to *count* the number of permutations, or different ways to arrange the people ($3 \times 2 \times 1 = 3! = 6$).

If you want to *identify* all the possible arrangements, you can make an organized list or a tree diagram.

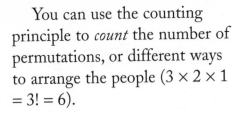

Organized List

1. mother, father, child
2. mother, child, father
3. father, mother, child
4. father, child, mother
5. child, mother, father
6. child, father, mother

Tree Diagram

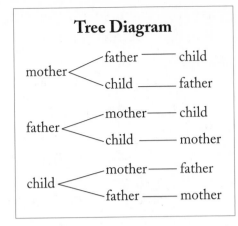

The expression $_3P_3$ represents the number of permutations for 3 people placed in 3 positions. Any set of permutations can be represented by the expression $_nP_r$, where n tells how many choices are available, P stands for permutation, and r tells how many places need to be filled. The expression $_nP_r$ is read "the permutations of n items taken r at a time." The number of permutations is calculated by dividing $n!$ by $(n - r)!$

To find how many ways 2 people out of 6 can line up for a photo, you need to find $_6P_2$.

$$_6P_2 = \frac{6!}{(6-2)!} = \frac{6 \times 5 \times 4 \times 3 \times 2 \times 1}{4 \times 3 \times 2 \times 1} = 6 \times 5 = 30$$

There are 30 permutations, that is, 30 ways to arrange 2 out of 6 people for a photo.

Combinations. Sometimes order is *not* important when you are choosing a number of items. A **combination** is an arrangement in which order is not important. Suppose a photographer wants to know how many different groups of 2 he can form out of 6 family members. The chart below shows all the ways that 2 out of 6 family members could line up.

In this case, however, you only need to find all the *different* groups of 2 family members, without regard to the order in which they are arranged. A choice in which the mother is on the left and the father is on the right (AB) is the same as one in which the father is on the left and the mother is on the right (BA). Therefore, the extra (duplicate) two-person groups are crossed out in the chart.

AB	AC	AD	AE	AF
BA	BC	BD	BE	BF
CA	CB	CD	CE	CF
DA	DB	DC	DE	DF
EA	EB	EC	ED	EF
FA	FB	FC	FD	FE

The expression $_6C_2$ represents the number of possible two-person combinations that can be formed from 6 family members. In order to eliminate the duplicate two-person groups, you need to divide the number of different ways 2 out of 6 people can line up for a photo ($_6P_2$) by the number of ways 2 family members at a time can be arranged ($2!$).

$$_6C_2 = \frac{_6P_2}{2!} = \frac{6 \times 5}{2 \times 1} = \frac{30}{2} = 15$$

Thus, fifteen two-person combinations are possible.

Another example of a problem that can be solved by finding the number of combinations is setting up a tournament in which each team plays every other team once.

EXAMPLE   Kevin is organizing a volleyball tournament in which each of 7 teams will play every other team exactly once. How many games will be played?

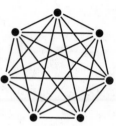

The diagram to the right represents this problem. Each point represents 1 of the 7 teams. Each line segment connecting 2 points represents 1 game. To find the number of line segments in the diagram, find the number of ways in which 2 points out of 7 can be chosen. Keep in mind that the order of the 2 points does not matter; they represent the same pair or combination of points!

$$_7C_2 = \frac{_7P_2}{2!} = \frac{7 \times 6}{2 \times 1} = \frac{42}{2} = 21$$

In this case, 21 games would be needed in order for each of 7 teams to play each other team once.

Meeting the Challenge

To answer the Challenge, first use the counting principle to find the number of possible ways to combine a shape and a topping. Then make a tree diagram to identify each possibility.

STEP 1:   To find the total number of possibilities, multiply the number of choices for the shape of the pizza by the number of choices of topping.

(2 choices of shape) × (3 choices of topping) = 6 possibilities

STEP 2:   Draw a tree diagram. Match each shape with each topping and list the possible combinations: R–M, R–P, R–O, S–M, S–P, S–O.

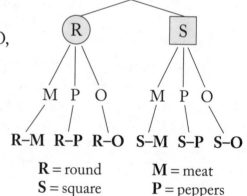

R = round
S = square

M = meat
P = peppers
O = onions

Another Way You can use the counting principle to find the number of ways you can arrange two people from six. To eliminate arrangements that are the same, divide by the number of ways you can arrange two people. For example, there are 6 × 5 = 30 ways to arrange two people from six people. There are 2 × 1 = 2 ways to arrange two people. Since $\frac{30}{2} = 15$, there are fifteen ways to choose two people from six.

Name________________________ Class __________ Date __________

Try It Yourself

5.7 Counting Strategies
Practice Exercises

A. Fill in the circle next to the correct answer to each multiple-choice question.

1. Which situation describes a permutation?
   - Ⓐ selecting 3 of 11 items at a salad bar
   - Ⓑ picking 3 children from a group of 10 to join the music club
   - Ⓒ arranging 4 people to line up for a family picture
   - Ⓓ packing 4 books in a box from a group of 15 books

2. You decide to pin the photos of 6 friends in a row on a bulletin board. In how many ways can you arrange the photos?
   - Ⓐ 6 Ⓑ 120 Ⓒ 360 Ⓓ 720

3. In how many different ways can 5 people line up at theater ticket window?
   - Ⓐ 5 Ⓑ 20 Ⓒ 80 Ⓓ 120

B. Complete the two parts below. Use additional paper if necessary.

The partially completed tree diagram below shows possible take-out lunch combinations.

Sandwich	Sides	Combination
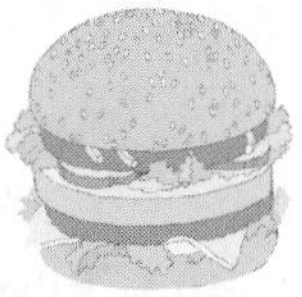 Burger	Fries	________
	Coleslaw	________
	Applesauce	________
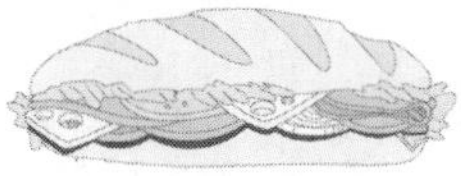 Chicken	________	________
	________	________
	________	________

Part A Complete the tree diagram.

Part B How many combinations are possible? If hot dogs were added to the sandwich choices, how would that change the number of lunch combinations? Explain your answer.

Try It Yourself

A. Fill in the circle next to the correct answer to each multiple-choice question.

1. Which situation describes a combination?
   - Ⓐ choosing 2 students from a class of 30 students to win an award
   - Ⓑ arranging 9 books on a shelf
   - Ⓒ selecting a president and vice president from 20 club members
   - Ⓓ finding all the ways to put 5 team members in 3 different positions

2. You are going to paint your room and add a wallpaper border. You have narrowed your choices down to 4 colors of paint and 3 different borders. How many different combinations of paint and border are possible?
   - Ⓐ 7
   - Ⓑ 12
   - Ⓒ 14
   - Ⓓ 64

3. How many numbers with one to four digits can you make with the digits 0, 1, 2, 3, 4, 5, 6, 7, 8, and 9? Digits may be used more than once. (Hint: There are 4 places for digits and 10 possibilities for each place).
   - Ⓐ 10^4
   - Ⓑ 9^4
   - Ⓒ 10^3
   - Ⓓ $9 \times 8 \times 7 \times 6$

4. A baseball coach is deciding on the batting order for his team. Which expression shows how many ways there are to order 9 players?
   - Ⓐ 9^9
   - Ⓑ $9!$
   - Ⓒ 9^2
   - Ⓓ 2^9

B. Complete the two parts below. Show all your work.

You are wrapping gifts for your friends. You have 5 wrapping-paper designs, 8 colors of ribbon, and 4 types of tags to choose from. You want to find out how many unique ways you could wrap the gifts.

Part A Would a tree diagram be a good way to solve this problem? Why or why not?

Part B What other method could you use that would be faster? Use this method to determine the number of different ways you could wrap the gifts.

Name________________________ Class __________ Date __________

Extended-Response Question Practice

Unit 5

1. For extra credit in health class, Maya agreed to collect information about the weight of her classmates' backpacks and to report her data in to the school nurse. She was supposed to gather the data from all 18 students in her homeroom class, but she did not allow herself enough time to weigh all the backpacks before the first period of classes began. Maya could collect data only for the first 9 students, who are listed in the chart below.

Student	Backpack Weight
Shanice	15 lb
Jenna	17 lb
Kayla	12 lb
Dolores	20 lb
Rebecca	10 lb
Ja'Lisa	18 lb
Marta	20 lb
Soon-yi	12 lb
Maya	8 lb

Part A Calculate the mean, median, mode, and range of the data. Show your work.

Part B Which technique would be most effective for displaying the data—a circle graph, a scatter plot, or a stem-and-leaf plot? Explain your answer, and then create that graph or plot on your own paper, using Maya's data.

Part C Is Maya's sample of her science class likely to provide a good representation of the whole class? Why or why not? If you were gathering the data, what might you do differently?

✔ If you have trouble with this problem, review the following lessons:
5.1, "Data Collection: Sampling"
5.2, "Displaying Data: Simple Graphs"
5.3, "Displaying Data: Line Graphs and Scatter Plots"
5.4, "Displaying Data: Histograms and Related Graphs"
5.5, "Central Tendencies and Box-and-Whisker Plots"

Unit 5

2. A new family with 4 children is moving into the house next door. You do not know yet how many are boys and how many are girls, but you have heard that 1 of the children is in high school, 2 are in middle school, and 1 is in elementary school.

   Part A How many different orders of boys and girls are possible? Calculate the number of possible arrangements. Name each one.

   Part B Assuming that boys and girls are equally likely to be born, what is the probability that the family next door will have a boy in middle school? Explain how you found your answer.

   Part C What is the probability that there will be only 1 girl in the family? Explain how you found your answer.

✔ If you have trouble with this problem, review the following lessons:
  5.6, "Introduction to Probability and Odds"
  5.7, "Counting Strategies"

Extended-Response Question Practice: Cumulative Review

For extended-response questions, you have to think through a problem logically, work through it step by step to find the answer(s), and communicate in writing your understanding of the process. These skills are very important, not only for math exams but also for solving problems in real-life situations.

In this section, you will find five extended-response problems. Although these problems are very challenging, all of them can be solved using the skills you have learned in this book. Each problem will make you think, but if you think hard enough and work through the problem one step at a time, you will be able to solve it.

These extended-response problems test many of your math skills, but each problem in this review section focuses on one major content area, corresponding to one of the five units of this book. If you have trouble with any of the questions, go back to the appropriate lessons in those units. (The lessons that cover the skills you need are indicated at the end of each problem.) Reread the instruction in Learning the Ropes. Go through the steps of answering the Challenge problem. Make sure that you understand each step before you move on to the next. If you do not understand any of the math terms used in a problem, look them up in the Glossary at the back of this book.

For each response, make sure that you

- show all your work in solving the problem.
- clearly label your answers.
- tell why you took the steps you did to solve the problem.
- write as clearly as you can.

Unit 1

1. For this problem, your challenge is to use five 3s to create expressions equal to each of the whole numbers from 1 to 12. Each expression should include exactly five 3s, used as integers, decimals, numerators, denominators, and/or exponents. You may use any combination of the four basic operations ($+$, $-$, $\times$, $\div$), in any order. You may also use powers, radicals, and factorials.

As you work on this problem, remember the properties of numbers and the identity elements for addition and multiplication. Think about the rules for exponents and roots. Remember that the factorial sign after a number means to multiply the number by each whole number less than the number. Follow the rules for the order of operations, and use parentheses to group numbers within the expressions as necessary.

There are many different ways to create the whole numbers from 1 to 12. Some examples are given below to get you started. Study the examples to get ideas about how to create the numbers. Then, on your own paper, write an expression for each whole number from 1 to 12.

EXAMPLES

$1 = 3^{3-3} + 3 - 3$

$2 = \dfrac{33}{3} - (3 \times 3)$

$3 = \dfrac{3^3}{3 \times \sqrt{3} \times \sqrt{3}}$

✔ If you have trouble with this problem, review the following lessons:
  1.4, "Fractions, Ratios, and Proportions"
  1.5, "Decimals and Percents"
  1.6, "Exponents and Radicals"
  1.9, "Properties and Identities"
  1.10, "Performing Operations"

2. You are canoeing on a river with a friend. You start at point A and paddle upstream against the current. It takes you 1 hour to get to point B, which is 2 miles away. Coming back, you paddle just as hard as you did going upstream. With the current pushing you, it takes you only 20 minutes to get back to point A.

> distance = rate × time
>
> rate = distance ÷ time
>
> time = distance ÷ rate

Part A How long would it take to drift with the current from point B back to point A? That is, what is the rate of the current alone? Use the information in the box below, and explain the steps you take to find your answer.

> Hints: First find your speed going upstream and your speed going downstream, in miles per hour.
>
> Your speed going *upstream* is your own rate of paddling (r_p) minus the rate of the current (r_c): $r_p - r_c$
>
> Your speed going *downstream* is your own rate of paddling (r_p) plus the rate of the current (r_c): $r_p + r_c$

Part B How long would it take you to paddle from point A to point B if there were no current? Show your work.

✔ If you have trouble with this problem, review the following lessons:
   2.1, "Variables, Expressions, and Equations"
   2.3, "Solving Equations with One Variable"
   2.4, "Solving Equations with Two Variables"
See also Lesson 4.10, "Measuring Rate and Velocity."

3. You have a square wooden box in which you want to store cylindrical metal canisters. Each canister is 8 inches in diameter. Two canisters will just fit in the box diagonally, as shown in the diagram below.

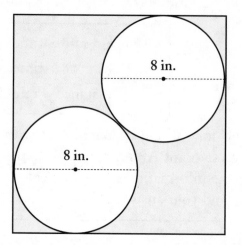

Draw a diagonal of the square. Calculate its length. Explain how you found your answer.

If you have trouble with this problem, review the following lessons:
3.2, "Two- and Three-Dimensional Shapes"
3.4, "The Pythagorean Theorem"
See also Lesson 4.4, "Measuring Length, Perimeter, and Circumference."

4. Gina is making a quilt out of squares cut from old T-shirts. She
   needs to cut out squares of backing material to iron onto the
   T-shirt material to make it stiffer. She has a roll of backing material
   that is 22 inches wide. She is going to cut out 14-inch squares and
   8-inch squares. She is going to cut out the smaller squares next to
   the larger squares, as shown in the diagram below.

   Unit 4

   Part A How many squares of each size can Gina cut from the
   backing material so that the bottom edges of the squares will line
   up exactly? Explain how you found your answer.

   Part B When Gina sews the pieces together, the larger ones will be
   12 inches on a side (to allow for the seams), and the smaller ones
   will be 6 inches on a side. Gina
   wants her quilt to be 8 feet long and
   5 feet wide. She is planning to have
   the same number of 6-inch squares
   and 12-inch squares. How many of
   each size does she need? Explain
   how you found your answer.

   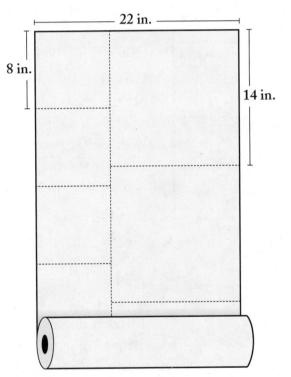

   Part C On your own paper, draw a
   rectangle to represent Gina's quilt.
   Set the scale of your drawing to be
   1 inch = 1 foot. Using a straight-
   edge, show how you could make a
   symmetrical pattern for the quilt
   using the same number of 12-inch
   and 6-inch squares. Draw the line(s)
   of symmetry.

✔ If you have trouble with this problem, review the following lessons:
   4.5, "Measuring Area"
   4.8, "Effects of Changing Dimensions"
See also the following lessons:
   1.4, "Fractions, Ratios, and Proportions"
   2.4, "Solving Equations with Two Variables"
   3.3, "Symmetry, Similarity, and Transformations"

Unit 5

5. The town officials of Lilyfield conducted a study to find out more about their community and its needs. To present their findings to the community, they prepared graphs showing different characteristics of the town.

Part A Which of the following would be the best way to display changes in the town's population over the last ten years: a line graph, a bar graph, or a circle graph? Explain your answer.

Part B Which of the following would be the best way to show how much money is spent on the items in the town's budget: a scatter plot, a circle graph, or a line graph? Explain your answer.

Part C The chart to the left shows the number of households of each size in the community. Why is a bar graph a better way to show this information than a line graph or a scatter plot? What household size is the mode in Lilyfield?

Number of Persons per Household	Number of Households
1	266
2	512
3	824
4	937
5	493
6	124
7+	109

Part D Here are the prices of homes sold in one Lilyfield neighborhood during the past year: $185,000, $142,000, $140,000, $131,000, $159,000, $215,000, $179,000, $128,000, and $204,000. What is the mean price of these homes? What is the median price? What is the range? Is this sample necessarily representative of the house prices in the whole town? Explain why or why not.

Part E At the town budget meeting, the voters have to decide whether or not to spend the money to do three projects: repair the town's swimming pool, install streetlights in a new neighborhood, and build a new train depot. They could choose to do all three projects, none of them, or any combination of them. How many different possibilities must the voters consider? Let P represent the swimming pool, L the streetlights, and D the depot. Show all the possibilities that the voters might choose.

✔ If you have trouble with this problem, review the following lessons:
    5.1, "Data Collection: Sampling"
    5.2, "Displaying Data: Simple Graphs"
    5.3, "Displaying Data: Line Graphs and Scatter Plots"
    5.4, "Displaying Data: Histograms and Related Graphs"
    5.5, "Central Tendencies and Box-and-Whisker Plots"
    5.6, "Introduction to Probability and Odds"
    5.7, "Counting Strategies"

Mathematics Posttest

On pages 282–310, you will find a practice test with 55 questions. Taking this test will show how much you have learned since you took the Pretest. To help you answer the questions, you may use a calculator and the Mathematics Reference Sheet on page 311.

This test contains four types of question. For multiple-choice questions, choose the **best** answer and fill in the bubble next to that answer. Give yourself about a minute to answer each multiple-choice question. Those questions are worth 1 point each. Other questions include a grid where you should record your answer. Short-response and extended-response questions require you to write your own answers.

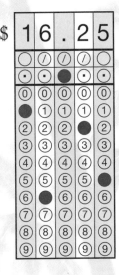

For gridded-responses, write your answer in the spaces at the top of the grid. Then fill in the correct bubble in each column. You can grid whole numbers up to five digits. When you grid fractions, use the slash symbol as the fraction bar between the numerator and the denominator. You can also grid decimals by putting a decimal point in the right position. If an answer should be a percent, there will be a percent sign after the grid. If an answer should be in dollars and cents, there will be a dollar sign before the grid. The example to the left shows how to grid the answer "$16.25." Allow a minute and a half to answer each gridded-response question. Those questions are worth 1 point each.

Extended Response

This symbol appears next to questions that require long answers. Allow 5–15 minutes to answer each of these questions. They are worth 4 points each.

Short Response

This symbol appears next to questions that require short answers. Allow 3–5 minutes to answer each of these questions. They are worth 2 points each.

Read each question carefully. Be sure to fill in each bubble correctly. Reread your short and long answers to be sure that they make sense.

MATHEMATICS POSTTEST

Directions: There are 55 questions on this test. Read each problem carefully. Think about ways to solve the problem before you try to answer each question. Then write or mark your answers in the book.

1. What can you do to the figure on the left to make it look like the figure on the right?

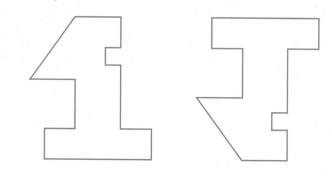

Ⓐ turn

Ⓑ slide and turn

Ⓒ flip and turn

Ⓓ slide

2. Which equation shows what operations you must perform on *x* to get *y*?

Ⓐ $x - 5 = y$

Ⓑ $\frac{1}{2}x + 1 = y$

Ⓒ $3x - 3 = y$

Ⓓ $\frac{1}{3}x + 1 = y$

x	y
9	4
45	16
63	22
360	121

3. Susan gives Aaron a math riddle: "I am thinking of a number that can be multiplied by $\sqrt{3}$ to get 6." What is Susan's number?

   Ⓐ $2\sqrt{2}$

   Ⓑ $3\sqrt{2}$

   Ⓒ $2\sqrt{3}$

   Ⓓ $2\sqrt{6}$

4. Niagara Falls is 55 meters high. Angel Falls, the highest waterfall in the world, is 44 meters higher than 17 times the height of Niagara Falls. Which equation shows the height of Angel Falls? (Use x for the unknown height of Angel Falls.)

   Ⓐ $x - 44 = 17 \times 55$

   Ⓑ $17x - 44 = 55$

   Ⓒ $x + 44 = 55 \times 17$

   Ⓓ $55x + 44 = 17$

5. If the height of a triangle were quadrupled, what would happen to the area?

Ⓐ The area would be twice as big as before.

Ⓑ The area would be four times bigger than before.

Ⓒ The area would be eight times bigger than before.

Ⓓ The area would be sixteen times bigger than before.

6. Tania, owner of Tania's Gift Shop, prepares a graph showing the sales of dolls for six consecutive years. What is the percent of decrease in sales from 2000 to 2001?

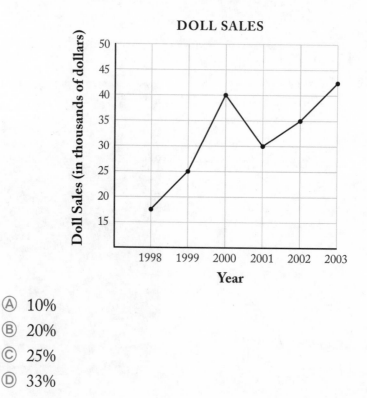

DOLL SALES

Ⓐ 10%

Ⓑ 20%

Ⓒ 25%

Ⓓ 33%

7. Amira is painting the top, bottom, and all four sides of a box that has a length of 3 feet, a width of 2 feet, and a height of 1 foot. How much area, in square feet, must she cover with paint?

8. After playing a board game, Jelena had x points and Miki had y points. The following equation compares the players' points:

$y = \frac{2}{3}x + 7$

If Miki earned 79 points, how many points did Jelena earn?

Ⓐ 48

Ⓑ $59\frac{2}{3}$

Ⓒ $86\frac{2}{3}$

Ⓓ 108

9. Ki-young learned that one of the largest elephants ever recorded stood a dizzying 150 inches high. She wants to know the measurement in feet. How many feet high was the elephant?

Ⓐ 0.8 feet

Ⓑ 1.2 feet

Ⓒ 12.5 feet

Ⓓ 47.7 feet

10. Nick is planning a party and wants to find out what kind of ice cream his friends like most. For her health class, Miko needs to calculate the average height of her classmates. Coach Stefan is forming the varsity and junior varsity swim teams. Half of the athletes will be placed on the varsity team and half on the junior varsity team, according to their times in the tryout race.

Extended Response

Part A Explain the measure of central tendency that Nick should use to meet his need and what he should do to calculate the central tendency.

Part B Explain the measure of central tendency that Miko should use to meet her need and what she should do to calculate the central tendency.

Part C Explain the measure of central tendency that Coach Stefan should use to meet his need and what he should do to calculate the central tendency.

11. Miguel measures the perimeter of a room in poxies, blips, and gurkles. One gurkle equals 7 blips, and 1 blip equals 3 poxies. He finds that the perimeter is 3 gurkles and 5 blips. How many poxies is that?

12. What is the equation for the line in the graph below?

Ⓐ $y = \frac{1}{2}x - 6$

Ⓑ $y = 2x + 6$

Ⓒ $y = \frac{1}{2}x + 3$

Ⓓ $y = 2x + 3$

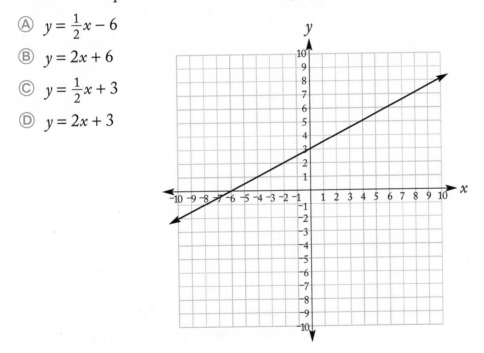

13. The students in Mr. Weinstein's class have to vote on whom they are going to send to a contest, Jorge or Marika. Marika and her friends in the class are unable to vote because of a water polo game that is scheduled the same day as the vote. Why should Mr. Weinstein reschedule the vote?

Ⓐ The vote might be biased toward Jorge.

Ⓑ There definitely would be a tie between Jorge and Marika.

Ⓒ There would not be enough people to vote.

Ⓓ The sampling technique would be too random.

14. In the picture below, what is the value of x?

Ⓐ 22°

Ⓑ 92°

Ⓒ 24°

Ⓓ 67°

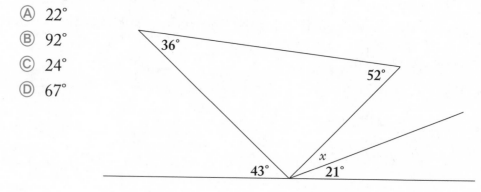

15. The students at Memorial Middle School sold magazines to raise money. The sixth graders sold $8,741 worth of subscriptions. The seventh graders sold $9,810. The eighth graders sold $7,195. Round each number to the nearest thousand dollars and estimate how many dollars worth of subscriptions were sold by all three grades.

Ⓐ $ 3,000

Ⓑ $17,000

Ⓒ $26,000

Ⓓ $30,000

16. The Richter scale measures the size of seismic waves produced during an earthquake. The scale is logarithmic, which means that a number on the scale is 10 times as big as the previous number. An earthquake of magnitude 7 has seismic waves 10 times as large as an earthquake of magnitude 6, and 100 times as large as an earthquake of magnitude 5. How much larger are the seismic waves of a quake of magnitude 7 than a quake of magnitude 2?

Ⓐ   1,000 times

Ⓑ   10,000 times

Ⓒ   100,000 times

Ⓓ 1,000,000 times

17. What is the sum of the interior angles of the stop sign?

Ⓐ   180°

Ⓑ   360°

Ⓒ   720°

Ⓓ 1,080°

18. When you pedal your bike, you move forward 6 feet, $6\frac{1}{2}$ inches every time the wheels go all the way around. What is each wheel's diameter in inches? Use 3.14 as an approximation of π.

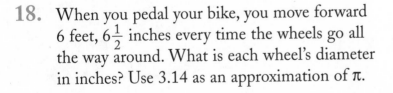

19. All 6 people in the Perkins family enter their names in a drawing. Altogether, 150 people have entered their names. What are the **odds against** someone in the Perkins family winning the drawing?

    Ⓐ 24 to 1

    Ⓑ 25 to 1

    Ⓒ 25 to 24

    Ⓓ   6 to 25

20. To keep a fence from falling down, a farmer ties a rope to the top of the fence and nails it to the ground. If the fence is 4 feet tall and the rope is 8 feet long, what is the distance from the nail to the fence? Round your answer to the nearest foot.

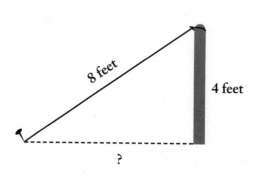

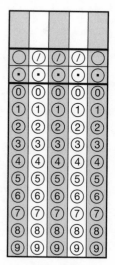

21. Georgette and Olufemi buy large juice containers so they can bring punch to a school dance. Georgette's container is rectangular, while Olufemi's is cylindrical.

Whose container can hold more punch? Find the volume of each container, using 3.14 as an approximation of π.

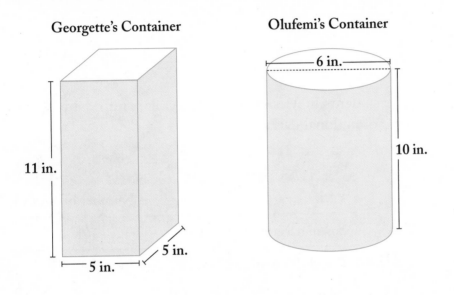

Georgette's Container   Olufemi's Container

11 in.   6 in.

5 in.   10 in.

5 in.

22. What value of *x* will make both of these equations true?

$2x + 3y = 41$
$-2x + y = 11$

23. Which of the following numbers is irrational?

  Ⓐ 33.3$\overline{3}$

  Ⓑ 0.981

  Ⓒ π

  Ⓓ -5

24. The students in Mrs. Wong's class collect information about the sizes of national parks.

SIZES OF NATIONAL PARKS	
Park	**Number of Acres**
Yosemite National Park, CA	761,266
Everglades National Park, FL	1,399,078
Yellowstone National Park, WY	2,219,790
Grand Canyon National Park, AZ	1,218,375
Mount Rainier National Park, WA	235,625

Round each number to the nearest hundred thousand. Which of the following is the best estimate of the mean area, in acres?

  Ⓐ 1,600,000

  Ⓑ 1,200,000

  Ⓒ 800,000

  Ⓓ 200,000

25. Marguerite studies a map that has a scale of $1\frac{1}{2}$ inches to 7 miles.
She finds that the nearest gas station is half an inch away from her
location on the map. How far away is it, in miles?

(A) $1\frac{3}{5}$ miles

(B) $2\frac{1}{3}$ miles

(C) $3\frac{1}{2}$ miles

(D) 21 miles

26. The basketball coaches create a diagram
of the new court that the school is
building. They want to paint the
shaded area with the school's colors.

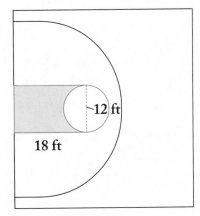

Short Response

Write and solve an equation you can use to find the area of the
shaded portion. Use 3.14 as an approximation of π, and give your
answer to the nearest square foot.

27. Kyra has *d* dollar bills, *q* quarters, and *p* pennies. Which equation shows how many dollars (*D*) she has?

    Ⓐ $D = 100d + 25q + p$

    Ⓑ $D = d + 25q + 100p$

    Ⓒ $D = d + 0.25q + 0.01p$

    Ⓓ $D = 100d + 0.25q + 100p$

28. Angela's track and field coach told her to walk 2 laps around the track, sprint 50 yards, and jog 2.5 miles. Each lap is 440 yards. By the end of practice, how many **feet** did Angela go?

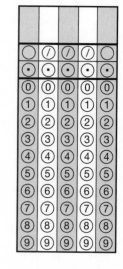

29. A quality assurance tester inspects 400 bulbs at random out of 48,000 bulbs. She finds that 5 of the 400 bulbs are defective. If she checked the entire batch of 48,000 bulbs, about how many defective bulbs would you expect her to find?

30. Which of the following properties does this equation reflect?

$x^2(y + z) = x^2y + x^2z$

Ⓐ associative

Ⓑ additive

Ⓒ commutative

Ⓓ distributive

31. How can you solve this equation for *y*?

$2 + y = {}^-3$

Ⓐ Subtract 2 from both sides.

Ⓑ Subtract 3 from both sides.

Ⓒ Add 2 to both sides.

Ⓓ Add 3 to both sides.

32.

Extended Response

The students of Evergreen Middle School want to start a bus route that leaves later in the day. Students who have rehearsals or sports practices after school can use this bus to go home. The students voted on what time the bus should leave the school, and the results are shown in the chart below.

Time	Number of Students
3:30	71
4:00	118
4:30	92
5:00	56
5:30	39

Part A On the grid below, create a bar graph for the data in the chart. Remember to label both axes of your graph and to give it a title.

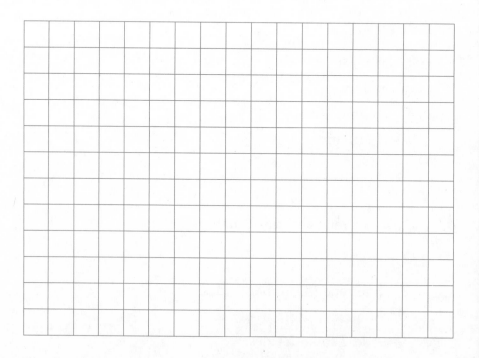

Part B On the grid below, create a line graph for the data in the chart. Remember to label both axes of your graph and to give it a title.

Part C Explain why a bar graph is better than a line graph to show the results of the vote.

 297

33. In rush-hour traffic, Mr. Nauman drove 40 miles at an average speed of only 30 miles per hour. How long did it take him to go 40 miles?

Ⓐ 133 minutes

Ⓑ 120 minutes

Ⓒ 1 hour, 33 minutes

Ⓓ 1 hour, 20 minutes

34. Crop circles are geometric designs that have appeared in large fields in various parts of the world. The origins of these strange designs are unclear. The diagram below illustrates part of a symmetrical crop formation found in England. If the diameter of the circle is 64 feet, what is the length of one side of the square?

Ⓐ 32 feet

Ⓑ $32\sqrt{2}$ feet

Ⓒ 64 feet

Ⓓ $64\sqrt{2}$ feet

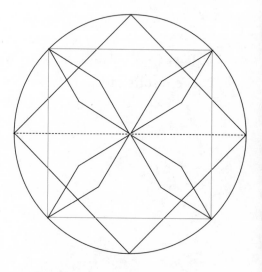

35. Dion is starting a new job at the local bookstore. He will work 20 hours per week and will get paid $8.00 per hour. He plans to put 10% of his paycheck each week into a savings account he just opened. At the end of every 4 weeks, his mom promises to add another 15% to the money he has saved. Calculate how much money Dion will have in his savings account at the end of 4 weeks (after his mom puts in the extra money).

36. Ms. Tilssen flips a coin 6 times and she gets heads 6 times. She says that if she flips the coin another 6 times, she is sure that she will get tails 6 times. Explain what is wrong with her logic. Tell the probability that she will get tails the next six times in a row.

37. In the graph below, point *A* is located at (0, ⁻3), and point *B* is located at (⁻9, ⁻6).

Short Response

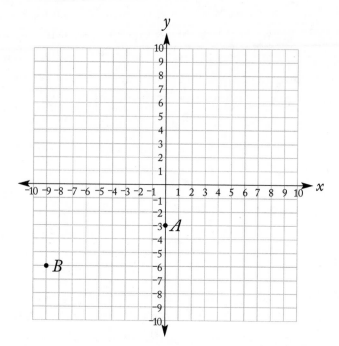

Draw a line that passes through points *A* and *B*. Write an equation that represents the line.

Name________________________ Class __________ Date __________

38. Alice, Bernice, and Carlos's grandfather bakes cookies. Alice takes one-third of the cookies on the plate. Bernice takes one-third of the cookies left over after Alice takes her cookies. Carlos then takes one-third of the cookies that remain. After all the grandchildren have taken their cookies, there are 8 cookies left. How many cookies were originally on the plate?

Ⓐ 45

Ⓑ 36

Ⓒ 30

Ⓓ 27

39. Haruki's scores on 4 math quizzes were 89, 82, 91, and 90, for an average score of 88. What score does he need on the next quiz in order to raise his average for the 5 quizzes to 90?

Ⓐ 92

Ⓑ 94

Ⓒ 96

Ⓓ 98

40. Elvin's lacrosse team won 4 times as many games as they lost. (There were no ties.) What percentage of their games did they win?

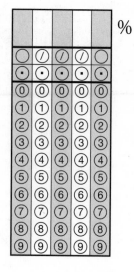

%

41. Find the area of the shaded region of the circle below if the circumference of the large circle equals 16π.

Ⓐ 8π

Ⓑ 16π

Ⓒ 32π

Ⓓ 64π

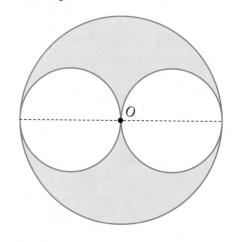

42. The shapes on each side of the first two scales are equal in weight. What shapes are needed on the right side of the third scale to balance it?

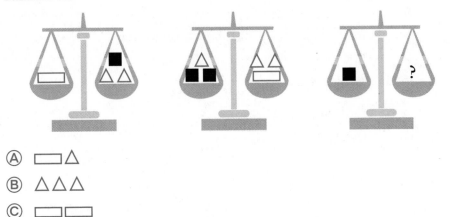

Ⓐ ▭ △

Ⓑ △ △ △

Ⓒ ▭ ▭

Ⓓ ▭ ■ △

43. When $x = 3$, what is the value of the expression below?

$4(x^2 + 5) - 7$

44. A study by the American Heart Association finds that 1 out of 5 Americans suffers from high blood pressure. The U.S. Census Bureau estimates that there are 15,100,000 people living in Florida. According to the statistic, which is a good estimate of how many people in Florida have high blood pressure?

　Ⓐ　　300,000

　Ⓑ　　600,000

　Ⓒ　3,000,000

　Ⓓ　76,000,000

45. In the figure below, triangle *ABC* is an equilateral triangle and triangle *ADC* is an isosceles triangle.

Short Response

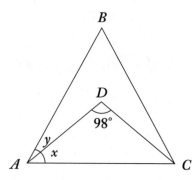

Calculate the measure of angle *x* and the measure of angle *y*.

46. Because so many townspeople were buying scooters from the Joy of Toys, the manager of the store decided to increase the price. Originally the store was selling the scooter for $80. The manager increased the price to $100. What is the percent of change of the scooter's price?

Ⓐ 20%

Ⓑ 25%

Ⓒ 40%

Ⓓ 50%

47. What is the 30th number in the number sequence below?

Position	1st	2nd	3rd	4th	5th	6th
Number	8	11	14	17	20	23

Ⓐ 33

Ⓑ 72

Ⓒ 92

Ⓓ 95

48. Domingo and Ursula are wrapping gifts to give to their grandfather. Domingo wants to wrap two tins full of cookies. Ursula wants to wrap a box containing a sweater.

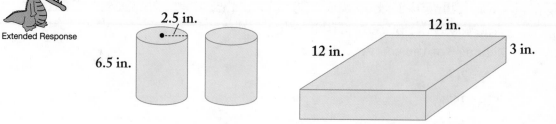

Extended Response

Part A What is the least amount of wrapping paper that Domingo needs to wrap his gift? Use 3.14 as an approximation of π.

Part B What is the least amount of wrapping paper that Ursula needs to wrap her gift?

Part C Domingo wraps his gift first and a piece of wrapping paper that is 4 square feet is left over. Explain why or why not the piece of paper is big enough to wrap Ursula's gift if she allows an extra 1 square foot for overlap.

49. Elyse and Ramiro are using flash cards to form sentences. Each card has one word on it. Each word belongs to one of five categories. The table below shows the categories and the words in each category.

Article	Adjective	Noun	Verb	Adverb
The	big	cow	hopped	happily.
A	strong	woman	barked	loudly.
	beautiful	robot	laughed	
		prince		

Elyse and Ramiro must choose one word from each category and combine them to make a sentence. How many different sentences can they make?

Ⓐ   4

Ⓑ   14

Ⓒ   24

Ⓓ 144

50. Lewis mixed 12 grams of a solid substance with 10 milliliters of water to make 15 milliliters of a chemical solution. How much solid substance and water must be mixed to make 240 milliliters of the chemical solution?

Ⓐ 192 g of solid substance and 160 mL of water

Ⓑ 160 g of solid substance and 192 mL of water

Ⓒ 120 g of solid substance and 100 mL of water

Ⓓ 240 g of solid substance and 160 mL of water

51. At the store, Diane can buy 4 tubes of Smile Right toothpaste for $7.68, or 6 tubes for $10.14. How much does she save per tube by buying the 6-pack of toothpaste?

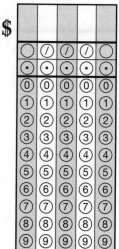

52. Justina has scored a total of 63 points in the last 7 basketball games. She wants to get enough points in the next game so that her average is 10 points per game. Which equation shows how many points she needs to score in the eighth game (x)?

Ⓐ $(63 + x) \div 8 = 10$

Ⓑ $(63 \div 8) + x = 10$

Ⓒ $63 \div 8 = x$

Ⓓ $63 \div x = 10$

53. Pieter goes to a carnival to play games. The first game has 48 red bowls and 8 blue bowls. If he sinks a ball into a blue bowl, he wins a goldfish. In the second game there are eight cups. Underneath one cup there is a marble. If he picks the cup with the marble, he wins a bag of marbles.

Tell which game he would be more likely to win. Explain your answer.

54. Tao makes a graph showing data about his radio-controlled car. Which of the following statements is true about the movement of his car?

MOVEMENT OF TAO'S RADIO-CONTROLLED CAR

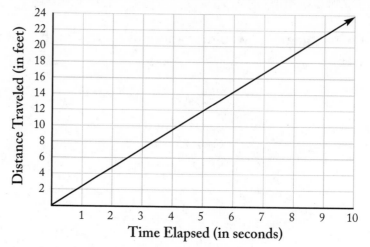

Ⓐ The car is moving at a constant speed.

Ⓑ The car is speeding up.

Ⓒ The car is slowing down.

Ⓓ The car travels a yard every 4 seconds.

55. Rebecca's tennis club membership costs $600 a year. It costs members $10 to rent a court. It costs nonmembers $30 to rent a court. To justify having a membership, Rebecca should play at least how many times per year?

Ⓐ 15

Ⓑ 20

Ⓒ 30

Ⓓ 60

Appendix A: Mathematics Reference Sheet

Area/Perimeter

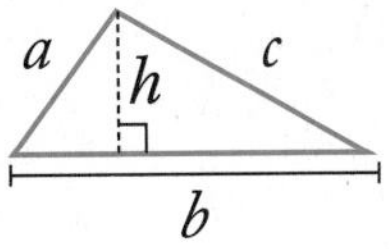

Triangle
$$A = \tfrac{1}{2}bh$$
$$P = a + b + c$$

Square
$$A = s^2$$
$$P = 4s$$

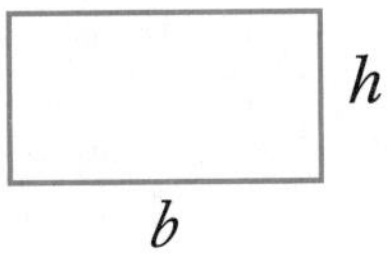

h Rectangle
$$A = bh$$
$$P = 2b + 2h$$

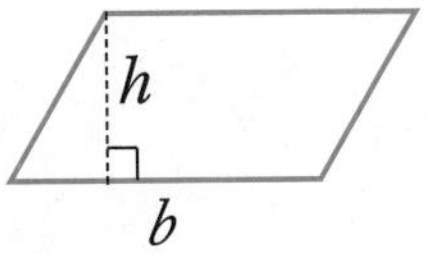

Parallelogram
$$A = bh$$

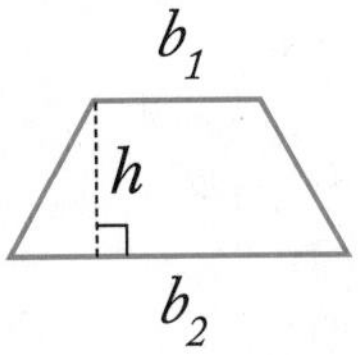

Trapezoid
$$A = \tfrac{1}{2}(b_1 + b_2)h$$

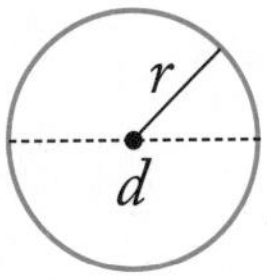

Circle
$$A = \pi r^2$$
Circumference of circle $= \pi d = 2\pi r$
$\pi \approx 3.14$ or $\tfrac{22}{7}$

KEY	
A = area	P = perimeter
b = base	r = radius
B = area of base	s = side
C = circumference	$S.A.$ = surface area
d = diameter	V = volume
h = height	w = width

Pythagorean theorem
$$c^2 = a^2 + b^2$$

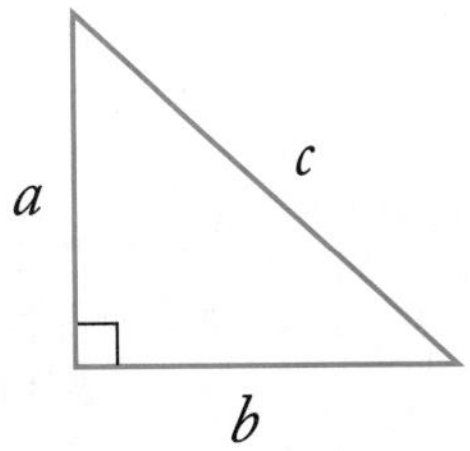

Total Surface Area   Volume

Cylinder $S.A. = 2\pi rh + 2\pi r^2$ $V = \pi r^2 h$

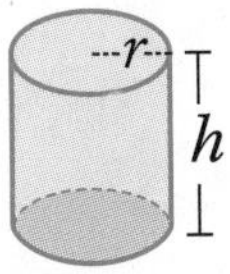

Cube $S.A. = 6s^2$ $V = s^3$

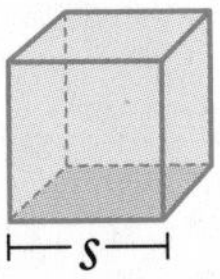

Other Formulas

Distance = rate × time

Rate = distance ÷ time

Sum of measures of interior angles of polygon = $180(n - 2)$, where n = number of sides of polygon

EQUIVALENTS

Customary (English) Units

Length

inch (in.)	smallest common unit
foot (ft)	1 ft = 12 in.
yard (yd)	1 yd = 3 ft
mile (mi)	1 mi = 5,280 ft

Capacity

teaspoon (tsp)	smallest common unit
tablespoon (tbs)	1 tbs = 3 tsp
fluid ounce (fl oz)	1 fl oz = 2 tbs
cup (c)	1 c = 8 fl oz
pint (pt)	1 pt = 2 c
quart (qt)	1 qt = 2 pt
gallon (gal)	1 gal = 4 qt

Weight

ounce (oz)	smallest common unit
pound (lb)	1 lb = 16 oz
ton (T)	1 T = 2,000 lb

Metric Units

Length

millimeter (mm)	smallest common unit
centimeter (cm)	1 cm = 10 mm
decimeter (dm)	1 dm = 10 cm
meter (m)	1 m = 10 dm
kilometer (km)	1 km = 1000 m

Capacity

cubic centimeter (cm^3 or cc)	smallest common unit
milliliter (mL)	1 mL = 1 cm^3 = 1 cc
liter (L)	1 L = 1000 mL

Mass

milligram (mg)	smallest common unit
gram (g)	1 g = 1000 mg
kilogram (kg)	1 kg = 1000 g
metric ton (T)	1 T = 1000 kg

Time

second (sec)	smallest common unit
minute (min)	1 min = 60 sec
hour (hr)	1 hr = 60 min
day	1 day = 24 hr
week (wk)	1 wk = 7 days
month (mo)	varies depending on the month (between 28 and 31 days)
year (yr)	1 yr = 12 mo = 365 or 366 days
decade	1 decade = 10 yr
century	1 century = 100 yr
millennium	1 millennium = 1,000 yr

Appendix B: Diagnostic Test

Part 1: Basic Facts

1. $36 \div 4 =$ _____

2. $77 \div 7 =$ _____

3. $8 \times 4 =$ _____

4. $16 \div 4 =$ _____

5. $6 + 5 =$ _____

6. $8 \times 5 =$ _____

7. $11 - 6 =$ _____

8. $15 \div 3 =$ _____

9. $16 - 7 =$ _____

10. $24 \div 3 =$ _____

11. $8 \div 4 =$ _____

12. $9 - 5 =$ _____

13. $3 \times 7 =$ _____

14. $6 + 3 =$ _____

15. $17 - 8 =$ _____

16. $12 - 9 =$ _____

17. $36 \div 3 =$ _____

18. $12 \div 4 =$ _____

19. $17 - 9 =$ _____

20. $20 \div 4 =$ _____

21. $28 \div 4 =$ _____

22. $5 + 5 =$ _____

23. $9 + 7 =$ _____

24. $32 \div 4 =$ _____

25. $13 - 9 =$ _____

26. $5 \times 6 =$ _____

27. $14 - 9 =$ _____

28. $8 \times 7 =$ _____

29. $4 \times 3 =$ _____

30. $11 - 9 =$ _____

31. $24 \div 4 =$ _____

32. $4 + 9 =$ _____

33. $30 \div 5 =$ _____

34. $5 + 6 =$ _____

35. $27 \div 3 =$ _____

36. $15 - 9 =$ _____

37. $8 \times 3 =$ _____

38. $6 + 4 =$ _____

39. $12 - 7 =$ _____

40. $8 \times 9 =$ _____

41. $18 \div 3 =$ _____

42. $5 \times 3 =$ _____

43. $5 + 4 =$ _____

44. $3 \times 3 =$ _____

45. $35 \div 7 =$ _____

46. $8 \times 6 =$ _____

47. $10 - 7 =$ _____

48. $7 + 5 =$ _____

49. $4 + 8 =$ _____

50. $2 \times 9 =$ _____

51. $14 - 8 =$ _____

52. $3 \times 5 =$ _____

53. $5 + 7 =$ _____

54. $3 \times 9 =$ _____

55. $56 \div 7 =$ _____

56. $4 + 7 =$ _____

57. $16 - 9 =$ _____

58. $8 + 6 =$ _____

59. $4 \times 5 =$ _____

60. $11 - 7 =$ _____

Part 1 subtotal: _____

Appendix B: Diagnostic Test (cont.)

Part 2: Basic Skills

Addition

1. 43   35
   +54   +29

2. 432   385
   +265   +667

3. 18   8
   +30   +16

4.   5   75
    +8   +8

Subtraction

1. 468   423
   −235   −286

2. 123   285
    −99   −63

3. 624   147
   −323   −20

4. 325   726
   −151   −349

Multiplication

1. 98   86
   ×56   ×45

2. 34   27
    ×2   ×4

3. 42   29
    ×3   ×3

4. 313   210
    ×4   ×15

Division

1. 3)639   4)516

2. 2)88   4)104

3. 7)455   6)5430

4. 5)255   6)4818

Part 2 subtotal: _____

Part 1 subtotal: _____

Grand total: _____

Appendix C: Using a Basic Calculator

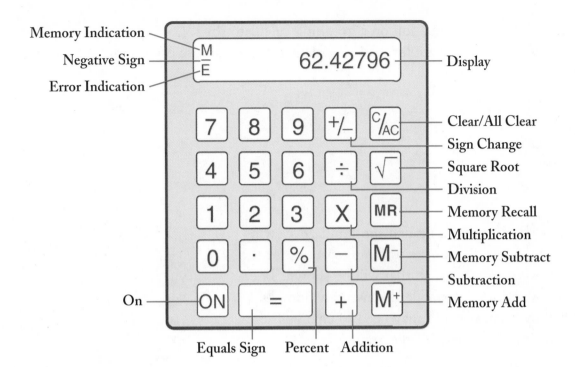

Memory Indication
Negative Sign
Error Indication
Display
Clear/All Clear
Sign Change
Square Root
Division
Memory Recall
Multiplication
Memory Subtract
Subtraction
On
Memory Add
Equals Sign   Percent   Addition

1. Always read and think carefully about each problem. Sometimes it is easier and faster to perform simple calculations in your head than on a calculator.

2. A calculator can help you to solve some, but not all, of the problems on the exam.

3. Well before your exam, practice using your calculator and learn what all the functions do.

4. Before you begin entering numbers on your calculator, make sure you clear your calculator first by pressing the "Clear/All Clear" (C/AC) button twice.

5. If you want to save a number to use later, you can put the number in memory by entering the number and pushing the "Memory" (M+) button. A little "M" will appear in the corner of the display. Then press the "Clear/All Clear" (C/AC) button once and proceed with your calculations. To recall the number you have stored in memory, push the "Memory Recall" (MR) button.

6. The "Memory Add" (M+) and "Memory Subtract" (M–) buttons add and subtract numbers to and from the number you have stored in memory. Practice using all the memory functions.

7. To clear the memory, push the "Clear/All Clear" (C/AC) button twice, or push the "Memory Clear (MC) button once. The "M" in the corner of the display should disappear. Always clear the memory before you begin a new set of calculations.

8. Do not rely on the calculator to do the operations in the correct order.

9. After completing a problem, always double-check your work and your answer. Make sure you have answered all the parts of the problem. You can use estimation or your calculator to make sure your answer is in the right ballpark.

Appendix D: Using a Graphing Calculator

You can graph a linear equation on a graphing calculator by following these steps. Although these instructions are for a TI-83 calculator, you can use other graphing calculators in a similar way.

Graph $y = 4x + 7$.

1. Press ON.

2. Press WINDOW. This is called the standard viewing window. It shows the domain and range values for the part of the coordinate graph that will be shown. The coordinate grid for the standard viewing window is $(-10, 10)$ by $(-10, 10)$. You may need to change these values to view other parts of the graph.

```
WINDOW
Xmin=-10
Xmax=10
Xscl=1
Ymin=-10
Ymax=10
Yscl=1
Xres=1
```

3. Press Y =. Then enter the equation by pressing 4 X,T,θ + 7.

```
Plot1   Plot2   Plot3
\Y₁=4X+7
\Y₂=
\Y₃=
\Y₄=
\Y₅=
\Y₆=
\Y₇=
```

4. Then press GRAPH. The viewing window shows a straight line on a coordinate grid. When a graph shows the origin and the points where the graph crosses the x- and y-axes, it is called a complete graph.

5. Press TRACE. Use the arrows to move the cursor. As you move the cursor along the graph line, new coordinates are shown for each location. One solution is $(0, 7)$.

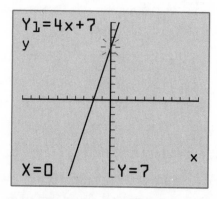

6. Press 2nd ON to turn calculator off.

Appendix E: Glossary

absolute value. The distance of a number from zero on a number line. Example: $|2| = 2$ and $|{-2}| = 2$

accuracy. The closeness of a measurement to the true value

acute angle. An angle that measures less than 90°

acute triangle. A triangle that contains three acute angles

addend. A number that is added in an addition problem

additive inverse property. A rule that states that the sum of a number and its additive inverse, or negation, equals zero (0). Example: $2 + {-2} = 0$

algebra. A generalized variety of arithmetic that makes use of letters (variables) to stand for numbers

algebraic equation. A mathematical sentence using an equality symbol (=), stating that two expressions containing at least one variable are equal in value

algebraic expression. A mathematical expression in which letters stand for numbers

algebraic rule. An equation or formula that uses variables to describe what is happening. Example: using a linear equation to describe a graph

alternate interior angles. Angles that are between two parallel lines and on opposite sides of a transversal

altitude. The height of a figure; the distance from its base to the opposite vertex

angle. The shape made by two rays extending from a common endpoint. The angle is measured by the number of degrees between the rays.

area. The measurement of the space covered by a two-dimensional shape, measured in square units

arithmetic progression. A sequence in which the difference between two consecutive terms is a constant amount

associative property. A rule that states that the way in which numbers are grouped in an addition or multiplication problem does not change the answer. Examples: $(3 + 4) + 5 = 3 + (4 + 5)$; $(7 \times 5) \times 9 = 7 \times (5 \times 9)$

axes (of a graph). The horizontal (x-axis) and vertical (y-axis) number lines used in a rectangular graph or coordinate grid system

axis of symmetry. See *line of symmetry*.

ballpark answer. An answer that is close to, but not the same as, the exact answer

bar graph. A graph that uses bars along one axis to show categories of data. The bars can be either horizontal or vertical.

base. 1) A side of a triangle or figure from which an altitude is drawn. 2) A polygonal or circular end of a three-dimensional shape.

base number. A number used as a multiple factor. The exponent shows how often it is used as a factor. Example: $2^3 = 2 \times 2 \times 2$. The base number is 2.

base quantity. The original amount to be considered when calculating a percent change

bias. A characteristic of a sample that makes it unrepresentative of the population as a whole

boundary line. The line that marks off the graph of a linear inequality, separating the values that satisfy the inequality from those that do not

box-and-whisker plot. A graph that uses a box to show the middle 50% of the data and "whiskers" extending from both ends to display the remainder

capacity. The largest amount that can be held by a three-dimensional container. See also *volume*.

Celsius, or **Centigrade, scale.** A scale for measuring temperature on which the freezing point of water is 0°C and the boiling point is 100°C

central angle. An angle formed by two radii of a circle

central tendencies. The mean, median, and mode of a data set

chart. A display of data in an organized form, often using rows, columns, and ruled lines

circle. A two-dimensional shape that is formed by connecting all the points at the same distance from a center

circle graph. A graph in the form of a circle that shows parts of a whole. Also called a *pie chart*.

circumference. The perimeter of a circle

closed figure. A two-dimensional figure whose beginning and ending points are the same. Examples: circle, square, rectangle

closure property. A rule that states that if an operation is performed on two numbers in a set, the result is a number in that set

coefficient. A number that is multiplied by the variable in a term

column graph. A graph that uses vertical bars to show categories of data along the x-axis

combination. A grouping of items in which order does not matter

common denominator. A number that is a multiple of the denominators of two or more fractions

commutative property. A rule that states that the order of the numbers in an addition or multiplication problem does not change the answer. Examples: $3 + 4 = 4 + 3$; $5 \times 2 = 2 \times 5$

complementary angles. A pair of angles whose sum is 90° (a right angle)

composite number. A number that has factors other than itself and 1

concave polygon. A polygon that has at least one interior angle greater than 180°

cone. A three-dimensional figure with one circular face and one vertex

congruent. Having the same size and shape. Said of two figures that differ only in location.

constant. A quantity whose value stays the same

conversion fraction. A fraction used to convert from one unit of measure to another. The conversion fraction has a value of 1 because the numerator and denominator, although expressed in different units, are equal in value.

convert. To change the unit of measure of a quantity to another unit of measure

convex polygon. A polygon that has no interior angle greater than 180°

coordinate grid. A network of evenly spaced horizontal and vertical lines used for locating points or displaying data

coordinates. Two numbers in the form (x, y) that give the location of a point on a coordinate grid

correlation. The relationship between two variables. The correlation between two variables can be positive (as one increases, the other increases) or negative (as one increases, the other decreases). Some variables have no correlation.

corresponding angles. 1) Matching angles in two similar polygons. 2) Angles that are in the same position relative to parallel lines and the transversal.

counting numbers. See *natural numbers*.

counting principle. When one event can occur a ways and another event can occur b ways, you multiply to find that both events can occur ab ways.

cross multiplication. Multiplying the numerator of one fraction by the denominator of another, and vice versa

cube. A three-dimensional shape that has six square faces. All the edges form right angles.

cubed. The third power of a number. Example: 2 cubed $= 2^3 = 2 \times 2 \times 2$

cubic centimeter. A cube whose sides are all one centimeter long; abbreviated cc; equal to 1 milliliter

customary units. Standards of measurement used mainly in the United States, such as inch, mile, cup, gallon, ounce, and pound. Also called *English units*.

cylinder. A three-dimensional shape that has a circular base and a congruent circular top

data. Facts, or a collection of information on a subject, especially facts expressed numerically

decade. A customary unit of time equal to 10 years

decagon. A polygon with ten sides

decimal. A number written with a decimal point. Examples: 1.0, 0.725

decimal fraction. Number or numbers that are to the right of the decimal point in a decimal number. Decimal fractions are less than 1. Examples: 0.7, 0.75, 0.003

decimal point. A symbol (.) that separates the ones place from the tenths place in decimals, or dollars from cents in money

degree. A unit of measurement for temperature or an angle

denominator. The part of a fraction that tells the amount of the whole or the total number in the group

density. Mass per unit volume. The formula for density is $D = \frac{m}{V}$.

dependent variable. The output value of a function, typically the y-variable. See also *independent variable*.

diagonal. A line segment that runs between two opposing vertices of a polygon

diameter. The distance across a circle through its center, equal to twice the radius

difference. The answer in a subtraction problem

digit. The single numbers 0, 1, 2, 3, 4, 5, 6, 7, 8, and 9. Every number is made up of digits.

dimension. Length, width, or height

direct measure. To use either standard or nonstandard tools to measure an object

distributive property of multiplication over addition. A rule that states that multiplying a number by the sum of two addends gives the same result as multiplying the number by each addend and adding the products. Example: $3(4 + 5) = (3 \times 4) + (3 \times 5)$

dividend. The number to be divided in a problem. Example: $54 \div 9 = 6$. The dividend is 54.

divisible. Able to be divided evenly, without a remainder

divisor. The number by which a dividend is divided. Example: $54 \div 9 = 6$. The divisor is 9.

domain. The individual elements that are all values of the independent variable in a set of ordered pairs

elapsed time. The difference between two times

ellipse. A closed symmetrical curve like an elongated circle (oval)

endpoint. The point from which a ray extends, or either end of a line segment

English units. See *customary units*.

equation. A number sentence that uses the equals sign (=) to show that two expressions have the same value

equilateral triangle. A triangle with three equal sides and three equal angles (60°)

equivalent fractions. Fractions that have different numerators and denominators but the same value

estimate. To find a number that is close to an exact answer

evaluate an expression. To find the value of an algebraic expression by replacing the variables with numbers and performing the operations

expanded notation. A way to write a number showing the place value of the digits that make it up. Example: $3,000 + 500 + 60 + 2 = 3,562$

exponent. A small number that is written to the right of, and a little higher than, a base number. It tells the power to which the base number is raised.

expression. A collection of numbers, symbols, and/or operation signs

exterior angle. The angle formed by extending one edge of a polygon. The sum of the measures of the exterior angles of a convex polygon always equals 360°.

extrapolate. To estimate a value or quantity beyond what is known

extremes. The highest and lowest data points in a data set

face. A surface of a three-dimensional figure

factor. A whole number that divides another number exactly, without a remainder

factorial. The product of all the positive integers from a given integer down to 1. It is represented by an exclamation point following the integer. Example: $3! = 3 \times 2 \times 1 = 6$

Fahrenheit scale. A scale for measuring temperature on which the freezing point of water is 32°F and the boiling point is 212°F

first-degree equation. An equation that does not have variables with exponents other than 0 or 1

flip. A manipulation that produces the mirror image of a figure. Also called a *reflection*.

fractal. A geometric pattern that repeats in increasingly smaller versions of itself

fraction. A portion of a whole. Example: $\frac{1}{4}$

frequency polygon. A graph that shows how often the points of a data set fall within certain intervals

function. The relationship between two sets of numbers in which each number of one set has one assigned number in the other set. See also *pattern*.

geometric progression. A sequence of numbers in which each term is multiplied by the same number to produce the next term

geometry. The study of points, lines, angles, and shapes and their relationships

graph. A picture that shows data in an organized way

greatest common factor. The largest number that is a factor of both the numerator and denominator in a fraction

grid. A network of evenly spaced horizontal and vertical lines

heptagon. A polygon with seven sides

hexagon. A polygon with six sides

histogram. A type of bar graph that shows the number of times, or the frequency, that an event occurs within given intervals

hypotenuse. The side opposite the right angle in a right triangle

hypothesis. A theory to be tested

identity element. A number that when combined with another number using a particular operation does not change the value of the other number. Example: Zero is the identity element for addition because when 0 is added to any number a, the value is still a.

improper fraction. A fraction in which the numerator is larger than or equal to the denominator. Its value is 1 or greater. Example: $\frac{5}{3}$

independent variable. The input into a function, typically the x-variable. It is used by the function to produce a corresponding value (y) as the output.

index. The number in a radical that tells how many identical factors are multiplied to give the radicand. Example: In $\sqrt[3]{8}$, 3 is the index.

indirect measure. Using an object whose measurement is known in order to measure an object of unknown size

inequality. A statement that shows that one expression is greater than (>), greater than or equal to (≥), less than (<), or less than or equal to (≤) another expression

integers. The set of numbers that includes positive whole numbers, negative whole numbers, and zero {..., –2, –1, 0, 1, 2, ...}

interest. An amount of extra money earned by deposits in a savings account or required to pay back a loan. For simple interest, the formula is $I = prt$, where I is the interest, p is the principal, r is the percent rate per unit of time, and t is the number of time units. Example: $100 is the principal deposited, the rate is 4% per year, and the time is 3 years. The simple interest would be $I = \$100(0.04)(3) = \$12$.

interior angle. The angle of a vertex inside a closed figure

intersecting lines. Lines that cross one another

inverse operation. An operation that cancels another operation. For example, multiplication is the inverse operation of division, and vice versa.

irrational numbers. Numbers that can be expressed as infinite decimals that do not repeat. Example: 1.1246…

isolate the variable. To perform the same operation(s) on both sides of an equation in such a way as to get the variable alone on one side

isosceles triangle. A triangle that has two sides of equal length and two equal angles

leg. One of the two sides defining the right angle in a right triangle

like terms. Terms that have the same variables with the same exponents

likelihood. See *probability*.

line. A set of points extending forever in opposite directions. A line has one dimension—length.

line of best fit. A straight line drawn through or close to points on a scatter plot to show the correlation between the sets of data. See also *correlation*.

line graph. A graph that displays data as points along a graphed line

line segment. A portion of a line that has a defined beginning and end

line of symmetry. A line drawn through the center of a shape such that one half is the mirror image of the other. Not all shapes have a line of symmetry. Also called *axis of symmetry*.

linear equation. An algebraic equation whose variables are raised to the first power only. The graph of a linear equation is a straight line.

lowest common denominator. The smallest number that can be the denominator for two or more fractions

lowest terms. The simplest form of a fraction, when it is expressed using the smallest numbers possible

manipulations. Changes to a shape made through turns, slides, and flips. Also called *transformations*.

mass. The quantity of matter in an object

mean. The average of a set of numbers, calculated by dividing the sum of the quantities in a data set by the number of quantities

median. The middle number in a set of ordered numbers. Half of the numbers are above the median and half are below it. If the set contains an even number of elements, the median is the mean of the two middle numbers.

metric system. A system for measurement based on the powers of 10 and used in most of the world. Metric units include meter, gram, and liter.

midpoint. The point on a line segment that divides it into two equal parts

mixed number. Any number that contains a whole number plus a fraction. Example: $3\frac{4}{7}$

mode. The number or data point found most often in a set of data

multiples. Numbers that result from multiplying a given number by the set of whole numbers. Example: Some multiples of 15 are 15, 30, and 45.

multiplicative identity. Multiplying a number by one (1) produces no change. Example: $2 \times 1 = 2$

natural numbers (counting numbers). All whole numbers except zero

negative exponent. A number raised to a negative exponent is the reciprocal of that number raised to the same positive exponent. In scientific notation, negative exponents are used to indicate numbers less than 1. Example: $2.04 \times 10^{-3} = 0.00204$

nonstandard units of measure. Units such as pencils, paper clips, blocks, fingers, hands, etc. that are used for making approximate measurements

number line. A line with evenly spaced numbers that shows the order of numbers

numerator. The part of a fraction that tells the number of parts of the whole or the portion of the group

obtuse angle. An angle that measures more than 90° but less than 180°

obtuse triangle. A triangle that contains one obtuse angle

octagon. A polygon with eight sides

odds. The relationship between the instances which an event occurs and the instances in which it does not occur, expressed as a ratio. Example: six-to-one odds

operation. A mathematical process, such as addition, subtraction, multiplication, or division

opportunity sampling. A method of taking a sample from a population in which items or people are chosen based on convenience. Opportunity samples are often biased.

order of operations. A set of rules that tell you which operations to solve first in an equation

ordered pair. A set of two numbers that tells you the location of a point on a graph. The first number is from the x-axis, and the second is from the y-axis.

origin. The intersection of the x- and y-axes in a coordinate grid, described by the ordered pair (0, 0)

outcome. One of several equally likely results

parallel lines. Lines in the same plane that do not cross. They are the same distance apart everywhere along the lines.

parallelogram. A four-sided flat figure with two pairs of parallel sides. Its opposite sides are equal, and its opposite angles are equal.

pattern. A predictable sequence of numbers or objects that repeat or follow an established design

pentagon. A polygon with five sides

percent. A fraction expressed in hundredths. The ratio is written as a whole or decimal number followed by a percent sign (%). Example: 30% means 30 out of 100.

perfect square. The product of a whole number multiplied by itself

perimeter. The sum of the lengths of all the sides of a polygon; that is, the distance around that polygon

period. A group of three places in a number. Periods are set off by commas, and the places within each period are hundreds, tens, and ones. Example: In the number 123,456,789, the digits 456 form the thousands period.

permutation. An arrangement of objects or events in which order is important

perpendicular lines. Lines that meet or cross at a right angle (90°)

pi. A Greek letter (π) that is the symbol for the relationship between the circumference and the diameter of a circle. Pi is always the same, no matter the size of the circle. Pi is approximately equal to 3.14 or $\frac{22}{7}$.

pictograph. A graph that uses symbols to show data

pie chart. See *circle graph.*

place value. The value assigned to the position of a digit in a number

plane. A two-dimensional surface that has no boundaries

plane figure. A two-dimensional figure that lies in a single plane

plot. To mark the location of a point on a graph

point. A single location in space. A point has no dimensions; it has no length, width, or height.

polygon. A closed plane figure formed by straight lines that do not cross. Polygons come in all shapes and sizes.

polyhedron. A three-dimensional figure in which all the surfaces are polygons

population. A whole group being considered

powers of 10. The numbers produced by multiplying 10 by itself. Examples: 10; 100; 1,000; 10,000

precision. How finely a measurement can be made; the number of place values to which a measurement is given

predict. To use logic to tell what might happen

prime number. A whole number exactly divisible only by 1 and itself

principal. The initial amount of money deposited or borrowed. See also *interest.*

prism. A three-dimensional figure with congruent, parallel bases and sides that are parallelograms

probability. The chance that something will happen

product. The answer in a multiplication problem

projection. 1) Prediction of future change based on trends in the current data. 2) In geometry, the image of a three-dimensional object on a plane.

property. A rule that numbers follow

proportion. A mathematical equation that relates two ratios

protractor. A tool for measuring angles

pyramid. A three-dimensional figure whose base is a polygon and whose triangular faces meet at a point

Pythagorean theorem. A rule that states that, in a right triangle, the sum of the squares of the legs (a and b) is equal to the square of the hypotenuse (c), as shown by the formula $a^2 + b^2 = c^2$

quadrant. Any of the four areas formed by the axes in a coordinate system

quadrilateral. A closed four-sided figure

quartile. The median of the lower half of a data set (first quartile) or the median of the upper half of a data set (third quartile)

quotient. The answer in a division problem

radical. An expression that has a root (square root, cube root, etc.). Any root can be specified by an index number, b, in the form $\sqrt[b]{a}$ (example: $\sqrt[3]{7}$). A radical without an index number is understood to be a square root.

radical sign. The symbol $\sqrt{}$ used before a number to show that it is a radicand

radicand. A number that appears inside a radical sign, of which you are to find the root. Example: In $\sqrt{2}$, 2 is the radicand.

radius. A line segment from the center of a circle to any point on the circle

range (of a data set). The difference between the highest and the lowest value in the data set

range (of a function). The individual elements that are all values of the dependent variable in a set of ordered pairs

rate. A ratio that describes one quantity per unit of another

ratio. The relationship between two quantities when one is divided by the other. Example: The ratio of x to y is $\frac{x}{y}$ or $x:y$.

rational number. A real number that can be expressed as a ratio of two integers

ray. A portion of a line that begins at a point and goes on forever in one direction. An angle is formed by two rays joined at a common endpoint.

real numbers. The set of all rational and irrational numbers

reciprocal. The inversion of a fraction. The numerator becomes the denominator, and the denominator becomes the numerator. The product of a number and its reciprocal is 1. Example: $\frac{4}{3}$ is the reciprocal of $\frac{3}{4}$, and $\frac{4}{3} \times \frac{3}{4} = 1$.

rectangle. A quadrilateral with opposite sides that are equal and four right angles

rectangular prism. A three-dimensional figure with six rectangular faces

reduce (a fraction). To make an equivalent fraction with smaller numbers by dividing both the numerator and the denominator by a common factor. See *simplify*.

reflection. See *flip*.

regular polygon. A closed plane figure in which all of the sides are equal in length and all the angles are equal

relation. A set of ordered pairs in which the two members have a defined relationship

relatively prime numbers. Numbers whose only common factor is 1

rhombus. A four-sided flat figure with sides that are all the same length. The opposite sides are parallel, but the angles are not necessarily right angles.

right angle. An angle that makes a square corner. It measures exactly 90°.

right triangle. A triangle that contains a right angle

rise. The vertical change of a line in a graph; the change in *y*-value between two points on a graph

root. A number that can be multiplied by itself a given number of times to produce a particular product

rotation. A manipulation of a figure by turning it. The amount of rotation is usually expressed in degrees clockwise or counterclockwise.

rounding. A strategy in which an exact number is changed into another number that is close to its value. Numbers can be rounded to any place value.

rule. A mathematical expression that describes a pattern or relationship

run. The horizontal change of a line in a graph; the change in *x* value between two points on a graph

sample. A selected part of a larger group

satisfy. To be a solution of, or to make a statement true

scale. To enlarge or shrink a figure, keeping the same proportions

scales. The numeric values on the axes of a graph

scale factor. The amount each dimension in the original is multiplied by to maintain the same proportions in the enlargement or reduction

scale model. A proportional model or drawing, based on a ratio of the dimensions for the model and the actual object it represents

scalene triangle. A triangle with all three sides of different lengths

scatter plot. A graph that displays points for ordered pairs of numbers on a coordinate grid. A scattergram shows whether or not there is a correlation between two sets of data. Also called a scattergram.

scientific notation. A way of writing a number as a number between 1 and 10 multiplied by a power of 10

segment. Part of a line between two points

sequence. A group of numbers or objects that follow a specific pattern

significant digits. The digits in a decimal number that are meaningful

similar. Having the same shape but not the same size

simplest form. A fraction written such that its numerator and denominator have no common factor greater than 1

simplify. 1) To combine like terms and complete operations in an expression or equation to make computation easier. 2) To reduce a fraction

skew lines. Lines that are not in the same plane

slide. A manipulation of a figure by moving it along a surface in a vertical, horizontal, or diagonal direction

slope. The steepness of a line; the ratio of change in the *y*-values to change in the *x*-values of the two points. The formula for slope is $m = \frac{y_1 - y_2}{x_1 - x_2}$.

solid figure. A closed three-dimensional figure

solution set. The set of all points that satisfy one or more inequalities

sphere. A three-dimensional figure shaped like a round ball

spread. See *range*.

square. A four-sided polygon with four right angles and four sides that are the same length

square root. A number that can be multiplied by itself to produce a given number. Example: The square root of 4 is 2, or $\sqrt{4} = 2$.

square unit. A unit of area that is one unit by one unit in size

squared. A number multiplied by itself. Example: 3 squared $= 3^2 = 3 \times 3$

standard measuring tool. A tool for measuring that has a fixed length everyone agrees upon, such as a ruler, yardstick, or meter stick

standard units of measure. The accepted measuring units of the customary or metric system

statistics. The gathering and analysis of data, usually presented as numbers

stem-and-leaf plot. A way to organize and display data in order from least to greatest, using the digits of the greatest place value to group the data

straight angle. An angle that is equal to 180°

sum. The answer to an addition problem

supplementary angles. A pair of angles whose sum is 180° (a straight angle)

surface area. The sum of the areas of the faces that make up a geometric solid (3D figure)

survey. A list of specific questions given to a group of people

symmetry. A characteristic of a shape such that one half is the mirror image of the other

table. A chart that organizes and shows information collected about a specific topic

temperature. The measurement of how hot or how cold an object is

term. One of the quantities in a ratio or expression. Example: In the expression $4x^2 + 3x + 5$, the terms are $4x^2$, $3x$, and 5.

tessellation. A repeating pattern of shapes that fit together without any spaces in between

tetrahedron. A three-dimensional figure that has four triangular faces

three-dimensional figure. A solid figure that takes up space and has volume. Its dimensions are length, width, and height. Examples: cube, sphere, cylinder

transformations. See *manipulations*.

transitive property. A rule that states that two quantities are equal if both of them are equal to a third quantity

translation. See *slide*.

transversal. A line that crosses two or more lines at separate points

trapezoid. A four-sided polygon with only two sides that are parallel

tree diagram. A diagram showing all possible outcomes of an event

trend. A pattern of changes in displayed data

triangle. A polygon with three sides and three angles

turn. See *rotation*.

two-dimensional figure. A polygon with only two dimensions—length and width. A two-dimensional shape does not have thickness, or height.

variable. A symbol, often a letter, that represents a number

velocity. An object's speed and direction

Venn diagram. A method of representing sets graphically in which each set is represented by a circle. Regions where two circles overlap have elements that are members of both sets.

vertex. The point at which two sides of an angle meet in a figure (plural: vertices)

vertical angles. The opposite angles formed when two lines intersect. Vertical angles are always congruent.

volume. The amount of space in a three-dimensional object. It is expressed in cubic units.

weight. The measurement of how heavy something is, or how strongly it is pulled down by gravity

whole numbers. The numbers in the set {0, 1, 2, 3,…}. A number that is to the left of a decimal point.

x-axis. On a graph, the axis that runs horizontally, left to right

x-intercept. The value of x on a graph when y is equal to 0

y-axis. On a graph, the axis that runs vertically, up and down

y-intercept. The value of y on a graph when x is equal to 0

zero property. A rule that states that multiplying by zero produces a product of zero

Index

A

absolute value, 57–58, 99
accuracy, 188
acute angle, 164
acute triangle, 164
addend, 99, 116
adding, 91–93, 99; decimals, 71;
  fractions with like
  denominators, 66; fractions
  with unlike denominators,
  66–67; inverse of, 93; positive
  and negative numbers, 98; real
  numbers, 107; vocabulary for,
  45
additive inverse property, 92, 94
al-Khwarizmi, 109
algebra, 109–111
algebraic equations and
  expressions, 110, 111, 115;
  constants in, 109–111;
  simplifying, 115–116; terms in,
  110–111; variables in, 109–111
alternate exterior angles, 159
alternate interior angles, 159
altitude, 203
analytic geometry, 143
angle(s), 158; acute, 164;
  alternate exterior, 159;
  alternate interior, 159;
  complementary, 158–159;
  congruent, 159–160;
  corresponding, 159, 171;
  exterior, 159, 163; interior,
  159, 163; obtuse, 164; right,
  158, 164; straight, 158; sum of
  exterior, 163; sum of interior,
  163, 164; supplementary,
  159–160; vertical, 159–160
angstrom, 77
approximation, 86
Archimedes, 203, 207
area, 78, 203–204, 216; of circle,
  203; of parallelogram, 203; of
  rectangle, 203; of square, 203;

of trapezoid, 203; of triangle,
  203
arithmetic, 109
ascending order, 85
associative (grouping) property,
  92; of addition, 92; of
  multiplication, 92
astronomical unit (AU), 81
average, 57–58, 255
axes (of a graph), 139
axis of symmetry, 165, 169, 174

B

back-solving, 40
ballpark estimation, 183–184
bar graphs, 238
base (of a figure), 164, 165, 171
base number (of an exponent),
  77
base quantity, 74
batting average, 124
bell curve, 256
benchmarks, 29
Bhaskara, 125
bias, 233
Bode's Law, 81
Bode, Johann, 81
bookkeeping, 53
Bouger, Pierre, 149
boundary line, 149–152
box-and-whisker plots, 256–257
Brahmagupta, 125

C

calculator, 315, 316; basic, 315;
  graphing, 316
canceling like variables, 116
Cantor, Georg, 133
capacity, 208
Celsius, 102, 144
central tendencies, 255–258. *See
  also* mean, 255; median, 256;
  mode, 256
certain, 261

circle(s), 199–200; area of,
  203–204; changing
  dimensions of, 215;
  circumference of, 199–200;
  diameter of, 199; lines of
  symmetry of, 169; radius of,
  199
circle graphs, 237
circumference, 199–200
closed figure, 163
closure property, 92, 107
coefficient, 115
column graph, 238
combinations, 269–270
common denominator, 67
commutative (order) property,
  91; of addition, 91, 94, 115,
  121; of multiplication, 91
comparing and ordering
  numbers, 85; absolute value,
  58; decimals, 85–86; fractions,
  65–66, 86; percents with
  fractions and decimals, 86;
  rational and irrational
  numbers, 88; ratios, 67
complementary angles, 158–159
composite numbers, 61–62
compound interest, 226
concave polygon, 163
cone, 165, 173, 207
congruent, 159–160, 171
constant, 109–110, 200
conversion fraction, 193–194
conversion tables, 195–196, 221;
  for capacity, 196; length, 195;
  mass, 196, 221; weight, 196
converting, 52, 194; between
  decimals and fractions, 54;
  between decimals and
  percents, 73; between fractions
  and percents, 73; monetary
  units, 184; temperature, 144;
  to decimals, 97; to scientific
  notation, 81, 97

with, 66–68; to express probability, 262

Fredn, William, 97

frequency, 250, 262

frequency polygon(s), 250; cumulative, 250; cumulative relative, 250

functions, 134–136; graphs of, 135; tables of, 135

Fundamental Theorem of Arithmetic, 61

G

Galileo, 169, 225

geology, 104

geometry, 61, 157

goal analysis method, 41

goal state, 41

Goldbach Conjecture, 38

golden rectangle, 163

graph(s), 135; bar, 238; circle, 237; column, 238; extrapolating from, 244; interpreting, 143–146; line, 243–246; of linear equations, 143–146. *See also* box-and-whisker plot, 256; frequency polygon, 250; histograms, 249–252; pie chart, 237; scatter plot, 244; slope, 143–146; stem-and-leaf plot, 251; Venn diagram, 239; *y*-intercept, 143–146

graph paper, 139

graphing, 135, 149; functions, 135; inequalities, 149–152; linear equations, 139–140

Graunt, John, 231

gravity, 65, 140, 221, 222, 225

greater than (>), 129, 149

greater than or equal to (≥), 129, 149

greatest common factor (GCF), 66

grid, 135; coordinate, 139

gridded-response questions, 29

grouping property, 92

H

Hamilton, William Rowan, 91

Harriott, Thomas, 149

heuristic, 39

hexagonal pyramid, 165

hexahedron, 165

histograms, 249–252

honeycombs, 170

hypotenuse, 177–178

I

icosahedron, 165, 211

identity element, 91; for addition, 92, 94; for multiplication, 92

impossible, 261

independence, 232

independent variable, 134

index (of a radical), 77

indirect measurement, 173

inductive reasoning, 37

inequalities, 129–130; graphing, 149–152; solving, 129–130

inequality signs, 129–130, 149

inferences, 37

infinite decimals, 53

infinity, 133

initial state, 41

integers, 52, 53

interest, 226; compound, 226; simple, 226

interior angle, 163

interquartile range, 257

intersecting lines, 158

intervals, 249

inverse, 77; additive, 92; multiplicative, 92; operations, 93, 94, 99, 120

irrational numbers, 53, 71, 85, 87

irregular polygon, 163

isolating a variable, 120–122

isosceles trapezoid, 164

isosceles triangle, 164

J

Johnstown flood, 129

K

Kanada, Yasumasa, 200

Kaplan, Robert, 51

Kramp, Christian, 267

L

largest common factor, 66

law of gravitation, 65

legs (of a triangle), 177–178

length, 199–200

less than (<), 129, 149

less than or equal to (≤), 129, 149

like terms, 115

likelihood, 261

line graphs, 243–246; data points, 244–245; predicting trends from, 244; projecting trends from, 244

line(s), 157; boundary, 149–152; intersecting, 158; parallel, 158, 159; perpendicular, 158; ray, 157; of reflection, 172; segment, 157; skew, 158; of symmetry, 165, 169

line of best fit, 245

linear equation, 139–140, 143

lowest common denominator (LCD), 67, 68

lowest terms, 66

M

Magellan, Ferdinand, 157

magnitude, 57

manipulations (transformations), 171–174

marketing, 262

mass, 65, 77, 221–222

matter, 221

mean, 255

measuring, 211; area, 203–204; circumference, 199–200; density, 222; estimating measurements, 183–184; indirect, 173; length, 199–200; mass, 221–222; perimeter, 199–200, 203; rate, 225–226; surface area, 211–212; weight, 221–222

median, 256
metric system, 193–194
microbiology, 82
mirror image, 169
mode, 256
Moore, E. H., 139
multiple(s), 62; of 3 and of 9, 62
multiple-choice questions, 29
multiplicative inverse property, 92
multiplying, 62, 91–93, 99; decimals, 71; with exponents, 82; fractions, 66; inverse of, 99; positive and negative numbers, 98; real numbers, 107; vocabulary for, 47

N

n-gon, 163
nanotechnology, 103
natural numbers, 51
navigation, 158
negative exponent, 78
negative numbers, 97, 125; in inequalities, 129–130
Newton, Isaac, 65, 221
newtons, 222
Nightingale, Florence, 249
nonlinear, 140
nonrepeating decimals, 53
nonstandard (measuring tool or unit), 183
normal distribution, 256. *See also* bell curve.
number line, 52, 58
numbers, 51–53; base, 77; composite, 61–62; counting, 51; even, 38; integers, 52; irrational, 53; natural, 51; negative, 97; perfect, 62; prime, 38, 61–62; rational, 52; real, 53; whole, 51
numerator, 54, 65

O

obtuse angle, 164
obtuse triangle, 164
octagonal pyramid, 165
octahedron, 165, 211

odds, 263; against, 263–264; calculating, 263; in favor, 263–264
operations, 97–100; with measurements, 189
opportunity sampling, 233
order of operations, 99
order property, 91
ordered pair, 133, 139
ordering numbers, 85; decimals, 85; fractions and percents, 86; rational and irrational numbers, 87
outcomes, 262; favorable, 262; possible, 262; unfavorable, 262
overgeneralizations, 37

P

paleontology, 216
parabola, 140
parallel lines, 158, 159
parallelogram, 164
parentheses, 99
Pascal, Blaise, 261
pattern, 136
pentagonal prism, 165
percent(s), 71–74, 237; change, 73–74; converting to decimals, 72–74; converting to fractions, 73; per centum, 237; to express probability, 262
perfect number, 62
perfect square, 79
perimeter, 199–200, 204
permutations, 268–269
perpendicular lines, 158
physics, 111, 140
pi (π), 86, 87, 200
pictographs, 238
pie charts, 237
plane, 157
plot, 135
point, 157
polling, 232
polygon(s), 163–164, 203; areas of, 203; concave, 163; convex, 163; irregular, 163; regular, 163; sum of angles, 164

polyhedron, 165, 207
population, 231–234
powers, 77; of ten, 78, 81
precision, 188
prediction, 244
Prime Number Theorem, 61
prime numbers, 38, 61–62; factors, 62; relatively, 62, 66
principal, 226
prism, 165, 207
probability, 261–264; expressed as decimals or percents, 262; involving simple random events, 262–263; of certain outcome, 261–262; frequency, 262; of impossible outcome, 261–262; range of, 261–262
problem-solving strategies, 39–42; back-solving, 40; diagramming, 40; divide and conquer, 39; equation method, 42; estimation, 41; goal analysis, 41; simplification, 39; trial and error, 40
projection, 244
proof, 38
properties, 91–94
proportional, 171
propotional representation, 66
proportions, 65, 67, 68
pyramid, 165, 207
Pythagoras, 52, 85, 177
Pythagorean theorem, 177–178
Pythagoreans, 52–53, 211

Q

quadrant, 139
quadratic function, 140
quadrilateral(s), 164; sum of angles, 164
quartile, first, 257; lower, 257; third, 257; upper, 257

R

radicals, 77–78
radicand, 77
radius (plural: radii), 199–200
randomness, 232

range, 134, 256; as opposed to domain, 134; of a data set, 256; in histograms, 249; interquartile, 257; of probabilities, 261

rate, 225–226

ratio, 65, 67, 68; to express probability, 262

rational numbers, 52, 71, 87

ray, 157

real numbers, 53

reasoning, 33; about math problems, 33–34, 37–42; deductive, 38; inductive, 37

reciprocal, 66, 77

rectangle, 163; golden, 163

rectangular prism, 165, 207

rectangular pyramid, 165, 207

reducing fractions. *See* simplifying fractions.

reduction, 172

reference sheet, 311–312

reflection (flip), 172

regular polygon, 163

regular polyhedrons, 165

relations, 133, 134

relatively prime, 62

relativity, theory of, 77

repeating decimal, 52

representative sample, 232

representing functions, 135; graphs, 135; tables, 135

Rhind Papyrus, 109

Rhind, Henry, 109

rhombus, 164

right angle, 158, 164

right triangle, 164, 177–178

rise, 145

roots, 77–78

rotation (turn), 172; around a line, 173

rounding, 103, 187

run, 145

S

Sagan, Carl, 61

sample, 232; size of, 232

sampling, 232; bias, 233; methods of, 233; opportunity, 233; principles of, 232; representative, 232; simple random, 233; stratified, 233; systematic, 233

satisfy, 139, 149

scale, 172; changes in, 215–218

scales (on a graph), 243

scale factor, 173

scalene triangle, 164

scatter plots (scattergrams), 244–245; correlation from, 244; line of best fit in, 245

scientific notation, 81–82, 97; converting into, 81

segment, 157

sequence(s), 135–136; Fibonacci, 135

Servois, François-Joseph, 91

set, 133

shapes, 163; congruent, 171; similar, 171; three-dimensional, 165–166, 173; two-dimensional, 163–164, 166, 173

Sierpinski Triangle, 134

Sieve of Eratosthenes, 62, 199

significant digits, 189

similar (shapes), 171

simple random sampling, 233

simplification method, 39

simplifying expressions, 115–116

simplifying fractions, 66; in expressions, 116

skew lines, 158

slide (translation), 172

slope, 143–146, 246

slope-intercept form, $y = mx + b$, 144, 152

Smoot, Oliver, 183

solid figures, 165–166. *See also* three-dimensional shapes, 173.

solution, 33

solution set, 150–151

solving equations, 119–122, 125–126; with one variable, 119–122; with two variables, 125–126

solving inequalities, 129–130

sphere, 165, 207

spread (of data), 249

square root, 78

squared, 77, 78, 140

standards, 29

statistics, 231, 234

stem-and-leaf plots, 251

Stevin, Simon, 71

stocks, 72, 243

straight angle, 158

strategies, 39; for problem-solving, 39–42

stratified sampling, 233

subtracting, 54, 99; decimals, 71; equations, 126; fractions with like denominators, 66; fractions with unlike denominators, 66; inverse of, 93; positive and negative numbers, 98; real numbers, 107; vocabulary for, 46

Sunshine State Standards, 29

supplementary angles, 159–160

surface area, 204, 211; of cylinders, 212; of rectangular solids, 211; of spheres, 212

symmetry, 169; axis of, 165, 169, 174

systematic sampling, 233

T

tables of functions, 135

temperature, 144; estimating, 184

term(s), 110, 115; coefficient of, 115; like, 115

tessellations, 170–171, 174

test-taking tips, 31–32

tetrahedron, 165, 211

theorem, 177

Think, Solve, and Explain questions on FCAT, 30

third quartile, 257

three-dimensional shapes, 165–166, 173